The Sutras of Abu Ghraib

THE SUTRAS
OF ABU GHRAIB

Notes from a
Conscientious Objector

Aidan Delgado

BEACON PRESS

BOSTON

Beacon Press
25 Beacon Street
Boston, Massachusetts 02108-2892
www.beacon.org

Beacon Press books
are published under the auspices of
the Unitarian Universalist Association of Congregations.

10 09 08 07   8 7 6 5 4 3 2 1

This book is printed on acid-free paper that meets the uncoated paper
ANSI/NISO specifications for permanence as revised in 1992.

Text design by Tag Savage at Wilsted & Taylor Publishing Services
Composition by Wilsted & Taylor Publishing Services

ISBN 978-0-8070-7270-7
Library of Congress Control Number: 2007924359

Endurance is one of the most difficult disciplines,
but the final victory comes to the one who endures.

THE BUDDHA

Contents

Prologue

How to begin? It's 2005, I've been back in the States for over a year, and nothing about my time in Iraq seems clear anymore. Ten thousand people have already weighed in on my story, and I am sagging under the weight of their words. I have never been a "man of principle" before, nor have I ever been a "communist" or "barking moon-bat," and never at the same time. Sometimes when I read about myself, I think, Was I even there? It fades in and out of focus. Did any of this really happen? Maybe I am a fraud, just as they say. The prison swells and recedes in my memory until it's just a dark blot on the camera lens. Maybe I'm just remembering it wrong, filling in the gaps, making it up . . .

Then it comes back into focus.

It's 2003: we've been at Abu Ghraib for only a couple of weeks. It's evening, just about sunset. There's no light or heat inside, so we gather to make a little fire. We're sitting around a fire barrel, reclining into bright red canvas chairs, just a couple of guys lounging around outside the barracks building. There are no showers yet, so everyone's dirty as hell and itching in the thermal underwear and field jackets we've just pulled out of our B-bags. It's late November; my birthday was last week. It's very cold. Shoe is trying to cook popcorn on a piece of sheet metal. Someone tosses another piece of crate on the fire and the popcorn begins to make noise. Sergeant McCullough wanders over, kneels down next to the fire barrel, and starts to talk. His face is young, bright, and friendly: a good guy, nicest sergeant in the world, everyone knows that.

You guys hear about the riot? he says in his agreeable southern drawl. No, we say, what happened? They killed some prisoners, shot one guy in the face, split his head open. Laughs all around.

Then we're all talking about the riot, asking about it. What happened, Sergeant? Details, details, details. They were throwing stones. Hit a couple of our guys, bloodied Pitts's face. It was fucking crazy, man.

He says they've got some photos of the riot in the TOC, the Tactical Operations Command, real nasty ones. You can see the looks on everyone's faces change. Wish I'd been there, someone says. The sun's gone down. People wander off. Shoe busts open the popcorn from his metal cup and it's wrecked; all but a few kernels are too blackened to eat.

What follows is a record of my time in Iraq, my own best effort at my story and my truth. Is it a transcript of reality? Hell, no. I defy anyone to produce one. Like any story, it is interwoven with my own reflections, wishes, judgments, and prejudices. Is every word I spoke, every word spoken to me during that year, exactly recorded exactly as it was said? No. It's a memory, recorded and set down as well as memory ever can be. But it's all true, to the best of my knowledge and the knowledge of some of the guys I served with.

In a larger sense, what happened to me in Iraq is completely irrelevant. The sights, the sounds, the tastes are all just curiosities that I present in an effort to paint the picture. I could give you an endless series of vignettes: what Iraq looked like, what we ate, the interesting characters in my unit, but it would all be meaningless. If you want to read about daring military exploits, there are many authors with stories more dashing than mine. It would be vain and empty merely to chronicle what happened to me, as if I were somehow so important that you needed to hear every event of my life in excruciating detail. I am not telling parlor stories. I wrote this book because I want to share a lesson I learned in the desert, in the hope that it will inform your view of the war in Iraq, of politics, of religion, of all the choices you make as a moral person. I can't bear to hear any more stories about battles and uncompromising heroes, with flags waving gently in the background. I want this book to serve as a hanging question about what it means to be an ethical soldier, to live an honest life. I want to give you a military life in shades of gray, filled with doubt, moral courage, and moral cowardice.

This book is not about who I am and what happened to me, even though you will read about who I am and what happened to me. It is a story about a struggle that we all face, a story about deciding what you believe is right and upholding that belief to the bitter end, come what may.

That's my invocation. Give me the strength to remember.

"Hey, that one sounded pretty close."

"Yeah, probably outgoing."

Another dull thump somewhere out in the dark, this one close enough to shake the room. The long fluorescent light dangling from the ceiling begins to swing. We've been at Abu Ghraib for a month now; we're getting used to this. We'd heard from other units since coming to the prison about the nightly bombardments—the incoming enemy fire and the outgoing return barrages from U.S. artillery batteries stationed inside the prison—and we'd been through a couple of light ones. We continue talking, Sergeant Toro, Shoe, Spangler, Sergeant Wallace, and I. We're all standing around our room in our physical training shorts or shirtless in our desert camouflage pants, getting ready to go to bed or watch a movie on the small TVs that have been our constant companions since Nasiriyah. Sergeants Toro and Wallace are visiting from their rooms downstairs. Sergeant Wallace has the tiny yellow notebook that he always takes notes in to give us during evening briefings. He cradles it in his huge black hands, its effeteness vastly incongruent with his massive height and bulk. We've wrapped up our business and now we're just chatting, commenting on the mortar fire like one might comment on the weather. I forget what we were talking about now; the next day's motor pool business or some other petty thing. I do remember what comes next.

The room we're in takes what feels like a direct hit; the mortar round impacts the other side of the wall. The roar is deafening, and the force of the thing knocks everyone off balance. The room shakes and all the junk on our shelves crashes to the floor. Suddenly the air is cloudy with plaster dust. Sergeant Wallace's baritone slices through the haze: "Get your shit on!" Then we're all moving in a frenzy, feeling around for our flak vests and Kevlar helmets. Sergeants Toro and Wallace bolt downstairs to get their own equipment. I remember this distinctly: I am wearing my shower shoes and an old pair of fatigue pants. I put on a shirt, throw my flak vest over it, and then sit down, trying to put on my boots in the midst of the bombardment. Shoe and Spangler are doing the same, grabbing their weapons and ammo and heading for the door. It's standard procedure during these things to grab your weapon and head downstairs for a head count, but I no longer have a weapon.

Shoe makes it out the door first and I'm right behind him. I lose track of Spangler in the confusion. I look down over the rails onto the first floor of the barracks, where everyone is yelling and running around aimlessly.

"Get your shit on!"

"Get downstairs!"

"Squad leaders, get your people!"

The scene is mass chaos.

I turn just as another round impacts nearby, and then the whole building seems to shake. Small pieces of plaster and concrete fall from the ceiling and the dust is everywhere. I watch as the building wobbles violently and unrealistically, as if viewed through a shaking camera. Wow, I think, it's like I'm in a war movie.

Then comes the long walkway around the second floor of the

prison to the stairs. My vest has no armor plates—they were taken back in Nasiriyah—and I start to think about shrapnel coming through the roof. Impulsively I cross my arms over my chest while I run, in some futile effort to protect my torso if I get hit. I start down the corridor with my arms wrapped around my body, probably looking goofy as hell, now that I think about it. All I can think is: fast, move fast, get downstairs where it's "safe." I start running, really running. For the first time, I know what it means to move as if your life depended on it. I am now at a full sprint. When I'm about halfway down the aisle, another mortar round pounds the building and the force of it makes me sidestep and nearly lose my footing. I'm going to die: the thought enters my mind suddenly and with peculiar force, as if someone were quietly whispering it in my ear. I am really going to die.

Of course, when you go to war you think about death abstractly. You are briefed about the dangers, you swap fears with your buddies, and in your quiet moments you contemplate it. But it's never quite real, at least it wasn't for me. I had thought about death more than most soldiers had; in fact, I was somewhat obsessed with death and my ability to face it. I had tried to prepare myself mentally; I had even tried to do an exercise I'd read in a book about samurai, a meditation on death. The practitioner sits and tries to picture, in as much detail as he can, being cut with swords, pierced with musket balls, thrown over high cliffs, and other terrible ways to die, in an effort to calm the mind. What's supposed to arise from this practice is an indifference to death and a resulting ability to perform on the battlefield with absolute equanimity. I had tried this, and still the thought of death horrified and repulsed me. I was not ready to die.

Despite all that theoretical preparation, it had never truly sunk in that I might actually lose my life in Iraq. I was incapable of conceiving that I could be killed; I was the protagonist in my own personal movie, and things like untimely death just don't happen to the protagonist. There in the corridor, in the midst of the bombardment, I realized for the first time that I might actually be killed, that this war was for real. I'd been in Iraq for more than six months, and I admit I had become careless and blasé about life in the war zone even at Abu Ghraib, currently the most dangerous square kilometer on earth (someone had said; it sounds more like a T-shirt slogan than a real statistic). Even near Baghdad, at the very heart of things, the war seemed somehow distant from my wrench and my little red toolbox in the motor pool of the 320th Military Police Company.

The feeling of being about to die is inexpressible. The roar and rumble of the falling mortar cuts through all your pretensions, all your thought systems, and communicates directly with your body on an animal level. You run. You sweat. You seek the low ground and the safe place. Your legs know their business better than you do, and they move you forward while your conscious brain is still processing the world of shit that you've suddenly entered. I'm running headlong down the corridor, stepping over coils of wire and ducking under low electrical cables. My legs are moving me. My brain is stuck on a loop: "Oh shit oh shit oh shit oh shit oh shit..." I had always imagined that when I was in a life-or-death situation, I would be strangely calm and luminous. I had imagined that my Buddhism would make me braver, stronger, and calmer at such a calamitous moment. But the ugly truth of that night is that it didn't. I wasn't ready to face my own death with anything resembling calm; all of my meditation, my imagined serenity, was gone. All I could think as I ran was, I don't want to die here. Over and over again. I don't want to die here.

I hit the stairwell. People are thundering down after me. On the ground floor soldiers mill about aimlessly, overloaded with weapons and clearly not knowing what to do or where to go. The older sergeants are barking orders, trying to make sense of the situation.

"Stay inside. Stay low. Squad leaders, get accountability of your people."

I head over to the doorway at one end of the barracks and find Shoe sitting down against the frame. He looks up at me with his crazy smile and says, "You know, they always taught us in school that during an earthquake you should take cover in a doorway." It seems like a great idea, so, knowing nothing else to do, I sit down beside him. There we are, sitting with our backs against the door frame, listening to the thuds and booms of incoming rounds as we watch the whole scene whirl past us. People rushing through the doorway look at us like we're crazy, and there is a sort of gallows humor to the scene. Being down low, close to the earth and pressed up against tons of concrete, gives me a profound sense of relief. I feel almost giddy in the midst of the hysteria.

Shoe and I keep looking at each other as if one of us is going to come up with a plan. Suddenly we're both grinning like idiots: Shoe's holding his M16 like he's going to shoot something and I'm crossing my arms over my chest like I'm holding a seat cushion in an airline-safety video. No armor plates, you see... we must look like a pair of fools. Tomorrow morning, guys in our unit will give us no end of grief about this sitting down in the doorway. They'll make fun of our "hiding," rib us about our "earthquake safety" during a mortar attack. But right now, we feel like the two smartest men on earth.

The first sergeant keeps coming in and out of the barracks area yelling, "Get your weapons, they're coming over the walls!" Both Shoe and I burst out laughing every time he says this. Clearly the command is just as confused as we are, shouting alarmist bullshit as if this were *The Lord of the Rings* and the Iraqis were going to scale the walls of the prison camp with ladders and siege towers. Shoe and I double up with laughter and start shouting, "They're coming over the walls!" in increasingly ridiculous imitation of the first sergeant. From now until we leave Iraq this phrase becomes our rallying cry, our secret password. Every time our superiors tell us something absurd and stupid, we whisper, "They're coming over the walls!" and remember this night.

Eventually the first sergeant comes in and stays to restore some semblance of order, his sharp voice forming an instant focal point for the confused soldiers. Shoe and I get up from our doorway and congregate around our sergeants and section leaders, who briefly jot down our names and then rush over to the TOC to give their report. Sergeant Toro waddles over under the weight of his machine gun and three huge bandoliers of ammo, in full uniform with his pant legs tucked into his boots. We all make fun of him for it later, laughing about how it's just like Sergeant Toro to take time out of a mortar attack to put on his full uniform and make sure his pant legs are tucked in, but right now we're just glad to see him. Sergeant Wallace ticks off our names with the end of his pencil and puts us down in his little yellow notebook. Lyons is missing.

Word spreads through the company; where is she? Have you seen her? We all experience a sudden cold feeling for the pretty little specialist who serves as our motor pool clerk. None of us knows where she is. Sergeant Black, her supervisor, is rushing around trying to contact her or get information on her whereabouts. After a while, word filters back that she's okay, stranded over in another part of the base when the attack began. She's fine.

A few minutes later, it's all over. The blasts have stopped and the base goes into reaction mode. Reports have to go up from each company to the base headquarters. Someone says there have been no KIAs; someone from the unit down the hall might have been wounded but no one knows for sure. Everyone in our unit is accounted for, so our medics leave for the Army clinic nearby in case anyone's been hurt. The area starts to settle down, but everyone is still jacked up on adrenaline. We get the order to keep our flak vests and helmets on and stay downstairs until the all clear signal. People start recounting where they were when the attack began and what they thought was going on. No one was scared, of course. After it's all over, everyone is a paragon of courage and bravado.

The all clear comes through and we're released for the night. It's late and we should go to bed, but we're all too excited to sleep. Shoe grabs his field jacket and heads out to the fire barrel. He stays up long after midnight, sitting and talking with a few others in hushed tones, strangely contemplative for his usual brash self. I talk to

Sergeant Toro for a while and then head back upstairs. Sitting down on my cot, I carefully place my helmet and flak vest on the shelf next to me for easy access, as will be my practice for the rest of my tour. The lights are off, but someone's TV is murmuring in the background and pulsing with harsh, white light, visible over the wooden dividers in the room. I stretch out on the hard, inflexible fabric of my Army cot and close my eyes mechanically, trying to sleep, but the events of the last hour keep playing in my head. Alone in bed, I can feel my heart still thundering in my chest and the blood rushing through my temples. It's all over now, and I'm safe, but I know that I wasn't ready, wasn't ready to die. I toss and turn and try to get comfortable, but sleep is a long way off.

Part One

HOME BY THE FOURTH OF JULY

KUWAIT CITY

MARCH 30, 2003 My war story is nothing like *Black Hawk Down*. It begins stupidly, boringly. Our giant passenger plane touches down on a landing strip on the outskirts of Kuwait City in the early morning hours. The flight was interminable, sandwiched as I am in a coach seat between one of the larger members of my company and piles of weapons and packs. Like every airline flight, it was tedious and uncomfortable, and all the gear piled around me makes me feel claustrophobic. In spite of the crowding, I managed to sleep through most of the flight. We made three long stopovers: one in Canada, one in Ireland, where we were segregated in a separate terminal watched over by armed security guards, and one in Cyprus, where we weren't allowed to leave the plane.

When we come to a stop, everyone gets up and pushes toward the doors, just as they do on commercial flights, but the passengers on this plane are soldiers in desert camouflage, carrying weapons and military gear as baggage. We're all tired and irritable and people are shuffling toward the door like zombies, their uniforms undone, dragging their packs and weapons behind them. I shuffle into the line. Before we disembark, the pilot's voice on the intercom deviates from the usual script, suddenly slow and deliberate with emotion: "On behalf of myself and all the crew, it's been a pleasure flying all you guys. Get the job done and come back home safe to us. We'll all be praying for you." It's touching. I feel his genuine care and affection, his pride. I reach the door. The flight attendant looks at me and at all of us with a tenderness and sincerity that is striking compared with the usual phony farewells. She is very young and very pretty. As we pass, she touches each of us on the hand or shoulder and mumbles something encouraging. It's sweet, even motherly, and it calms me down. I take a deep breath and let it out, closing my eyes and trying to center myself, as has been my custom since leaving Cairo, more than three years earlier. I shoulder my bags and step out the door into the night air of Kuwait.

There is a smell to the desert and desert cities, and it hits me full in the face. The air is dry and fragrant, harsh with sand and fine dust. The smell is somehow comforting, familiar. This is not the first time I've been to Kuwait City: I came here a handful of times in high school, when I lived in Cairo as the son of an American diplomat, seemingly a lifetime ago. The airport is the same—the same low buildings and the distant greenish glow of the deserted terminal—and the smell is the same. The Middle East, the desert, Cairo, they all smell the same, and it reminds me of home, of happier days. The airport is completely deserted, or perhaps we're just in an isolated section. I walk down the exit ramp, tottering under my two large bags, flak vest, and heavy machine gun. We assemble beneath the nose of the plane and a detail is selected to unpack the cargo hold. I volunteer, hoping to start the deployment by making a good impression on my superiors. We spend a good forty-five minutes in the plane's underbelly, heaving duffle after duffle down onto the tarmac. The work is close and strenuous, and the cargo hold is soon steamy with our sweat and grunted curses. In a way it's welcome, though; the methodical nature of the task helps me get my mind off things. When we finally finish, the night air feels cold and crisp on our soaking uniforms.

We wait around for at least another hour before several small Kuwaiti buses arrive, their windows tinted and curtained for our safety while we drive through the city. I remember the same small charter buses taking me to the American School of Kuwait for a trivia tournament in middle school; goddamn, everything is so familiar, it's eerie. We pack ourselves in and depart, peeking out through the black curtains as we traverse downtown Kuwait City and then the barren desert roads. It truly is the witching hour: long after midnight but too soon for dawn. The city is deathly quiet. We don't pass a single car and no one on the bus talks much. No one knows exactly where we're going, either; we just know it's some U.S. military base in the middle of nowhere. I relax back into my seat and let the memories flood over me. I let myself go back, back to Cairo, to the Middle East . . . to the desert . . .

Tonight I'm in Kuwait City again, but I'm no longer a student. I'm not carrying my backpack and homework. No trivia games await me. My old friends are gone. I'm a soldier now; under my feet is a duffel bag and at my side a belt-fed machine gun. I've come to join the war. We're not supposed to be here long; they say it will all be over quickly, we'll be back before the end of summer. This bus will take me to a military base, and from there into Iraq. The memory of Kuwait City seems timeless and distant, as if it had happened to some other boy, some other Aidan in another universe. How have I come here, to this moment? The last time I saw these streets, I was just a kid with acne and a bad haircut and glasses pushed up high on my face. Now I'm a young man, fully grown, in desert camouflage, still with a bad haircut, one of 140 soldiers in the 320th Military Police Company. Yet I'm *here,* on the very same streets, on the very same buses. I feel the circularity of it, the deeply unsettling feeling of my destiny curving in front of me, bending back on itself like a Möbius strip. I've returned, back to the very point I started at more than eight years ago.

The bus ride lasts more than an hour. What I remember most about it is the wind. I am leaning against my duffle bag, looking out through a crack in the curtains as the bright city lights recede farther and farther into the distance. The window in front of me won't close all the way, so the wind creeps in and blows uncomfortably cold in my face. As it passes through the narrow opening, it makes a whistling noise that's hypnotic. I remember the sound of that wind, rising and falling in shrill peaks as we head out into the night.

CAMP WOLVERINE, KUWAIT

The bus unloads us at the forward base just before dawn. After an endless series of "orientations," we are finally dismissed to find our way to the tents assigned to us. Ours is large, supported by a line of poles running down the center, with a wooden floor and two flaps for entrances on each side. The interior of the tent is a dusty yellow and lit with a trio of fluorescent lights dangling from each of the support poles. The flaps do little to keep out the desert, and inside the tent is hazy with dust and the body heat of over a hundred soldiers. Once inside, everyone collapses onto piles of their gear and most are fast asleep in minutes. I find it difficult to relax in the stifling interior of the tent and my mind is racing, so I borrow a sheet of paper, take out one of my many pens, and begin to compose my first letter home.

> *Dear Amy,*
>
> *I'm writing to you from a tent in Kuwait. We touched down at 0200 in the morning and unloaded all our gear. We then proceeded to a replacement station where we are waiting to be sent out to various camps . . . At the moment I'm reclining on a dusty piece of plywood inside a dull yellow tent with 140 other soldiers. Things are very quiet and each seems absorbed in their own thoughts. Most are dozing or trying to shut out the light and the dust by burrowing under their equipment. Yet I am wide awake . . .*

Amy . . . I miss her. It's been weeks since I last saw her. Brown skin, brown eyes, black hair . . . I have a picture of her in my helmet, the soldier's oldest good-luck charm. She's Indian, raised in a traditional family from a small, remote province on the country's eastern border, sheltered from the outside world. I've been a world traveler most of my life, but she comes from a place I've never heard of, and this intrigues me. I make a big deal of it, even though she was born in the States and unlike myself has spent her entire life there. We've been together more than a year, but for much of that time we've been separated because of my military training. She's reserved, studious, shy. We're both in college and I'm her first boyfriend. Now, against her will, she's wrapped up in the drama of this war as much as I am. She cried softly when I left, but tried not to let me see. I imagine her holding this letter, straining at it, trying to understand my chicken scratch. Already the word "reclining" is an undecipherable mass, unreadable to anyone but me. I hold the pen straighter and try to concentrate on my handwriting.

> *I am struck by my sudden similarity to a newsreel. The base camp, the blank expressions, the dusty armed figures milling about all could have been ripped from any CNN update. It seems strangely familiar. It was a pleasure to hear Arabic again and a comfort to remember the vastness of the open desert. Our plane's trajectory took us directly over Cairo, giving Iraqi airspace a wide berth, and I recognized the tiny lights of the city I had flown to so many times before. Somewhere far below, my friends in Cairo lay asleep and I continued on...*

After writing these lines, I get up and decide to accompany some of my company in hunting up some breakfast. Thinking of the first sergeant and his hawklike vigilance for uniform infractions, I reconsider breakfast and decide to try my hand at shaving. For some reason, I mark this moment as the real beginning of my deployment; not getting off the plane or arriving at the base or even entering Iraq, but this, sitting on a sandbag outside our tent, trying to shave with a bottle of water and a canteen cup. (It's probably because that's the only time I shaved during my military career without having been directly ordered to do so.) I do a rush job, enough so I can probably slip by the first sergeant at long range, and hurry after the group that went for breakfast.

We file into a cavernous tent staffed with Kuwaiti cooks and workers and go down the assembly line, heaping our paper trays with pancakes, potato wedges, scrambled eggs, and milk boxes, mango juice instead of orange juice. All the typical American breakfast foods are there but the taste is just slightly off, the eggs a slightly grayish color, and I don't get much pleasure out of breakfast. It doesn't help that I've recently become a vegetarian and am just getting used to life without meat. After breakfast, I hurry back to my company tent to finish my letter home.

Went and retrieved chemical gear and put it in my laundry bag for easy access. Sign seen in mess tent: "There will be no more Scud exercises. The next time you hear the alert it will be for real." Got a kick out of that . . .

In the unit, we joke about everything, and laugh off most of the threat of Iraqi forces. The one thing we never joke about is NBC: nuclear, biological, and chemical weapons. A few terrifying, graphic briefings before we left the States gave us an enormous respect for these. "Your protective mask won't filter out blood agents." Our eyes get wide. "If a nerve agent hits, you have about thirty seconds to give yourself the antidote before you're incapacitated." Oh, and by the way, the antidote is a two-inch needle you have to stick into your own thigh and it will only keep you alive for a short while before they get you to a hospital. Even at this first base camp, we all are imminently aware of the possibility of chemical attack, and carry our chemical suits and masks with us wherever we go, even to the showers. After all, the president had assured us that Iraq had a massive arsenal of chemical and biological weapons.

Don't know what I'm feeling about this deployment yet, very calm and collected for the moment but morale always comes and goes. Not stressed at all but that will change when we actually get our mission and get down to business . . .

Only has been a few days and already I miss your voice. I am sorry we didn't get to speak before I left. Feeling a little tired so I will adjourn for a short nap and continue writing afterwards. Hope to mail this out by evening.

I shove the unfinished letter in my hip pocket to finish later that day but I don't get the chance. Our instructions have come down unusually fast—we're moving out. By evening, we've been loaded onto buses heading for the largest coalition base in Kuwait and our last stop before the front.

CAMP ARIFJAN, KUWAIT

MARCH 31, 2003 Camp Arifjan is a complete change of scene from the makeshift tents of Wolverine. This is a serious place. They say that this is a Kuwaiti military base being lent for the war effort, and we see occasional signs of the previous occupants, and a mysterious cordoned-off area for the Kuwaiti military. The scale of Arifjan is truly enormous. A four-lane highway divides it into sections, with a separate housing area for each of the nations of the Coalition. The transit from the perimeter of the base to our housing area takes at least half an hour. As we rumble along the gravel service roads we catch glimpses of the overall structure of the place. It is a massive collection of corrugated steel warehouses and portable concrete barriers. Inside the metal buildings, troops are packed tightly. The base is a clearinghouse for all the troops entering Iraq, and tens of thousands must be processed through en route to the war. There are construction crews everywhere, laying power and sewage lines and dealing with every other necessity. Massive renovations are under way; the base seems to be expanding.

Arifjan is drab and sand-colored but otherwise not so different from the barracks life back home. Concessions to our comfort have been made. Inside the dining hall, they serve ice cream, and lobster or crab on alternate nights. A shame; I used to love lobster but I'm a vegetarian now. The guys get a good joke out of my two grilled cheese sandwiches and bowl of cauliflower next to their snow crab legs or surf and turf. Lucky bastards, I laugh, and drizzle my pale cauliflower in steak sauce. This is not so bad, we say to one another, I wonder how long we'll be staying? We quickly adjust to sharing a hangar bay with five hundred other soldiers, picking our way between the closely spaced cots with a flashlight after dark. The line to get into lunch is an hour to two hours long, depending on how early you arrive. The trick is to go to meals before you're hungry, knowing that by the time you get in you will be starved. Near the dining hall, there is a haphazard collection of fabricated buildings run by the locals and Army contractors: souvenirs, pizza, coffee shops, barbers, and tailors, all the usual businesses that follow in the wake of the military. We spend countless hours strolling up and down their shelves, examining the same inventory and stocking up on cheap souvenirs. Everyone must get an official pack of Saddam playing cards and requisite Operation Iraqi Freedom T-shirts and cigarette lighters.

We're sitting in the cafeteria, dozing or chatting during our welcome briefing, paying little attention to the base commander and his overly theatrical sergeant major. They've been haranguing us for more than an hour, outlining the rules of the camp: no drinking, no leaving base, no going anywhere without your gas mask, no . . . and most of us are bored and sleepy after a large lunch. They literally have just finished reviewing the procedure for a Scud attack when the camp loudspeakers crackle to life and blare: "LIGHTNING, LIGHTNING, LIGHTNING," the signal for an incoming missile. Instantly the cafeteria erupts in chaos. With one enormous sound of ripping Velcro, soldiers tear open their hip bags, reaching for their gas masks and fumbling into their protective suits. I remember having read in some book that 80 percent of all last words are "Oh shit," and those are exactly the words that cross my mind. Something like a hallucination flits over me, and I visualize a shell breaching the roof, bursting, me breathing in mouthfuls of yellow gas, doubling over and bleeding from the mouth. I blank out for a second, frozen in place, and only a nudge from my sergeant jerks me back to reality. I see across the table from me that the infamous leech of our company, the woman who can't do anything or be trusted with anything, has forgotten her mask and is struggling with another soldier, trying to take his mask from him. I spare a second to think, That bitch, and then everything goes blurry as I throw off my glasses and cinch my mask down around my face. Struggling into my chemical suit, I stumble after my sergeant and throw myself against the cafeteria wall for additional cover. As I finish securing my suit in place, I suddenly feel a deep, cold hardness in my stomach as I realize that I have forgotten my protective gloves. Desperate, I thrust my hands up into the sleeves of my jacket and stand as close to my sergeant as possible, in case he knows what to do. The world outside my foggy lens seems like it's under water; the corrective inserts for my mask haven't arrived yet, and without my glasses I'm blind. The walls are plastered with blurry green figures, looking ominous and ghostlike in their face masks and hazmat suits. We're all waiting for the sound. No one breathes.

Long minutes later we receive the all clear signal; the missile struck Kuwait but missed us by miles. That was the thing with Scuds: deadly but entirely inaccurate, especially when fired by the ill-trained Iraqi army. We breathe a collective sigh of relief and pry off our sweat-soaked masks. When I have my glasses on again I can see that people are dressed in an odd patchwork of protective gear, some without their hoods, gloves, or boots. Many soldiers are sniffling and red-faced, their cheeks streaked with dirt and tears and sweat. I look out at this motley assortment and realize that it's just an ordinary crowd, frightened and disordered, panicked. *Panic*: the word rings ominous in my mind, the antithesis of our training, the one thing soldiers are not supposed to do, are trained *not* to do. The supremely disciplined and professional units of the United States Army dissolved into a hysterical mass at the first sign of danger. I have to laugh, mostly at myself and my preconceptions about being part of an invincible tide. But in truth I feel acutely mortal and frightened, made more so by the fact that obviously everyone around me is frightened too. I never want to be part of that mass again, the instant chaos of one thousand people gone mad with self-preservation. My thoughts go back to that female soldier in our company, the person who can't seem to do anything right, the one who'd tried to take another soldier's mask. It's the first of many revelations about who we are as an army. People eventually collect themselves and disperse to go about their duties, but after today we all take the gas-mask order very seriously.

We relax. We do our laundry. We spend the long, hot afternoons dozing on our cots or taking three-hour lunches as we wait for more orders. No one seems to know what's going to happen in the next few days. The military police (MPs) begin cleaning their weapons obsessively, over and over, until every speck of carbon has been polished and ground out of the barrels. Then they do it again. A detail of younger soldiers is called over to begin loading magazines, hundreds of magazines for pistols and M16s. I spend the better part of a day breaking open boxes of pistol and rifle rounds and pressing them into magazines until my fingers are raw.

Then we get the word. Not definite yet, but good enough. We have a date and a mission: we're finally going over. The unit is electrified with fear, adrenaline, and rampant speculation. People begin making those last little adjustments: tying back the straps on their vests, double-checking their weapon sights, making sure their first-aid patch is still attached, writing their blood type on their boots, tucking dog tags under the laces. I pull out the letter I began to Amy, now crumpled and creased, and scribble out the last few pages so I can mail it before we leave.

> *Sorry it's been more than a day since I last worked on this letter but things have been moving really fast. We already moved to a different camp and got some additional anthrax shots. I decided to cut my long letter-writing short and get this out right away because we've just received word that we're going to the front on Friday. Just like that everyone has started packing bags and loading weapons. I am being sent forward with the first group because of my dubious Arabic ability of which I grow more doubtful day by day. I reviewed a book of the Iraqi dialect and discovered that it is 95% different than the [Egyptian] Arabic I am somewhat familiar with. Yet I am still going as a sort of "translator" on this mission.*

I had received notice that we would be sending a small group over the border to set up operations at the base camp, and that I would be given the questionable honor of being part of this "advance party." Our elderly platoon sergeant came over to my bunk, tapped me on the shoulder, and said, "Delgado, you're going on Friday along with Stevens and Sergeant Toro." Those words made me want to vomit. I was so excited and nervous that I couldn't get a bite down all that day. I instantly became the envy of all the young guys in the unit, who to a man were dying to "go over" and get into the action. My fellow mechanic Schumacher—Shoe—was so jealous I thought he would burst from indignation; HE wanted to go, HE was ready, HE was dying for this. Honestly, as excited as I was about finally seeing the grand spectacle, I would have been happy to let him go in my place. But it was a foregone conclusion; we had seven mechanics but only one person in the company spoke a word of Arabic.

I had become a victim of my own big mouth; when rumors of war had broken out back at the Reserve center in St. Petersburg,

I had unthinkingly volunteered the information that I spent my middle school and high school years in Cairo, seven years in all, and knew something of Arabic. It was an offhand comment that would later return to haunt me. What I knew was a mixture of slang, Egyptian idioms, and street Arabic that had served me well enough to get around Cairo, but I had no idea how it would fare on the streets of Iraq. Still, I was one of two in the entire battalion that could speak or understand the language at all. Back at Fort Stewart, the first sergeant ordered me to put together an impromptu Arabic-language course for the unit. I tried, but to them the words and sounds I conjured up were so much gibberish. After the language class even my superiors treated me with a certain grudging respect, realizing that Arabic was no easy subject. The attention had given me a brief sense of superiority, but now as we drew closer to the actual test my confidence was rapidly evaporating.

> *As the man next to me grimly pointed out: every convoy into this region of Iraq has met enemy resistance. I am pretty nervous about this whole "going to the front thing," as you might imagine.*

I remember the circumstances in which I wrote this. It was during the infamous "threat briefing" the night before we crossed the border. What a presentation that was; one for the history books. Master Sergeant Carlson gathered the six or seven of us from Headquarters Platoon that were going over and had us stand around in a semicircle just outside the barracks. He pulled out a little camouflage flip-book and began reading us the "intel" passed down from command and Military Intelligence: Possibly up to five thousand explosive-laden white pickup trucks coming down from Baghdad. Possibly. An unknown number of Iraqi military units. An unknown number of partisans and civilian militia, possibly in white pickup trucks. An unknown number of suicide bombers. "Every convoy going up so far has gotten hit, so there's a very high chance of enemy contact." Absolutely no idea who or what the enemy might be, though. Approximately forty-five seconds into this exercise I folded up my own little camouflage notebook and stopped trying to take notes. There was nothing to note. It was obvious that Military Intelligence had not the foggiest idea what the conditions were or what we might be facing once we crossed the border. They were just conjecturing. There was no intel to report, not a smoke signal, not a fucking clue. Don't take that for bravado; I wasn't laughing. I was scared, we all were. I remember watching the white-haired master sergeant's hands trembling as he read each line of the intel report, and then how his eyes would dart up and travel around the circle, looking at each man apologetically. After he finished he wished us a good night, told us to be ready at 0530 on Friday, and wandered off as if in daze, as if he himself couldn't quite believe the briefing he'd just given.

Most of our little group hung around in a knot for a while after the briefing, talking each other up, trying to work through our jitters. Unknown everything? Every convoy got hit? Shit, I better try to call home tonight. No, the lines are too goddamn long, takes like three hours to get ten minutes on the phone. Almost everyone goes outside to smoke or walk off their nerves. I go back to my cot and lie down. Shit... five-thirty Friday morning.

I wanted to write and tell you right away because I heard mail takes a long time to get there. I still don't have an address so you can't write me till I send you another letter, which I will as soon as possible.

I know this news is going to upset Amy; she'll be more scared than I am. I hate doing it to her, and the military always tells you to write nice letters home so that you don't put your loved ones through hell, but somehow I just can't bring myself to censor my own letters. I want Amy to know what's really going on with me, because that's what I'd want if I were in her place. I know she's going to take it hard, though.

I'm heading into the thickest part of things and I wanted to write and tell you one more time that I love you and not an hour passes that I don't dream of being with you. I love you so much. I will write again when I can.

Truest line I ever wrote. I think about her in every quiet moment and fantasize about coming home; her absence feels like a physical knot in my stomach. I talk about her constantly until all the guys in the motor pool are sick of hearing about her, just as I am sick of hearing about their girls.

I was never much for writing letters, and even this seven-page handwritten one has taxed my patience. I don't have the will to write a separate one to everyone back home. I give up, I surrender, let Amy send them a copy. Hope the letter reaches her soon so she'll have something of mine to hold on to. I seal the envelope, mark it "free postage," and sign the return address as "Mission Top Secret, Destination Unknown, don't even know if we're ever coming home," a line from an old army cadence that seems poetically appropriate. On my way to the phone center, I drop it in the mail slot.

It's midnight inside Camp Arifjan, and I am unable to sleep. I get out of bed, strap on my gas-mask bag, and paw around for my red-lens flashlight. Using the light, I try to maneuver my way through the dense rows of cots and not bump into anyone on my way to the bathroom. I fail. Every two steps I whisper, "Sorry, sorry..." and hear muffled curses wafting up from the sleeping bags: "Goddamn it, I'm trying to sleep..." and "Watch where you're going!" I make it to the exit on the corner of the building and step out into the open air. I hobble to the bathroom in my plastic shower shoes and wander around for ten minutes trying to find my way back to the right warehouse, Number 10, I believe.

Just outside the entrance to our barracks, I pause and lean against the bunker of sandbags that has been constructed for cover in case of air attack. They are elegant little structures: functional arcs of concrete covered in a layer of new, tan sandbags. They look like they would be pretty safe in the event of a Scud attack, but mostly people use them as places to smoke or have clandestine sex. I take a seat on the outside of the bunker, my feet dangling over the side.

There's a fresh breeze blowing in from the sea; I can smell the salt. There are no lights on outside, blackout conditions for wartime, and the skyline of the base stands out in sharp contrast. Here in the desert, far away from the light pollution of the city, the stars seem unusually sharp and clear, brilliant even. Not a sound on the whole base and no one else awake that I can see. Just me, out here by myself, sitting on these sandbags. For the first time since arriving in the Middle East, I feel totally calm, passive, focused. I'm happiest when I'm out here alone, away from the bitching and the hierarchy, with no one demanding my attention. The panic of Fort Stewart is gone, the feelings of inadequacy, the "I'm not going to be able to deal with this"—gone. I feel intensely, undeservingly peaceful. The breeze washes over me, shockingly cool after the humid air of the barracks. At this moment, leaning against a wall of sandbags in my T-shirt and shorts, it is impossible to visualize a war going on around me or conceive of the possibility that I might have to join it soon. Everything seems remote and serene, as if Iraq and all the bullshit of the Army were a million miles away.

The morning of our departure comes suddenly and rudely, with a sergeant staring down at me, shaking me vigorously, jerking me out of my cocoon. Groggily, I and the others headed for the front dress and begin to fold up our cots, trying to make as much noise and commotion as possible for the benefit of all the bastards not going. If we're not going to get any sleep, neither are they. We load our bags into the few trucks and Humvees designated for the mission and then we wait for the final checks and clearances before we can leave base and cross the border. Our friends and fellows have all gotten up to shake hands one more time and slap us on our backs, wishing us good luck and good hunting, once more unto the breach, dear friends, and all that ... As the convoy begins to lurch forward I wave a last farewell to those staying behind and see Shoe scowling with envy. The trail of vehicles rumbles out the main gate and onto the near-deserted highway. Kuwaiti street signs direct us north, getting less and less frequent until abruptly the street signs end.

KUWAIT-IRAQ BORDER, DEMILITARIZED ZONE

APRIL 4, 2003 Iraq looms ahead in the distance, just over a double wall of pressed earth and razor wire. Here it is at last. The sun is just beginning to rise as we pass the small checkpoint manned by Kuwaiti soldiers. There are a few small tanks and armored personnel carriers parked nearby, U.S.-designed vehicles stamped with the crossed swords and palm, the seal of the Kuwaiti royal family. The Kuwaiti soldiers seem relaxed and nonchalant, lounging around in no great number. They smile and wave us on without stopping us. We roll past an earth wall, then a wide, deep trench extending out to both sides, then the chain-link fence topped with razor wire; one more rammed-earth barrier and we're over the border, we're in Iraq proper now. Was that all it was? I had been expecting some kind of overture, some thunder or flashes of lightning as we entered "enemy territory." Nothing but an absolutely still and placid desert morning. As we pass through the invisible line separating Kuwait and Iraq, I nudge my way over to the rear of the truck bed and lean out with my disposable camera to snap a picture of the border crossing, for posterity.

Looking out over the crossing I am struck by how the sun has risen high enough to illuminate the tiny figures of men and tanks in silhouette over the wall. It's an incredible sight, stark and beautiful. I frantically snap several pictures from the back of the moving truck, but I will manage to capture none of the striking qualities of this sight. When I look them over more than two years later, I will smile at these terrible, pedestrian photos of a sun peeking out over a mound of dirt, because I will remember how awe-inspiring the scene was in person. As the border grows smaller and smaller in the distance, I put my tiny camera back into my vest pocket and resume my place as a side gunner. For the first time since Fort Stewart, I pull a belt of ammunition from the green drum underneath me and lock the first round into place, then pull back the bolt and let it slam forward, chambering the round. My shoulder settles on the stock, and I place the weight of my helmeted head against the rear sight. For the first time since training, my finger settles on the trigger of a fully loaded machine gun, its safety off.

The morning remains cool and overcast for the first few hours of our journey into southern Iraq. I scan the horizon obsessively. My first impression of the country is that it isn't so much a desert as a scrub wasteland. There are none of the dunes and open stretches of sand we had expected but rather a barren expanse dotted with bushes and stunted trees. A checkerboard of little two-lane asphalt roads seems to branch off everywhere and trail away into the bleak plain. The whole landscape seems scarred: pockmarked with trenches, dry canals, and stubby hills. Even this far south, just miles from the border, we spot wrecked and ruined Iraqi tanks, perhaps relics from the first Gulf War, lying gutted by the side of the road. Here and there we see more-modern ordnance, artillery and anti-aircraft guns, still recognizable although twisted and burned. Our apprehension intensifies as we note that the ground around these machines is still black and scorched: recent kills. My hand tightens on the stock of my weapon. I hadn't expected to see signs of the fighting this far south. The tension is overwhelming, physical. I wish I were in the same vehicle with Sergeant Toro and Stevens. Somehow it would be easier if my fellow mechanics were nearby. I'm in a truck with people that I don't know very well.

A few brave Iraqis are still on the roads; an occasional bus or cargo truck passes us by, the occupants giving us either a solemn nod or a halfhearted thumbs-up. Every vehicle displays a prominent white cloth or handkerchief signifying noncombatant status. I am fascinated by these convoys, these crowded vehicles, white rags fluttering from every window and antenna. An old wreck of a bus coughs and splutters its way alongside us, its rusty orange frame packed to bursting with passengers and luggage. For a moment we are traveling side by side, the gaps in the canvas covering of our truck and the barrels of our weapons eye to eye with the windows of the bus. We're sitting in the middle of the truck bed on our duffel bags, our rifles facing outward as we look directly across at the Iraqis. Scanning these faces as they linger beside us, I see a whole cross-section of Iraqi society: from white-bearded old men to handsome teenagers to frowning middle-aged women wrapped head to toe in black. The younger men in particular seem to be excited by our presence and wave or point; the older people are more reserved, sitting back in their seats and at most nodding slightly when I make eye contact. Their faces are inscrutable, crisscrossed with age and hard life. I long to see one of those weathered faces break into a smile. At every opportunity, I bow my head slightly, in accordance with Arabic custom, mumbling *Sabaah al- heer*—good morning, literally, "morning of bounty"—more to myself than to them, to get back into the feel and rhythm of the language. They seem not to notice me.

The Iraqis appear unconcerned, going about their daily business and travels, a small white handkerchief their sole concession to being in a war zone. Most are old enough to have lived through the Gulf War, and some had experienced the ruinous Iran-Iraq War. I marvel at their casualness, their aloofness, as my stomach churns and boils with fear. I wonder if war has become so routine for them that it has ceased to be noteworthy, or perhaps they are just too poor and desperate to care. No, that's not it, it's something else, a disinterest, a kind of blank resignation.

Their seeming passivity and disregard for danger reminds me of something I saw over and over again during my years in Cairo: fatalism. When a car broke down, the driver would often attempt repairs in the middle of traffic as other cars swerved around him.

Egyptian friends explained to me that such individuals believed that God had stopped their car exactly at that spot, that it was pointless to oppose the will of God. People sidestepped between speeding cars and took terrible risks in their everyday lives, secure in the belief that if it was not their time, they would not be injured, and that if they *were* fated to die that day, no amount of caution on their part would prevent it.

I see that same stoicism, that same acceptance, in the expressions of the Iraqis around me. Something I will always remember about that long ride north, in the first weeks of the Iraq war, is the sense of symmetry: the faces I had seen slipping between cars in Cairo were now staring back at me out of bus windows, resigned to their destiny.

The trip wears on, the sun climbs to its zenith, and the heat becomes irritating at first, then uncomfortable, and finally stifling. We haven't seen anything hostile: no soldiers, no explosives-laden vans, just a few buses of Iraqi civilians and the occasional family car. Tension and wariness give way to monotony and eventually to boredom. We begin to sag against each other or half-doze, our heads drooping against our gun sights. My helmet in particular is plaguing me. Every soldier has a few favorite padding materials and tricks for easing the discomfort. The Kevlar, as we call it, weighs several pounds, and over a long ride these few pounds become very heavy. Mine begins to weigh on me, producing a throbbing headache that vibrates in time with the thrum of the engine. My head sags forward, the brim of my helmet resting on the stock of my machine gun. Periodically someone reaches over and taps me. "Keep your head up Delgado, stay awake." I am awake, too awake. Sweat begins to roll down my shirt in the space under my vest, which I have surreptitiously loosened, in defiance of procedure. They say the flak vest raises your body temperature by ten degrees. I'm burning up, nauseous and sleepy at the same time. The solid mass of the helmet insulates my head, making it even hotter. The truck's suspension and the action of the powerful diesel engine cause the vehicle to vibrate, rattling me down to my bones. The misery begins to set in. Somewhere among these moments, during this timeless crawl, I realize that I will be spending several months in this place, and the feeling is like being tied to a boulder at the edge of a precipice. For a moment the rope is slack and you can almost believe that you're safe, but then the rope snaps taut and you know that you're falling, being pulled inexorably downward by forces beyond your control. You are utterly helpless. There is no escape.

Evening finally comes and dusk falls like a blessing. The heat recedes, but we're still hours from our destination. The convoy commander had figured conservatively, not wanting to chance a night run through southern Iraq. We will hole up for the night at a military checkpoint called Navstar, little more than a patch of desert fenced off with concrete barriers. The dust inside the barriers has been churned and stirred by so many vehicles that it is now powder-fine and ankle deep. The evening winds sweep it up into everything: our clothes, mouths, and eyes. Soon we are coated in it. By the time the vehicles come to a halt, we are all exhausted past talking and our first thought is sleep. We can't leave the vehicles and there isn't space to set up cots or tents so we shove our duffel bags to the side and curl up in the bed of the truck. I spend the most uncomfortable, sleepless night of my life in that truck. I am sandwiched between two other soldiers: Kosinski on my left and the fearsome Sergeant JP on my right, dreaded matriarch of the clerical section. I lie as still as possible in the truck, terrified that I will bump her or disturb her and so provoke her wrath. Both are still total strangers to me and here we lie, so close it would have been intimate under any other circumstances. I finally manage a slightly less uncomfortable position atop my duffel bag and succumb in the predawn hours to sheer exhaustion.

In the morning, the trucks churn up another coating of dust as the entire convoy revs its engines. Before leaving we cut open our Meals Ready-to-Eat (MREs) and I enjoy the first of many Cheese

Tortellinis. At this point, field rations are still a novelty and mostly we enjoy them and their curious preparation. I am less enthused about the MREs, because there are only four vegetarian flavors and one of them is exceedingly vile: the untradable Pasta with Alfredo Sauce. Over the next few months I will come to so loathe these four flavors that I will never touch another MRE again, no matter how desperately hungry.

The second half of our journey is not substantially different from the first, save that we are all now thirsty, exhausted, and irritable from lack of sleep. We are down to our last few water bottles and the bottles that remain offer little refreshment; they are hot as tea and brackish. Everyone is on edge now, ground down by all the petty annoyances and discomforts. JP seems to be simmering at a low boil, making everyone wary. We sit in defeated silence for hours.

As we near the end of our journey we suddenly glimpse an enormous mud-brick pyramid looming on the horizon. It is the Ziggurat at Ur, a temple from Babylonian times, built to honor the god Sin. The ziggurat is named Etemennigur, meaning "the house whose foundation creates terror." The imposing structure rises atop a steep plateau commanding the plain, visible for miles around in any direction. We turn off the main road and head onto an unpaved desert track passing within a half-mile of the monument, and from this distance we can see tiny figures—later we would learn they were our own Special Forces—moving atop it. Our destination lies in the ziggurat's shadow.

Part Two

ETEMENNIGUR

TALLIL AIRBASE, SOUTHERN IRAQ

APRIL 5, 2003 We arrive at the main gate of Tallil, passing an Iraqi kiosk peddling sodas, knock-off watches, and brands of candy we've never heard of. Just past the gates, our convoy takes the first right and parks in a sun-drenched vacant lot between two clusters of buildings. The base has the feel of a frontier encampment or ghost town; all of the buildings are crumbling and broken, cobbled together in no real order as if they had never been designed to be permanent. Everywhere, paint and plaster are sloughed away by the desert, leaving bare concrete exposed. Coalition forces had captured Tallil only a few weeks earlier, and the base is still a disordered wreck. Garbage and debris are strewn across every street and field, scattered by the wind. Fine dust swirls across the landscape, stirred by invisible siroccos. In the middle distance, we can see the unmistakable peaks of green Army tents and clusters of olive drab vehicles: other units. Camouflage netting punctuates the nondescript architecture, springing up between vehicles and off the sides of buildings like dusty green cobwebs. Everyone is eager to get out and stretch their legs after the cramped journey. The convoy commander and the other senior staff dismount from our trucks to await further instructions.

The concrete is hot, even hotter than the trucks, and it reflects sunlight onto us. Water is passed around and everyone tries to drink but it's too hot for more than a mouthful. The command emerges to tell us that we'll be stationed right across the street, in a former Iraqi barracks. The building is underwhelming: two squat stories of white-daubed cement, every window shattered, a pair of Swiss-cheese doors hanging on a hinge. The ground in front of the barracks has been plowed in neat rows like a vegetable garden, and a rank assortment of weeds and stunted palms grows amid the furrows. It looks like a parody of a small farm. We begin slowly unloading our bags and weapons and piling them along a covered walkway that leads to the barracks entrance. We snap to it only when the first sergeant's voice rings out: "Get your shit and get inside!"

I am waddling toward the entrance of the base under the weight of two heavy duffle bags and my own weapons and armor when I hear a sudden commotion behind me. I turn and see Morida, a stocky Asian with a crew cut and a pencil mustache, struggling with his bags and making odd noises. His friends are crowding around him and asking if he is all right. His eyes take on a glassy look and he suddenly collapses, vomiting thick white mucus all over the front of his vest. His head lolls back as dozens of hands swarm over him and begin to unfasten his vest and jacket. "Get back." "Give him some air." He is unconscious before his head comes to rest on the fine Iraqi dust. Damn, just like that, he falls right in front of my eyes. The heat really is that dangerous: drink too little and you faint straightaway, too much and you sweat out all your salt and get sick anyway.

I struggle through the doors and up a flight of collapsing stairs. I hope Morida's okay, but the journey has taken its toll; right now all I can think about is getting inside before all the best rooms are taken.

The motor pool takes the room on the end, the last room on the left side of the second floor. There is a good two inches of sand on the floor when we arrive, intermingled with shards of broken glass from the nearby window frame. An unbearable reek emanates from the small room. The first hours of my war are spent meticulously sweeping the floor with a palm frond and my hands. We bring up sealed boxes of rations and the precious crates of bottled water, one crate per room. The day is a blur of carrying and fetching, moving and unloading as we go through the routines of setting up a temporary home. Weapons, food, and supplies all have to be secured and counted and most of our equipment hasn't even arrived yet. As evening falls, Sergeant Toro, Stevens, and I unfold our green canvas and aluminum cots and unfurl our sleeping bags over them. After a day of punishing light and heat, dusk comes suddenly and completely.

The first night is inky and starless. Our small room is bathed in eerie colors: green glow-sticks, the blue flames of our small water heater, and red-lens flashlights. The three of us sit facing each other, our bunks pressed against the walls. Stevens is making coffee while we talk in low, hushed voices. Stevens has been collecting tiny packets of coffee grounds from each ration and hoarding them in a plastic bag he keeps bundled up in his rucksack along with packets of sugar and nondairy creamer. He breaks them out now, emptying each packet with enormous care into his steel canteen cup. His weathered machinist's hands tremble as he places the cup on the metal prongs of the heater, where it teeters precariously. As the water starts to bubble he squats beside the heater and slowly stirs the cup's contents, like an old-world craftsman or an alchemist.

In his late thirties, Stevens has already lived a full and hard life. The deployment doesn't seem to faze him. He seems as much at home in this little room in southern Iraq as he did back in Sarasota. Now and then the flames of the heater illuminate his craggy face and he is smiling in pure joy, revealing missing teeth. He offers to share his coffee packets and expend some of the precious gas in his heater to make us each a cup, and Sergeant Toro and I accept with honor. I have never been much for coffee but I hold out my cup eagerly, knowing what those little packets mean to him. When the coffee arrives it is black and frothing with tiny undissolved crystals of sugar, scalding hot, fragrant with hospitality. As the three of us sip it together we talk in muted tones of home, of our wives and girlfriends, of cheerful, familiar things.

As we relax, the talk turns to our expectations for the deployment, how long we think we'll be here, whether we'll see fighting or not, how long it will take to overthrow Saddam. We are all in agreement that the war will be over in less than six months and we'll probably be rotated out once the fighting's done. We keep repeating this like a mantra, as if saying it often will ensure that it happens, six months . . . six months . . . It's something we can hold on to, and talking about it makes me feel better. Both Stevens and Sergeant Toro are much older men than I, and hearing them talk about the deployment in concrete terms is calming. They've both been in the military for more than ten years and seem accustomed to the routines, and Stevens was deployed during the Gulf War. I've only been to the weekend drills since I left training. I haven't even gone on a field exercise with the unit yet, so I'm still one of the new guys. I speak a little Arabic, I know the Middle East, I can quote volumes of literature and religion, but I'm no soldier yet. It's nice to have people around me who know what they're doing and can look out for me. That night I actually feel pretty good about the deployment. It feels like everything will be all right.

That first night we leave the windows uncovered to allow a little bit of breeze into the room. This is a grave mistake. Instead of a fresh wind, the open window admits a gale of sand and dust, burying us in our sleeping bags. We awaken in the middle of the night to a quarter inch of dirt covering us where we sleep.

The next morning, it is unclear what we're supposed to do. The military police in the unit will be assigned to work at the prison camp on base and some of us will be rotating in as guards and radio operators, but the rotation hasn't quite been worked out. The only directive seems to be to make ourselves useful around the barracks. Sergeant Toro, Stevens, and I are mechanics without tools or vehicles. In the coming days we will spend an hour or so each morning giving a cursory inspection to the two or three vehicles we have been temporarily assigned. Without our regular duties to occupy us, Sergeant Toro has us take over most of the maintenance and construction tasks around the barracks. Much has to be done in short order to make the place livable.

After finishing up some odd jobs around the barracks, I retire to my room that first morning and spend the rest of the day reading on my cot. In the coming weeks I will read anything I can get my hands on. It had been months since I'd sat down and read an entire book. In these first weeks in Iraq I have nothing but time. I consume every book I brought with me, and every book sent overseas in a care package. Even Sergeant Toro, not much of a reader, borrows one of my books and spends the rest of that first day sitting on his bunk, glued to a Grisham novel.

That night, all three of us take out our treasured letter-writing kits and begin to draft letters home, Sergeant Toro to his wife and daughter, Stevens and I to our girlfriends. I sketch out an imperfect letter to Amy about nothing in particular, just to let her know that I've reached base camp safely. Something about the war, the pageantry of it all, the extremity of the situation, draws the language out of me.

> *I miss you so sharply. I feel like a part of my body has been cut off … you have become so necessary. This war has shown me the utter failure of everything in my life except for your love and steadfastness.*

I recognize my words as stilted and overwrought, quintessentially corny, and I hope she doesn't laugh at these love letters, sitting at home reading them in a world apart from the place where they were written.

These early weeks in Iraq are an idyllic time for me, with few responsibilities. Stevens is assigned to night shifts at the prison camp to help out the medical section, as he was trained as a field medic. Sergeant Toro and I awaken casually every morning around seven and take a slow, comfortable stroll around the barracks, inspecting each of the large generators that have been assigned for the company's use. The rest of the day is ours, and as long as we keep a low profile we can spend it reading quietly in our room under the pretense of "guarding the weapons" that are stored there. At night we tune in Stevens's radio and listen to garbled broadcasts of the BBC to track the progress of the war. Another city taken, another push north by the Third Infantry Division . . . the periodic reports blend into the background noise of our leisurely existence.

Sergeant Toro and I become constant companions, and I find that despite our difference in rank, he is as affable and friendly a superior as one could hope for. A barrel-chested Hispanic whose dark skin becomes almost black under the merciless desert sun, Sergeant Toro loves to lift weights, and becomes one of the largest and strongest members of our company. Although professionally a workaholic, he laughs and jokes constantly, his stocky frame doubling over and convulsing with mirth. He wields his authority over us, which is considerable, gracefully and leads the motor pool with a light touch. Although he has been a soldier for some ten years, he dreams of finishing school and becoming an architect. This aspiration is one of the first things that humanizes Sergeant Toro for me; previously I had seen him only as my superior. He dreams of improving himself and the lot of his wife and young daughter. Like Stevens he is an artisan, skilled in drafting and carpentry and, of course, mechanics. At first glance, we seem like unlikely candidates for friendship. He is married with a child and I am single. He is Puerto Rican and fiercely patriotic, while I am half Cuban and ambivalent with respect to my heritage. He speaks fluent Spanish and laughs at my halting "high school Spanish for beginners," jokingly calling me a bad Hispanic. We both love to talk politics even though he is a staunch Republican and I a lifelong Democrat. We laugh at the same stupid puns and delight in creating mocking nicknames for the commander and other antagonists. When he or I let loose a particularly good remark, his face splits open in an enormous grin and he giggles like a schoolboy. Although he is my superior and supervisor, we always act more like friends than coworkers. In time, we become as close as brothers.

At first Iraq seems manageable, even diverting. Here in the south of the country, it is relatively safe and we are mostly "playing Army." Our daily lives are concerned with minutiae like cold water and electric fans rather than any pressing military matters. Some soldiers in boredom begin to hoard and construct, erecting wooden signs and elaborate murals and flags to decorate their living areas. A favored sport of some MPs is staging gladiatorial combats between scorpions and camel spiders. The loser is eaten and the winner is crushed or discarded. Some of the Air Force security have taken to hunting wild dogs with their rifles from the back of four-wheelers.

This is something that sours me very early in the deployment. The sight of ragged, starved Iraqi dogs running desperately from packs of gun-toting men in four-wheelers is pathetic. I've never hunted, myself, and I never will. I have never understood the pleasure of killing an animal; even the killing of insects bothers me in an abstract way. Even Shoe, an avid hunter with both bow and rifle, will come to find this dog hunting distasteful. To him it is both cruel and disloyal to kill a dog. To Shoe, as for many avid hunters, the hunt itself is a near spiritual event: one man walking silently through the forest with a single rifle or bow as much for the serenity that the experience offers as for the theoretical kill. For him, this raucous slaughter is the antithesis of what it means to be a hunter.

One day, Shoe is visiting the base on a convoy mission and we watch a pair of Air Force security corner some bag-of-bones canine near our barracks and fire repeatedly at it. Silently at first, then out loud, we are rooting for the dog as it desperately jinks back and forth out of the way of rifle rounds. The dog is cut down by a limb shot but manages to hobble back to its feet and limp out of sight over a dune. The four-wheelers buzz off in pursuit of their prey. Shoe shakes his head in disgust, saying, "Someone ought to hunt their ass for a change." The riders disappear over the horizon. It doesn't look like fun to me; it looks primitive and ugly. I am quite a good marksman myself. An expert in Squad Automatic Weapon (SAW) gunnery, I can shred a paper target, but I never pictured it as anything more than the abstract challenge of pointing and aiming. There is a certain satisfaction in doing anything proficiently, and rifle marksmanship is no exception. Yet I never had the desire to "upgrade" and see my target explode in a mist of blood, or scream, or crumple with a well-placed shot. Rifle instructors sometimes talk about target animation, the idea that it is easier to train people to be marksmen with "fun targets," because shattering plates or splattering milk jugs is more viscerally satisfying than drilling holes in a piece of paper. This dog hunt is just killing for the sake of it, because you like to hurt and crush things, because a moving, whimpering, bleeding target gets your blood pumping harder than a paper cutout.

There is something primal in witnessing an act of violence. Something about it stirs the soul in vague and subtly erotic ways. We all experience the rush, the first time we fire a rocket or unload a belt of SAW ammunition. It is something deeply rooted in male identity and consciousness, an instinct for violence. I will come to see this dog hunt as the Iraq war in miniature. Witnessing it stirs up feelings of empathy that I didn't expect, but I don't want to talk about it with the other guys much, because in the Army you can't be seen to not enjoy guns, soldiery, killing; it makes you a crybaby, a pussy. So you just keep quiet about it, and that's what lets the dog hunters carry on with their fun.

The games we soldiers play are innocuous at first: drawing murals, playing stickball, building desks and chairs and collecting pinup girls from *Maxim*. They grow in intensity and stake. One moment we're in our room catching flies and the next we're crowded around a cinder block watching two camel spiders hiss and goad each other to the inevitable bloody finish. Hunting rats becomes hunting dogs. Driving outside Tallil, someone throws a piece of garbage at an Iraqi from his Humvee window and they make a game of it down the road. Fuckin' hajjis. It escalates. Time skips forward, and suddenly we're at Abu Ghraib and there are no more spiders to play with, so people invent new games . . .

Boredom is a constant menace, for with boredom comes loneliness and depression. By 6 p.m. we might as well be living in preindustrial times, and for me life of any kind ends when the sun goes down. We mechanics are starting to form a collective friendship that makes the situation more bearable. Although there are only three mechanics in Iraq at the moment, Sergeant Toro, Stevens, and myself, the others are soon to follow: Patterson, Shoe, Spangler, and Sergeant Wallace. Together the seven of us form probably the most rigid clique in the unit. As Stevens becomes more involved in his medical duties and spends less and less time in the motor pool, the tally dwindles to six. In the months to come, we coalesce into a single communal body: eating, working, and relaxing together at all times. From the time I wake up till the time I go to bed I am never away from someone in the motor pool for more than an hour.

One day the monotony is broken by a new assignment: Sergeant Toro and I will rotate in and out of the prison camp on the night shift as guards and radio operators. I am thankful for a change of pace. The long nights at the prison camp after midnight are as leisurely as sitting in my room, and with the prison's electric lights I can read easily there. I'm thankful that the command hasn't contrived something more onerous for us to do while we wait for the vehicles to arrive from the States via container ship. Unfortunately, the first night I'm assigned to the prison camp I am late for the transport, and running down the corridor in a hurry, my SAW swings off my shoulder violently, shattering my glasses to fragments with the butt of the weapon and nearly knocking me unconscious. Now I'm down to my backup pair of glasses.

The new prison camp is haphazardly built next to a large, dilapidated sporting complex. Tallil was previously an Iraqi Air Force base and as such was equipped with a modern indoor basketball court and track, complete with stadium seating for thousands. Whether the building had fallen out of use before we got there or the desert reclaimed it in the weeks after the invasion, the place is a ruin. The doors are rotting off the hinges, where they still exist, and a thick layer of dust hangs in the air even inside the stadium. The military police had taken over the basketball court as a holding and segregation area for prisoners entering the camp and had strung the foul lines with triple coils of razor wire. In the middle of this makeshift pen a few Iraqis sit sullenly with hemp sacks over their heads, alone or in small clusters. Military policemen pace the perimeter of the court and perch in the nosebleed sections of the bleachers, peering down on the prisoners with weapons at the ready. The adjoining offices and small side-rooms are swept and cleaned for use as the prison camp headquarters. Just outside this complex, a dirt enclosure houses most of the prisoners.

A bulldozer has rammed up out of the ground three earthen walls that form an elongated C shape in which the prisoners are corralled behind a line of razor wire. In the center of the enclosure, the guards and medics sit uneasily, facing the prisoners or pacing back and forth along the outer edge of the wire. The entire area is brightly illuminated by a ring of enormous generators around the outer edge of the earth walls, facing inward to deter any possible escape. The outer edge of the C is the "final protective line," where guards are stationed in wooden shacks atop steel shipping containers, with orders to shoot to kill any prisoner crossing that line. Although my duty is inside, at the radio, I have some free time to walk outside and survey the camp. The bored guards are more than eager to give me a guided tour, regaling me with stories of the latest incidents with prisoners. Here, within those three dirt walls, I encounter my first enemy soldiers at close range.

They are mostly young men, slightly older than myself. They are dressed in ragged *galabeyahs*, the long, traditional robes worn by most Arabs, and odd combinations of formal and casual clothing: occasional suit jackets thrown over ragged, stained robes or a pair of pleated slacks atop sandaled feet. Some are hooded in brown sacks, with numbers stapled to the front, but most of their faces are visible, and they stare directly at us without seeming cowed or frightened. I find Iraqi people in general to be very handsome: dark and complex, with swarthy faces and striking beards and mustaches as black as the rich, hot tea treasured in that part of the world. The men before me are obviously impoverished and fatigued to the limits of their endurance, yet they do not seem overly agitated, or even much concerned. They, like the passengers we saw on the bus during our journey here, radiate extreme nonchalance. They lounge around their tents, seemingly unconcerned with their plight, propped up on one elbow, talking and talking animatedly. Others stroll along the inside of the razor wire arm in arm with their fellows, chatting calmly and gesturing outward at the tense American soldiers. If anything, they appear to be biding their time, waiting for their fate to be decided. I try again to make eye contact but their expressions are impenetrable walls of reserve and quiet disdain. The two groups, soldiers and prisoners, pace around their respective territories, eyeing each other cautiously, as if in a standoff. The atmosphere is quiet, but a subtle tension bubbles beneath the surface.

After a quick circuit around the yard, I head back inside. The prison camp is depressing and I don't like the sensation of being a jailer. The immutable looks and world-weary faces of the prisoners fill me with something like reproach. I don't know why, but I feel almost guilty to see them caged, even though I know that they are "enemy" soldiers. Lying around in dusty tents, numbered and tagged, hemmed in by glaring spotlights, they don't look at all threatening. They look like tired, hungry farmers forced into a conflict they never had any say in. They talk to each other, they pick their teeth, they dig through their MRE bags looking for the candy, just as we do. They don't appear to have any special animosity toward us, and I can't say I feel any toward them. Most of the prisoners are young, in their early twenties, but a few of them are older men, seasoned; the others seem to defer to them. These men have long white beards and heads grizzled with silver and gray. Their blank gazes are unnerving. When the wind catches the hems of their robes, in the shadows between the tents and floodlights, these elders look like wraiths.

Inside the stadium building again, I sit down beside the large field radio and place the handset around my neck. It's going to be a long night. For hours I stare out into space, counting dust particles.

The night passes quietly and uneventfully with little more than eight marks in the radio log to note the passing of the hours. I return to the barracks bleary-eyed and tired just as dawn is breaking. In Iraq, the dawn is always gray and hazy as if seen through thick palls of smoke. Color doesn't seep into the world until early afternoon. The effect of the dawn is dreary and somber rather than inspirational. I have another night shift at the prison camp and things begin to fall into a routine: morning rounds, the afternoon off to read, late-night shift at the prison camp, stumble off the back of the transport truck to collapse in bed and do it all over again the next day. I have no desire to work or do anything other than read. The bubble-universe of each book seems more vivid to me than my actual life; Iraq is the dream world. What am I doing here? What are they paying me $1,200 a month for? My role seems utterly pointless and futile: nineteen weeks of training and two years of Reserve duty to come halfway across the world and carry cans of diesel fuel. I plod through the days, marking time until the rest of the motor pool arrives with our vehicles from the States. Then the real work will begin.

The night is hot and stagnant, just as it is every night. We're all stripped to our underwear, lying on top of our bundled sleeping bags, trying to get some air. I'm drifting in and out of a hazy sleep in which I can make out the contours of the room but everything in it is shifting and dreamlike. I remember the sensation of turning

over and feeling a layer of dust slide off the edge of my face and drift
down onto my shoulder. In the half dream, I see figures moving in
and out of the room, blurry and indistinct. I hear the sound of heavy
boots pounding across the floor between Sergeant Toro and myself.
Clank ... clank ... clank ... clank ... Someone is moving weapons.
Even half-asleep, I can recognize the sounds of rifles clattering
against each other and belts of SAW ammunition being lifted.
Shapeless figures loom over me, their heads seeming enormous and
their faces lost in pools of shadow. "Delgado ... Delgado ... wake
up ..." Words cut through the dream state and a hand comes to rest
on my shoulder, then a vigorous shake. I awaken only slightly and
sit up on my elbow without getting out of bed. It's Kosinski, standing over me in full battle-rattle, wearing a strikingly incongruous
helmet and flak-vest over shorts and a T-shirt.

"What the ... ? What ... What's going on?"

"Wake up, Delgado. Get your shit on. We're under attack."

Without further explanation, Kosinski grabs his SAW from its
resting place in the corner of our room and waddles off down the
hallway at a full-armored trot. After he shuffles off, a steady stream
of figures enter and leave our room, each pausing to gather up his
weapons. I spot the first sergeant among them. Across the room
from me, Sergeant Toro is awake now; he asks the first sergeant what
is going on.

"The base is under attack. A guard post near the gate popped a
flare ... it looks like the enemy is trying to breach the perimeter.
We're going to have the Quick Reaction Force get their weapons and
report to the roof to defend the barracks. Have you and your mechanics stand fast and wait for further instructions."

He vanishes as abruptly as he appeared, leaving Sergeant Toro,
Stevens, and I sitting half-awake in our underwear. Stevens begins
to dress frantically, throwing on his desert uniform bottoms and
a brown shirt. Sergeant Toro and I are more measured in our re-
sponse. Technically we are supposed to stay where we are, and Sergeant Toro doesn't seem to be in any particular haste to get out of

bed or get dressed. I'm not either, and I am leaning toward rolling over and going back to sleep. I slide my SAW over next to the foot of my bed and fit a drum of ammunition into it. With the weapon loaded, I slide my rubber chem boots over my bare feet and reach over for my Kevlar. I'm not sure what else to do, really; I don't see any real point in running anywhere. A brilliant light suddenly illuminates the room through the open window.

"Holy shit," Sergeant Toro exclaims, "that's the battle right there!" Through the open window, far off in the distance, we can see brilliant streaks of color from tracer rounds and the fading light of a flare floating gently down on a parachute, illuminating the desert like a tiny, falling star. The light of a flare at full intensity is almost as bright as day if you're near it; even from this distance, with the flare fading rapidly, we can make out the contours of the land between us and the perimeter. The "base" is not much more than a cluster of buildings hemmed in by erratic patches of chain-link fence and a few standing posts, and the "perimeter" is really an imaginary line drawn around the base from guard post to guard post. All the action seems to be taking place about six hundred meters away, to our right side, just beyond the small arches that comprise the main gate. Somewhere out there, nestled among hills and gullies, are the dug-in fighting positions that form the real perimeter of the base, and it is one of these posts that has reported enemy contact and sent up the flare. It might even be a trip-flare, a kind of illumination booby trap that the enemy set off themselves, trying to enter the base. The three of us stand there awestruck, watching as the light from the flare fizzles and burns out, knowing full well that we should be doing something, but not knowing what. A bizarre paralysis sets in: here is the very thing we have fantasized about and dreaded for so long, and all we can do is stand around and watch.

That is how I came to be standing at an open window just outside Nasiriyah, wearing only my underwear and a pair of rubber boots, watching the Iraq war roll past me. As far as I can tell, I am actually seeing the war; the battle has come within view of where I am standing. It would be a thrilling and almost religious experience were it not so absurd. The plain below is unbelievably broad and desolate, the peak of the ziggurat looming in the distance. Above us, the brilliant light of the flare rising into the sky is almost biblical, like an old woodcut of the star of Bethlehem. Then it hits me: in this case, the only Wise Men in attendance are the three of us in our underwear. Despite the seriousness of the situation, I begin to chuckle to myself as I imagine the scene as viewed from the ground below. If someone were to look up from the perimeter line with night-vision goggles or binoculars they would see a trio of nearly naked men standing in the window, wearing helmets and rubber boots, their mouths agape like idiots. My first sight of battle is not a stirring, patriotic moment but a farcical one. Eventually the flare goes out and the scene is once again obscured by darkness. When a half hour passes with no further sounds or illuminating flashes, it appears that whatever was happening has passed. No one comes back to the room to tell us to go anywhere, but down the corridor we can hear the shouts and stomping of everyone else running up and down the stairs in a frenzy, and we hear a shout from down the hall. "The base headquarters just radioed: Stand down! Stand down!"

Stand down, everything is under control. I fall back on my bed with my helmet on my chest.

APRIL 13, 2003 Assigned to the prison camp again, I settle in as usual, but something is different tonight. I'm different; my mood is darker. The faces of the prisoners shuffle past me into the central holding area, drained of vitality, led by young guards whose faces seem equally grim and lifeless. A bitter taste rises in the back of my throat. It all seems so pedestrian and unheroic, nothing at all like Army commercials or those brilliantly colored war movies. This is just bureaucracy. The world around me seems to have no color at all: gray walls blending seamlessly into gray dust, populated with the ashen figures of prisoners squatting amid razor wire. This is not at all the way it's supposed to be. But what was I expecting? I wrap the radio around my neck and begin a letter to Amy.

> *I'm writing to you from one of the destroyed and abandoned offices that the military has claimed for its own use . . . I'm sitting here, terribly bored, and suddenly very lonely. Maybe it's the sight of all these prisoners: ragged, dirty, half-starved, with looks of utter bewilderment and confusion on their faces. I watch them being herded into barbed-wire cages and I can't help but feel terribly sorry for them, no matter who they are or were, no matter how black their hearts have been. Something stirs in me when I see them. They're not being abused or beaten or anything, but I just feel this deep, abiding sorrow for them. They seem so utterly wasted and defeated.*

I set down my pen for a moment. My handwriting has become erratic as I scribble the words as fast as I can, trying to match the volume and forcefulness of my thought. The words flow out in a torrent, unplanned:

> *The other day, I was told, a seventeen-year-old boy came in [to the prison camp] and cried from the moment he was led in till the time they released him. He was a civilian whose parents and entire family were killed in the war, and he had been walking along with his donkey when I guess he wandered into the wrong place and time. He was arrested and taken to our prisoner camp. He wept so bitterly because he thought he was being taken to a death camp. One of our chaplains, a Christian who spoke no Arabic, sat down with the boy and comforted him, even cried with him . . .*

It occurs to me that I'm no longer writing to Amy at all, I'm writing to myself. On the window next to me there are thousands of dead insects crammed into every cavity. Dried-out husks of moths and beetles litter the windowsill and the floor, and ants cart these forms away to cannibalize them. Just over my head, tilting lazily under the ceiling fan, is a strip of putrid yellow paper coated in glue, on which a dozen insects are held fast in varying degrees of slow death. Some still struggle, and their feeble attempts to free themselves make the flypaper ripple like a spider's web. I fixate on their tiny, delicate legs, the armored shells twinkling like shards of reflective glass. The moths look as soft as feathers, covered in pale down, stuck fast to the brittle yellow paper. They fight impossibly hard, ripping their bodies to pieces and tearing holes in their soft paper wings to be free. They want so badly to live.

I'm too soft for this business, the sight of defeated enemies depresses me and fills me with pity and loathing ... Even in this room, there's a strip of flypaper hanging from a window and on it a moth is helplessly stuck, its antennae waving feebly. When I look at it I want to cry. A trapped and dying insect moves me almost to tears and here I am in this great and victorious war. I'm supposed to be a soldier, some kind of tough guy and here I am writing about a poor moth. I hate it. I hate seeing any living thing suffer, I can't stand it, it's like needles in me and the worst thing of all is to be surrounded by pain and unable to do anything. I feel wretched and hypocritical. I can honestly say that I am the worst Buddhist in the world....

Here, writing atop one of the empty crates in a dusty corner of the old sports stadium, I am hopeless. I despair. The Way seems so impossibly distant, an unreachable dream. Reading the sutras makes me feel almost physically ill, so far am I from the ideal. I feel like there is nothing Buddhist about me, except that word, hovering over me like a badge of hypocrisy. Compassion ... Loving-Kindness ... Although I call myself a Buddhist, I know that I am no follower of the Way, soldier and jailer that I am. How did I ever come to be here? A Buddhist ... can I even call myself that? I have come so far from what I wanted to be.

My [Buddhist] practice is weak and irregular, my will is deficient and lazy and I have gotten myself into a situation where, far from preventing suffering, I am actually adding to it. I had not realized how important to my identity it was to think of myself as a Buddhist, and now I feel that I cannot honestly claim that. I am a dissolute and irreligious man. I know what I want to do and be, but I can't muster my strength enough to do it. I am irrelevant as a human being and as a Buddhist. I can't even master my body enough to sit upright and meditate for a few minutes. Without the truth that Buddhism represents for me, my entire life is meaningless and sinful, and my every pretense at Buddhism that much more laughable and deceptive. I can't even bear to read a word out of the Buddhist bible [Dwight Goddard's A Buddhist Bible, *originally published in 1932] I brought because it only drives home to me how far I am from sincere, how Buddhism is still so intellectual for me and not natural or spiritual. What a waste my life has been... I can't see how my frail, undisciplined self will ever advance along that path into the kind of man I want to be. I can keep the Precepts,[1] but the actions have no value without the mind-set that goes with them.*

This letter has gone on too long already. What will she think when she reads it? It will be weeks before my next letter arrives and she'll be worried about me. I shake out my hand, which is burning from the fatigue of nonstop writing, and draw in a long, slow breath. Breathe in, breathe out. You're okay, you're in control. I pick up the pen again and close the letter with words of affection and longing.

The act of writing the letter leaves me drained. I know what I believe. What am I going to *do* about it? In the days to come I will spend countless hours sitting on my bed, working underneath trucks, or staring out into the sunset thinking about this question. I will agonize over it and burn for it, night after night. I will speak with my sergeants, my friends, and my superiors about it; it will not go away. In Zen, the koan is a puzzle, a paradox; "like a ball of red-hot iron in your throat," you can neither swallow it nor disgorge it. My question is like that, a koan: I live with it; I cannot push it out of my mind. *What are you going to do about it?* It dangles like the sword of Damocles over every night I spend in Iraq, every page I thumb through in my Buddhist texts. This question, and my answer to it, will become the defining spirit of my deployment, of my Iraq war ... and like all great questions it begins with something small, as tiny and inconsequential as a strip of flypaper.

My longest night at the prison camp ends, and I believe it is my last. By fate, I'm never reassigned there again. The other mechanics will soon arrive from Camp Arifjan, and I will be needed full-time as a mechanic. I bid farewell to the prison camp without regret. The next morning I feel better, as mornings always allow me to do. The world seems brighter and more manageable, with Sergeant Toro groaning his way out of bed as Stevens mixes and pours his predawn coffee. I breathe in, and the world seems more manageable. I breathe out, and I can get out of bed and begin the day. Last night's crisis recedes in my brain as I set my two bare feet down on the tile. As always, at the end of each crisis I find some reservoir of balance that I didn't know I had, a base of calm that I always return to.

I am still new to the Way, but this sensibility has been with me all my life, it seems. Buddhism ultimately comes from India, from a little kingdom in the north that vanished thousands of years ago. It also comes from Japan. And, of particular meaning to me, Buddhism comes from Thailand.

Bangkok, Thailand

1987 I am a little boy standing in the street. In my restlessness I pace back and forth or walk quickly in a circle. There are only a few people out today. Once I saw a man frying grasshoppers in an iron skillet, right next to our house, but today I see the monks again. I'm not sure who they are or what they do, but I know that they are monks because one day I asked my mother who the people dressed in bright orange robes were; they're the brightest colors on the street and you can see them a long way off. They travel with a little boy around my age; the boy wears normal clothes but has a shaved head. My father explained that the monks aren't allowed to touch money, so the boy goes with them to pay for their taxis and things and to take the money when people give it to them.

Most of the monks I've seen are young men, teenagers. They have dark brown skin and shaved heads that are darker than the rest of their bodies; you can see that before they shaved it off, their hair was black, like all Thai people have. Sometimes their hair is short and stubbly, like they haven't cut it for a while. They walk around with big brown bags and they stop at all the Thai houses on the street. At each house, they knock on the door and bow when a person answers it. Then the person gives them some rice from a big bowl, or some folded baht. The monks stop at every house on both sides of the street but skip ours. The monks never approach Westerners. That's what we are. Everyone else is very nice and respectful to them. When they pass by, people on the street put their hands together and bow. This kind of bowing is how Thais wave hello to each other, and I know how to do it. You put your hands together like you're praying, bend forward, and say *Suwaadi kap* if you're a boy and *Suwaadi kaa* if you're a girl. Thai people do this instead of saying hi; they bow to each other, but it's different when they do it for the monks. They press their hands together hard and bow very low. Sometimes the monks bow back and sometimes they just keep walking. This is because they are Buddhists, and that is very serious, and the Thai people respect them a lot. This is because Thailand is *a Buddhist nation*, I've heard the Thai culture teacher say over and over again. The monks come from pretty far away and they live in temples, which have huge, arched roofs decorated with green, red, and blue dragons.

Once, my dad and my brother and I helped carry rocks to build a temple. It was an old temple that they were building back up. It was at the top of a very tall flight of stairs in the side of a mountain.[2] Everybody who went up the stairs had to carry two plastic bags of gravel up to the top and leave them there to help build the temple. We went up the stairs but halfway up Dad started carrying my rocks. The stairs went up so high on the mountain that you couldn't see the temple from the ground, you could only see clouds. It took us all afternoon to climb to the top and on the way up we passed by clouds floating right next to us on the staircase. When we finally got to the temple, we couldn't see it until it was right in front of our faces, it just seemed to appear out of the clouds. That's why in Thai they call it Cloud Temple. Right in front of the gate, there's a huge green statue of a sitting man without any head. That's probably why they're rebuilding the temple. Even though there's no head, I know that this is a statue of Buddha, because there are millions of them everywhere in Thailand. Buddha is very, very serious and most Thais have a picture or a little statue of him in their house or store.

Buddha mostly sits there, although sometimes he lies down on his side with his arm propped up. There are statues of him covered in gold, made out of green jade, or carved in old, crumbly stone; big statues and little statues and giant statues over fifty feet tall. They are all over the place, in the country and inside the temples in the city. This is because Thailand is very old and has a *very rich history,* the Thai culture teacher says. Buddha has long, stretched-out ears and funny little buds of hair that look like bumps. He has a little smile on his face, like he knows a secret about someone in the room. When he's sitting up, Buddha always has his hands in front of him, either pressed together like he's saying *Suwaadi kap* or flat with his thumbs touching. At big statues, Thais leave plates of food and flowers or wrap the statue in bright orange cloth as if it was a real monk. Buddha is everywhere in Thailand, pictures on windows and buses, statues left in the middle of the jungle.

The monks on my street don't look much like Buddha, except for the robes. For one thing, they are too young and too skinny and their faces don't look quite the same. Buddha doesn't have much of a nose and his cheeks are flat like two mirrors, and he hardly has any lines at all on his face. The monks' faces are covered in lines. They always smile at me, and they have lots of wrinkles around their mouths and foreheads. They look like they are going to split open from smiling. Even though they are young, their faces make them look like they're very, very old. This must be because they're so wise from sitting around in temples all day. There's something nice and friendly about the monks in their bright orange robes. They look like they're really, really happy, but quiet about it too, never shouting or talking above a whisper. My brother Aaron likes to talk loud and be around lots of people, but Mom says that I am an introvert. The monks are like me. You can just kind of let out your breath when you see them and stand there and not talk. You feel like you don't have to say anything and they don't have to say anything back. I felt the same way standing at the top of those longs stairs in the clouds, looking up at the huge green Buddha without any head. Like it was enough just to be there, to be still.

Sarasota, Florida

Summer 2000 I'm a young man now, living in America for the first time. Like Cairo, Sarasota is all sun and palm trees, but with well-manicured islands of grass instead of sand. Oh my God! Girls are walking around in shorts and tank tops here, everyone speaks English; I have arrived at last! I've come here with my parents, and will attend New College of Florida, the state honors college. It's a steal, because I'm Hispanic. As far as I can tell, if you're Hispanic and want to go to college in the state of

Florida, they all but cart wheelbarrows of money up to your door to get you to go to their school. I'm going to school for free because my name's Delgado, yet I had to study Spanish in high school. What a joke. My parents unload my few belongings quickly and without much ceremony and deposit me in my four-person dorm room, shared by my brother and two others.

Within a month, I hate the place with a passion. Everyone around me is my enemy, and I feel the workings of a vast conspiracy to isolate and vilify me. It's the *people* here, they're political correctness fascists, I think to myself; it's not me. But it *is* me. I am the problem. The people here are *different*, to say the least. The school is liberal, progressive, even counterculture. The students, as a general rule, tend to be the smart, weird outcasts of high-school life. Coming from the extreme conservatism of Egypt and the sheltered world of Cairo, I feel awkward and uncomfortable here. Rumors start to circulate, true and false, about the horrible things my brother and I have said about people or the boorish ways we've behaved. People start to avoid us, or they say, "Oh, you're one of the Delgado brothers" when they first meet one of us. I spend my first year marinating in negativity. I just want to graduate from this stupid school so I can get back to the "real world." Classes aren't engaging, so I am often absent, or if I do go, I sleep through the lecture. On a whim, I sign up for a class on Buddhism: Daoism, Chan, Zen. That sounds interesting. However, I skip most of the classes, until Professor Newman takes me aside one afternoon and asks me what I think I am doing coming to class since I have no chance of passing the course. My face burns with shame as I am kicked out of my Buddhism class by a professor so relaxed and calm that he seems nearly inert. He's kicking *me* out? I feel victimized. I think of high school: captain of the wrestling team, Model United Nations, dating the prom queen ... college seems a pale shadow of my vibrant high school years. He's kicking *me* out? I've got to get out of this place for a while, get my head together.

One day I see an Army climbing wall in the school parking lot. A handful of recruiters are standing around it, inviting students to climb the wall. A thought enters my mind, later reinforced by my friends who sign up with me: Maybe *that's* the change of scene I've been needing... maybe I should join the Army Reserve, you know, get away from school for a while, get some discipline, get my life in order. Become an army of one.

Military Entrance Processing Station, Tampa, Florida
September 11, 2001 I'm enlisting today. My recruiter is a gorgeous blonde who looks like Kim Basinger: Sergeant Bennet. She didn't even need to do the sales pitch. I had walked up to her in the parking lot of New College and said, "I'm interested in joining the Reserves." She administered the ASVAB test the next day, in the dining hall on a laptop. I scored an 88 on the practice test and she was very pleased. She told me in general terms about the Army and I only half-listened, because I had already made up my mind. Straight talking, faint southern accent: she gave me a fair deal, told me everything I needed to know, and I'd asked few questions. I had read and downloaded so much information, I thought I knew everything there was to know about enlistment.

Now I'm standing in the processing station waiting to sign my contract, to determine what job I'll have in the military. I suppose I could sign up for cryptography or languages or military intelligence, but I've been doing intellectual things like that my entire life; I already know I'll be good at those things. I want a job I know nothing about. I select light-wheeled mechanic because that seems like it might have some application to real life. All my life it's been books, computers, games, study. Let me learn something that will get my hands dirty. I'm tired of college life, tired of the elitism, the petty sophistication. I don't want to be a college boy and pseudo-intellectual; for once I want to be just like everyone else: a common soldier, a mechanic, nobody special. A Light-Wheeled Vehicle Mechanic; that should be fine.

It's midmorning, sometime around nine. I sign my name to the contract. There's no puff of sulfur, no fanfare, no sense of crossing any threshold; just exhaustion from a long day of standing in lines. Signing the papers is just the last formality in a long process. Now I want to go home and sleep.

My recruiter walks into the small office where I'm sitting and says, "Hey, you should come see what's on TV. Something just hit the World Trade Center." In the other room, a small group of soldiers and entrants are standing in front of the TV set, staring in idle curiosity at the clouds of smoke pouring out of a hole in the side of the Twin Towers. An accident, I'm sure, some idiot in a private plane flew too close. Dumb ass. Just as I think this, another plane streaks across the screen and hits the second tower in a plume of fire. Holy shit, that was no accident. "I think we better go," my recruiter says, and leads me toward the door as five hundred people simultaneously drop what they're doing and fix their eyes on the TV screen.

As the processing station explodes into pandemonium, Sergeant Bennet hustles me back into her government car and hits the road south toward Sarasota, with the local radio station turned up to maximum as updates pour in. "The Pentagon has been struck by a plane." She floors the accelerator. "The towers have collapsed." We cross the Howard Franklin Bridge. "A plane has deviated from its course and may be headed for the White House." Sergeant Bennet is agitated. "I gotta get you home and report to my unit." The business of the day is forgotten, enlistment is forgotten. The long bridge between Tampa to Sarasota, the Sunshine Skyway, fades into obscurity. The water is a blur beneath us, hundreds of feet down. The only sound is the voice of the radio announcer, crackling over the dial on every station, voices in an increasing state of alarm. The world contracts . . .

the whir of the engine, the clacking sound of the tires, the rush of air past my face through the crack in the window.

I feel a swirl of emotion: confusion, fear, excitement, adrenaline. We're under attack. We're under attack. America. The country is under attack and I'm in the Army, sort of. This is the reason we have an Army, and I joined *before* it happened. After this, everyone is going to come flooding into the military to protect the country. Whatever happens from this point on, I will always be able to say: "I signed up before it was popular." I'm proud of myself. Everyone who told me not to join the Army will see now, they'll see why what I did was right. My father, who pleaded with me not to enlist, my mother, who said, "I hope you know what you're doing," my brother, who told me I was making the biggest mistake of my life, they were all wrong. I've been vindicated. I'm nineteen years old, I'm going to be a soldier, and I joined *before*...

Stupid fucking kid. I'm officially inducted one week later.

Sarasota, Florida

Fall 2001 I withdraw from school for the semester, telling everyone I've joined the Army and will be leaving for basic training at the end of October. Everyone is still in shock and mourning over the terrorist attacks; they nod gravely when I tell them my plans. God bless you, school will be waiting for you when you get back, the kindly administrator tells me. Just like that, my schedule is clear. I no longer have anything to do: no classes, no papers, no homework. I have a month and a half to kill before I leave for training. For the first couple of nights, I can't sleep. I'm a bundle of nerves. My enlistment keeps playing over and over in my head, signing my name on the dotted line. I've seen movies of basic training, but what will it actually be like? Will I make it? Will I wash out? I can hardly eat or concentrate because I'm so nervous. I need to get my mind in order before I leave for basic, I know that much. I've got to get my head right or this will be a living hell. All my classsmates are engaged in school and have little time to spare for my post-enlistment angst. One evening, on a whim, I wander over to the school library and check out an armful of books on Buddhism. I've got nothing but time now. Maybe I'll actually read some of those books that Professor Newman assigned.

It's dark outside; everyone else in the dorm is asleep. There's a single lamp on in my room, illuminating a cluster of boxes and half-packed crates. I set the load of books down on my desk and pick up the top one because it looks like a quick and easy read. It's a slim volume, just 150 pages or so, called *It's Easier Than You Think: The Buddhist Way to Happiness* by Sylvia Boorstein. It's easier than you think? What a weak title, I think, as I climb onto my sheetless bed and open the book to the first page... just to glance through it...

I sit up. It's after midnight. I've read the book cover to cover without looking up. I sit and ruminate for a moment. I'm a Buddhist. I didn't *become* a Buddhist, I've been a Buddhist for a long time. I don't experience a sensation of *conversion* to Buddhism, only a sense of homecoming, a return to something I had always known, something buried in me as fractured images of monks, and statues, and the Cloud Temple jutting out of the side of a mountain. I take up the next book in the pile, then the next... Every work is brilliant, elegant, insightful. *The cause of all suffering is our own selfish desire: craving things we do not have and clinging to things we cannot keep.* I read the words, simple, straightforward words, and each one tears into my consciousness like a bullet. Every day of my life, I hurt and agonize because I don't have the things I feel I *deserve:* money, popularity, sex, academic success. I literally ache inside because I crave these things so badly. On the other hand, I can't let go of things that are past. My high school years, my popularity, my old girlfriend, my success in school and sports; I cling to all these things as if they were still real, but I know inside that they are gone, truly gone. I always want to feel the way I did in the past: winning a gold medal in wrestling or making highest honors in school, but I can't, because those moments are gone forever, gone like this sentence, gone like the last three seconds of your life, never to return. I feel the truth of suffering descend over me: I know exactly what The Buddha meant when he said that suffering was *clinging* and *craving*. They say in Zen that when you experience a moment of enlightenment you no longer have to theorize or study, you see the truth face to face: "You can read volumes of books about the sea, but simply get up and walk for some days in any direction, dip your finger in the water and drink, and suddenly you know the taste of all the oceans." Buddhism is what I have believed my whole life, and I never knew it until today. My mind is seething, wide awake until dawn, reading and scribbling on a scrap of computer paper.

After that first glimpse comes details, then theory, then study. On one level it's the simplest thing in the world, but the more I read, the more I discover how much there is to learn. Entire libraries are filled with volumes on Buddhism, as befits a great world religion. There are countless pages of sutras, teachings, and only a tiny fraction have ever been translated into a modern language. In part, they comprise the teachings of a man, Siddhartha Gautama, who may or may not have lived about twenty-six hundred years ago in India, the prince of a tiny kingdom that no longer exists. The core teachings of Buddhism are the Four Noble Truths, which express the fundamental problem of human life—suffering—and propose a solution.

The First Noble Truth: Life is full of suffering. The world we live in is imperfect and we as imperfect beings are subject to sickness, old age, and death. Even those moments that we call "happiness" or "contentment" are tainted because they cannot last forever and we cannot hold on to them. All things in life are transient. Happiness cannot last.

The Second Noble Truth: The cause of suffering is a fundamental misconception of the self, the wrong belief that we are distinct, permanent, and essential. The consequence of this wrong belief is negative attachment: either *craving* for things we do not have and believe that we need, or *clinging* to things that cannot last forever. Since whatever we desire is itself transient, the loss of what we desire is unavoidable and suffering will inevitably follow.

The Third Noble Truth: The end of suffering is possible through the elimination of selfish desires and attachments, the cessation of *craving* and *clinging.* This state of total equanimity is called *Nirvana,* a Sanskrit term literally meaning "extinguish," as in extinguishing the "flames" of desire.

The Fourth Noble Truth: The means to end suffering is through a discipline of gradual self-improvement called the Noble Eightfold Path. This system is often called the Middle Path or Middle Way between the two extremes of excessive luxury (hedonism) and excessive austerity (asceticism). Through the cultivation of morality, discipline, and wisdom one can overcome the root cause of suffering: misconception of the self.

That's it. That's the heart of it, the heart of what I realize on that one sleepless night in Sarasota. Later, long after my tour of duty in Iraq, I'm sitting in a small red-carpeted room, listening, with about twenty other people, to a Buddhist teacher. The teacher is English, his voice is gentle and lilting, drifting over us in a steady stream. "What is Buddhism in a nutshell?" he asks rhetorically, and then shares a quotation from one of his Tibetan teachers, the central theme of all his teachings:

> *Cease to do negative actions,*
> *learn to do positive actions,*
> *control your mind,*
> *and benefit others,*
> *that is the teaching of The Buddha.*

I learn later that these words are a famous proverb found in many Buddhist texts from many different cultures. It is often said that those simple lines summarize the traditional eighty-four thousand teachings of The Buddha. I guess they're what you'd call the "short answer." The long answer involves a few hundred thousand pages of text, mostly in Sanskrit and Pali, and those are just the words attributed to The Buddha himself. But that's all extra, the real root of it is simple: Do no evil, do as much good as possible, and purify your own mind. Oh yeah, and one more little thing: *Don't believe a word I say, just because I say it or anyone else believes it. Only believe it if it is true for you.* Another favorite phrase of that English teacher, words he attributes to The Buddha himself. The anti-dogma, Buddhism isn't about following or parroting or letting someone else tell you what's right and wrong, it's about the monumental task of sitting down by yourself and working things out *for* yourself, something most people aren't ready to do. According to the legendary accounts of his life, when The Buddha lay dying, his last words were: *Decay is inherent in all compound things; strive diligently for your own enlightenment.* Meaning that The Buddha, like everything else, must pass away and dissolve in accordance with the transient nature of the world. I read his words as, *I won't be here to guide you any longer; from now on you must work out your own truths for yourselves,* and for me that was his most profound teaching.

I continue reading, studying, voraciously swallowing up any texts on Buddhism I can find. I read principles and ideas that are nearly three thousand years old and yet seem absolutely fresh and modern. Ideas swirl around me and I feel them coalesce into a huge, glittering framework: a philosophy, a way of looking at the world. I feel my own style of Buddhism beginning to emerge from all the texts I've read: Zen, an ancient style of Buddhism, transplanted to Japan. Zen to me is directness and tranquility, bundled together with that succinct Japanese eloquence, that *style*. In the misty intersections of history and myth, Zen begins like this:

The Buddha stands on a bridge, overlooking a large gathering of monks and followers. He is famous across India as the greatest teacher mankind has ever seen. Everyone has gathered to hear what profound sermons he is going to preach. The audience falls into an awed silence as The Buddha steps forward to address the crowd. Without speaking a single word, The Buddha reaches into his robe and pulls out a single lotus flower and holds it up to the audience. Everyone is confused, except for one man named Kashyapa who smiles. The Buddha sees this and smiles back and Zen is born: a direct transmission of understanding, heart-to-heart, outside of words and signs.

The word *Zen* means "meditation"; it is a Japanese rendering of the Chinese word *Ch'an*, which is itself a pronunciation of the Sanskrit word *Dhyana*. When Buddhism faded in India, an enterprising monk called Bodhidharma took the teachings to China, where they flourished and became more refined. From China, missionaries carried the new philosophy to Japan, where it took root and has been largely preserved unto the modern day. That is the transmission: from India to China to Japan. Modern Zen traces itself back through a long line of teachers and patriarchs, back to that original moment of The Buddha holding up a lotus flower and imparting the whole of his teachings without saying a word. It is called Zen because it focuses on the practice of meditation as a means to train the mind and overcome delusions: to see directly into the nature of things without filters or judgment. That is one of the fundamental truths of Zen, that the greatest and most profound power in the universe is simply being able to see things for what they are.

The morning after that sleepless night during which I discover my own truth, I eat breakfast and jostle with my roommates as usual. I continue to freak out about basic training, and worry and fret and lose my temper, but something on the inside has shifted, subtly, almost imperceptibly. I come back to a root, a steadiness, an inner baseline. I'm getting ready to leave. At New College's little bay-front, a tiny concrete dock opening onto the Gulf of Mexico, I spend hours staring out into a wind-tossed sea. All around me I can feel the waves rising and crashing, but somehow my inner sea seems calm, tranquil, pacific.

So here I stand: an American Buddhist in Iraq. Now, with our unit beginning to settle in for the long, slow crawl, I have some time and empty hours to brood. I can feel depression and hopelessness on the edge of my mind, gradually intruding, increasing in volume, like static noise in the background. My idyllic days of reading and loafing end suddenly with the arrival in early May of Sergeant Wallace and the rest of the company from Arifjan. It's good to see Shoe and Patterson again after so long apart, but part of me mourns to see the column of vehicles pulling into our courtyard, knowing that the long days of leisure, of falling asleep in the sun, are gone forever. Sergeant Wallace is a fiend for work, and with all our vehicles here, battered and broken from being shipped and convoyed across half the earth, there will be plenty of it. I slap Shoe and Patterson on the back as they shuffle into our room with their baggage, and we swap stories of what we've all been doing in the meantime.

Shoe and Patterson are like mirror images of each other: in their early twenties, both rail thin, one the whitest white you've ever seen and the other a dark Jamaican. Shoe is bone-white and near skeletal. He's a proud country boy who loves fishing, hates school, and chews tobacco. He has nothing but disdain for "college boys" and places great stock in "common sense." Sarcastic, cynical, and bold, he is a constant target for Sergeant Wallace's "character lessons." He has a bear claw tattoo on his chest, another bear on his calf, and the word WAR tattooed in six-inch letters across his stomach. Eventually, he wants to get it filled in with full color and a Native American warrior across his side. He's full of piss and vinegar and we are fast friends. The two of us are often singled out as "bad influences on each other" by Sergeant Wallace, because once we get going in one of our bitter rants, there's no stopping us.

Patterson is a Jamaican, college educated and a formidable ladies' man. Before we left the States, he'd amassed three or four "girlfriends" in the unit that he'd see on a rotation. In Iraq he adds a few more. The details of his exploits are the stuff of motor pool banter and the basis of his solid bragging rights. He's slim, good-looking, and a smooth talker. When he wants to, he can lapse into a Jamaican accent so thick you'd think it was a foreign language. He calls all of us "son" and pretty soon we're doing it too, ending every sentence with "son," in his distinctive tone. Although we joined the unit together, he as a private E-1, the lowest rank, and I as a private first class, he's already made up the two ranks and looks poised to surpass both Shoe and me by making specialist first.

I'm even glad to see Sergeant Wallace, clapping him on the shoulder and joking with him even as I realize that his arrival is the death knell of my free time. The last member of our section, Spangler, I'm not glad to see. We are a motley group, we mechanics: college boys and country boys, two whites, two blacks, two Hispanics . . . and Spangler: a short, stocky man with a crew cut and prominent mustache. Somehow Spangler doesn't fit in. In some ways I pity him, because it must be terribly lonely to be an outsider in the tightly knit group, and yet the man resists every effort to get along with him. In truth, I dislike him intensely. We all bully him and he bullies us back wherever possible, until his little brown mustache twitches with fury. Despite our personal conflicts we absolutely need him. He has the most experience and is the most skilled mechanic by far, having worked on U-Hauls and trailers for years. There are some repairs we cannot accomplish without him and I resent him all the more for it, because as a less-experienced mechanic I am forced to bow and scrape to borrow one of his tools or ask his advice. I am ashamed to remember how often I did something to make him more miserable, as we all did.

Spangler is the only dim spot on our reunion. With the motor pool together again I feel a surge of adrenaline and purpose—as long as we're in it together it can't be that bad. We are a unit unto ourselves, rarely fraternizing with the other members of our company and, in fact, holding most of them in quiet disdain for the way they mistreat their vehicles. The motor pool eats together, works together, and sticks together always.

The next morning, instead of a leisurely awakening in the sun, the enormous shape of Sergeant Wallace looms in the doorframe. "All right, get up, y'all, it's time to go to work."

SPRING 2003 My Iraq war is stasis, sameness. The vastness of my year in Iraq fuses into a single day of sun and diesel fuel until I can no longer speak of individual days and nights but only of periods and seasons, unending cycles of sleep, feeding, and toil. When I began work on this story, I asked Shoe if he could remember anything from those days. He said, "Man, I only remember two days in Iraq. One long day in Tallil and one long day at Abu." The entirety of my six months at Tallil seems like one unit, indivisible save for a few peaks and troughs of memory. My life is the motor pool: Every aspect of my day revolves around the hour when I must report to it and the instant when I am excused from it. Diesel mechanics... At first it's a diversion, a series of interesting problems to be solved, a pleasant change from the undemanding work of filling generators and sitting by the radio. Then it becomes drudgery, an unending dull pain of Sergeant Wallace goading and threatening us into work beneath a relentless sun. It becomes my continual barrage of sarcasm and Shoe's dull, resentful expression, it becomes our reason to resent the sergeants. Finally, terribly, mechanics becomes so intrinsic to life that we know nothing else. Our routine beneath the maintenance tent becomes the daily clock of our lives, and on the rare days we are given off, we find that we no longer know what to do with ourselves.

In a way, we all come to resemble our supervisor, Sergeant Wallace, the man who defines that vast stretch of my war service. A staff sergeant whom we address simply as "sergeant" in everyday speech, Vernon Wallace is a man who proudly attests to having no hobbies. He lives to work and to make us work; the sole recreation he admits to is reading the Bible and attending church. He seems not to understand our desire to do anything outside work and is newly confused each evening when we beg to be released from the motor pool. He is an unusually large man, with dark, blue-black skin and a thin mustache. He is country, deep country, and it comes out in the way he speaks and writes, full of odd phrases and bizarre religious exclamations. At times of excitement or joy he is prone to bellow, "Glory! Glory!" at the top of his lungs, paralyzing all lesser beings within earshot. Shoe claims that Sergeant Wallace comes from a little town called Sulphur Springs, where he works as a supervisor at a furniture factory, but I never find out for sure and Sergeant Wallace enjoys telling tall tales about himself. It's one of the things we love about him. He often tells us how he worked as an undercover agent for the Army Criminal Investigation Division, which in his telling involves flying a jet and infiltrating a pilot school. He jokingly claims that he possesses a rare Excalibur automobile and an original Picasso. He mock-seriously confides to us that the long scar on his forehead is the result of running into a helicopter blade during the invasion of Grenada. He is friendly, fatherly, and vastly entertaining. He views all of us in the motor pool as his surrogate children and continually vows to "teach us some character." We all, I think, have a love-hate relationship with Sergeant Wallace. He takes all our sarcasm and mockery with gentle good humor, smiling and humming like a benevolent giant in desert camouflage, yet he works us to the bone.

Our prison is the maintenance tent, a twenty-foot-high canvas frame large enough to accommodate two vehicles and all of our tools and supplies. Our day begins just as dawn breaks, so we have a cool hour or so in the morning before the heat becomes maddening. Walking outside in Iraq at midmorning is like opening the door of a pizza oven and taking the blast of superheated air full in the face. We routinely park the vehicles under the maintenance tent several hours early to let them cool off before we start working on them. We drink so much hot, fetid water that we come to loathe the taste of it, the smell of it. Men in the unit will kill for a packet of Kool-Aid, a scoop of Tang, a canister of Gatorade, anything to break the monotony of bottle after bottle of vaguely mineral-tasting water. The heat and stagnant air turns even the simplest chore into a nuisance, and the business of vehicle repair into a test of endurance.

Ten weeks of mechanics school at Fort Jackson and two months at Fort Stewart and I still have never really gotten down into the guts of a diesel engine before. Until I joined the Army, I'd never worked on a vehicle in the slightest way. In mechanics school, I somehow finished as an "honor graduate" but still had no idea how to check the radiator fluid. The Humvee and by extension all large machines were a powerful mystery for me, propelled as far as I could tell by the circulation of ghosts within. Sergeant Toro and Sergeant Wallace were ten-year veterans of Army maintenance, Stevens was a machinist, Spangler a truck mechanic, and Shoe a "shade-tree mechanic" working on his old trucks. Only Patterson and I were uninitiated college boys, but like everything else he put his hand to, Patterson proved to be a natural at Humvee repair. Not me. I am quickly relegated to changing tires, tie-rod ends, and other simple, straightforward tasks. I am happy with my make-work assignments, content to do the easy stuff and endure the abuse of Spangler for my "uselessness." I *am* useless. Naturally, Sergeant Wallace takes it upon himself to bring me up to speed—teach me some character—reassigning me to work on every complex job. How I hate him for that … and yet, eventually, I can do it. I learn that each end of a tie-rod tightens in the opposite direction, so you need two different kinds. I learn to fear dropping a needle bearing because you can never get it back together again. I learn to install a half-shaft. I become competent. After the initial satisfaction of being able to fix something wears off, I come to realize that I will be doing these same repairs a dozen times a day, every day, for the duration of my deployment. There's something oddly comforting in that: every day when I wake up and for every moment after that, I know what's coming next.

At night Sergeant Lewis, the cook, lets me listen to his portable radio, and the BBC reports that the Third Infantry Division has pushed all the way to Baghdad. The war is going to be over soon; we're about to take the capital. Home by the Fourth of July, just like the commander said. My letters to Amy speak of nothing but how much I miss her, and pleasant thoughts of a future with her, because of the present there's nothing to tell.

Eventually the company command feels "settled in" enough to begin running missions into the city of Nasiriyah and up the service road of southern Iraq: patrol, peacekeeping, and resupply. Each mechanic starts riding along on missions, but none as often as I. "Delgado!! Get your shit on, you're going to Nasiriyah at 1400," is the periodic call that plucks me out of the motor pool and deposits me like so much baggage in the back of a Humvee. It seems the command and the MP platoon sergeants have not forgotten my idle comments back in St. Petersburg about speaking Arabic, and every mission now wants to take me along as a *translator* so they can interact with the locals. Shoe is so jealous. He yearns to go on these trips, patrols, rambles, anything to get out of the motor pool and get a rifle back in his hands. In a way even I welcome the opportunity, if only to do something different. With the start of missions into Nasiriyah, things begin to change.

I'm in the back of a Humvee, my SAW unloaded across my lap, my translation books tucked into my vest pockets. More often than not, I hold the pocket-size Arabic-English dictionary in my hand close to my smudged glasses so I can read it through the glare. I'm reviewing the vocabulary I'll need for this mission, specific words that might come up: *air conditioner, medic, roast chicken, resistance fighter, dry cleaning,* and most importantly *ice,* although I already know the word for that. I've reviewed the same words before every mission, I should know them by now, but each time we go out I'm fraught with nerves. When the pinch comes every member of the team expects fluency and I have to try to fake it. These missions aren't exactly "combat operations"; once the command learns that most of the locals are friendly to the Coalition, our forays revolve around purchasing luxuries for the company: food, fans, and ice, always ice. The first couple of times out, I manage to hem and haw my way through a few simple Arabic exchanges with Iraqis and the company is dazzled. I develop a reputation for being useful on an "ice run," and thereafter I am included in just about every trip.

Nasiriyah is what you would expect: buildings caked with soot and sand, open sewers and piles of garbage, the occasional donkey-cart blending in among the traffic of old junker cars from the late 1980s. Nature pokes through here and there: stands of tall water rushes beside a slow-moving stream, date palms with pictures of local clerics nailed to them, undeveloped lots of open sand. Dogs are everywhere. It's not very different from Cairo, not very different from the dozens of third world cities I have lived in and visited. Wherever you go outside the U.S., poverty and want look the same. Combining the memories of my childhood and adulthood, I could piece together patches of urban sprawl from Bangkok to Nasiriyah to Dakar, and nothing would change except pale skin to brown to black, Thai to Arabic to French. One long slum across two continents ... The only thing that stands out about Nasiriyah is that every so often along the road you see a pile of rubble where a building once stood, and you *know* what destroyed it. The city is dotted with these ruins. Sometimes whole streets have been leveled; in other neighborhoods individual buildings have been picked out and flattened, with almost surgical precision. Almost. Most of the buildings show pockmarks of bullets, or pieces of wall torn away by the bigger, high-velocity rounds. Ours or theirs? You can't really tell.

In spite of the residue of war, the city of Nasiriyah seems almost to have returned to life. People are out on the street, the bazaars are crowded, there's fresh fruit in the stalls, and vehicles zip up and down narrow lanes, blaring their horns in lieu of signaling or stopping. White flags still flutter on every car antenna and rooftop, but the people of Nasiriyah seem to be carrying on with their lives. Iraqi men working in shops look up at us and wave, or regard us sternly until our convoy passes them by. Hordes of children crowd the sides of the street as we pass and every time that we stop, calling out in chorus: "Mister . . . mister . . . give me water. Give me food. Give me money." We hear this "mister, mister" so often, some of the MPs start referring to Iraqi children as "mistah-mistah's." We have our guns up, the brims of our helmets down, looking for trouble, but we never find any. Once or twice far in the distance, we hear a pistol shot and everyone goes ramrod stiff, but nothing ever befalls us. This isn't really enemy territory; the Coalition units passing through left only a token presence, and it seems to me that the war has mostly passed Nasiriyah by.

The Iraqis in this city don't seem hostile or even particularly sullen. On the contrary, they are curious about their new neighbors and even jovial. Within minutes of stopping our vehicles, the convoy is quickly surrounded by a crowd of onlookers, making the MPs particularly nervous. In turn, members of the crowd shout any words of English they know, usually, "Hello, what is your name?" or "Hello, what time is it?" and occasionally "Hello, what time is your name?" Typically, the mood is light and festive, with the Iraqis laughing at one another's English as often as we do, trying to shake our hands, and whispering conspiratorially at our female soldiers.

When I break away from the group to talk to one of them, usually to ask directions to a particular souk, or market, the Iraqis are beside themselves with glee. They are so stunned and pleased that a high-and-mighty U.S. soldier is actually trying to speak their language that they help me through my halting pidgin Arabic and patiently try to decipher my gestures and pantomimes. In spite of my faulting attempts to communicate, the Iraqis make themselves understood and do their best to piece together what I am asking: "Where ice?" "Where market?" "Where air conditioner?" They love it and they love me, constantly hugging me, shaking my hand, and asking again and again if I am a Muslim. "La-ah, la-ah, abu safaraga, bil Masr, tamanya sana," I tell them—"No, no, father ambassador, in Egypt, eight years." My father was not an ambassador, but I lack the word for "diplomat" and this one gets the point across.

The moment they hear me speak, the Iraqis know I learned in Egypt. The way I use *la-ah* for "no" instead of *naam*, the way I say *kuwayyis* to mean "good," slang like *maalesh* ("never mind") are all dead giveaways that I am a *Masri* or Egyptian, even though I'm not. Since the Egyptian dialect is used in media throughout the Arab world, they have no trouble understanding me and laugh with bemusement at my "Egyptian accent," but I have to strain to understand their Iraqi Arabic, which uses many of the same words in unfamiliar ways. In Egypt, *naam* was a question meaning "What?"; here it means "no." This and a thousand other minor differences means I must throw what little Arabic I know out the window and start over by piecing together the words we have in common and trying to learn the local variants. It is arduous, frustrating, and slow, but no one else in the company has even a breath of Arabic so it all falls to me. I find that young men are the most helpful. I single out the teenagers in a group when I need help with directions or a certain phrase. I say a word, they say another word, I pantomime a chicken, and they say the word for "roasted" and tell me where I can find one. They point to the bullets in the ammo belt of my SAW and say *rrosaas* and now I know that Iraqis call bullets the same thing we do: "lead." They make me feel comfortable, and I get my voice back. The more they laugh and tug on my shoulder, the better my Arabic gets. I come to cherish these brief interactions.

The change soon becomes its own routine: motor pool work and shopping trips to Nasiriyah, back and forth, an orderly rhythm. In quiet order, three months pass, leaving only vague markings like footprints in sand, fading as soon as they are made. A spit of chickens roasting in a glass window in Nasiriyah, skin crisp and blackening, with blood-rare bones visible through slices in the meat. The clicking sound of the ratchet as it spins, my elbow working in a steady rhythm. Schumacher carrying a crate of pineapples some stranger sent him from America. Shoe's thin arms hacking the small pineapples apart with a machete. Somehow they're still cool to the touch. All of us standing shirtless, gorging on pineapple, the juice running down our faces and arms. Sergeant Gott washing his clothes in a bright plastic tub outside our window. His back and arms are covered in a single large tattoo, Japanese, a three-quarter sleeve. The coiling dragons and Buddhas are so bright he looks like he's wearing a Hawaiian shirt.

Ninety dawns and ninety sunsets pass, and yet there is a framework to it all. Looming over everything is a growing dread and a doubt, a vague and insubstantial longing, somewhere between physical pain and depression. I miss my girl. I miss waking up in the morning and going where I please. When we roll through the streets of Nasiriyah I increasingly feel a sense of hypocrisy, growing to horror and guilt: did we not come here to bring ruin and war? I am an outsider. I do not belong here. Our missions accomplish nothing, my repairs accomplish nothing except to allow more missions. It's circular, leading nowhere. I feel like a mechanism, a single cell, completely without autonomy. My desires and fears move me. Every time I think about Buddhism or try to read a line from my Buddhist books, I am stopped dead by an overwhelming sadness and loss. If it is so sweet and noble to serve one's country, why does my time here feel so meaningless and dishonest?

There's not really anyone I can talk to about it, this vague feeling of dread, almost everyone else in the unit seems at ease in their military duties. No one in the motor pool ever talks about "depression" or anxiety or ennui, they just go about their business, keeping their thoughts to themselves. The military police seem positively *thrilled* about their jobs, getting psyched up each day to go on their patrols and guard shifts. It's in their nature.

Ask any soldier what they think of military police. Unless they are military police themselves, you're bound to hear colorful answers. Military police have a reputation. They're not bad guys; they just love their jobs, I mean really *love* their jobs. Most of the MPs in our unit are young guys from central Florida, a mixture of eighteen-year-olds, college students, and older, more experienced types. A large percentage of them are police or corrections officers back home, so being a police officer in the military is just a variation on their usual job. After getting off work at Fort Stewart we would watch in fascination as they practiced handcuffing each other and loading each other into the backs of trucks, relishing in the practice of their skills. They never failed to remind us that they were the *law* and we were there to serve them.

But they're good guys, guilty only of thinking that their job is the greatest, like every other profession in the Army. We mechanics do it too, bragging that we're the only thing keeping this company going. Since Fort Stewart the four platoons have divided into virtual armed camps, competing for prestige and notice, each platoon of MPs against the others and all MPs against us, Headquarters Platoon. Going on convoy missions with each platoon, I begin to get a sense of the distinct character of each, along with the sergeants who lead them. At the head of each platoon is a commissioned officer, but the sergeants run the show. Each MP platoon fancies itself the hardest and toughest, deriding the skills, manliness, and courage of the other platoons whenever possible.

Rivalries over turf and authority have increased since we've been at war, and the longer we're away from home the more we grate on each other's nerves. Members of each platoon ask me when I'm finally going to be permanently assigned as their designated translator. I always smile and change the subject, because truthfully, I like all of them. They're not the kind of guys I would usually hang out with at home, but the more I spend time with them, the more affection I feel for them and come to appreciate their style. This is one of the reasons I joined the Army, after all: to meet people I might not otherwise have a chance to know; police officers, career soldiers, people who love Nascar. I like them, they're good solid people, far from the ivory tower.

One day I'm sleepwalking through a trip to Nasiriyah: chicken, sodas, ice, the same old deal. We're stopped at a large roundabout near the city center, pulled off to the side of the road while I ask for directions. There's a crowd, as usual, people curious to see all the guns and helmets and armor up close. Nothing to worry about, just spectators. But there's something unusual about today, something ominous. The usual conversation has died down, and when people speak it's in short, clipped phrases. Traffic and crowd noises reverberate off the densely packed buildings, rising to a dull roar. The MPs seem on edge, continually scanning the rooftops and blind alleys, uncharacteristically vigilant. There's a tension in the air that hasn't been there before: a buzzing in the crowd and the stiff, contorted movements of the soldiers. The MPs are scowling, cross, irritable. It's hot as hell today and the sun is bearing down directly overhead. The mission's taking longer than expected. Tempers are bound to flare.

"Get the fuck away from me, you fucking hajjis!"

I know the voice: a good guy, a friend of mine, Nick Sollugob.

We met back at the unit because we enlisted together. Funny guy. I turn and see the barrel of his rifle pointing at the face of an Iraqi.

"I swear to God, one of these days I'm going to shoot one of you fuckers."

Something seizes up inside me. I've heard things before, little flashes of aggression toward the Iraqis, but this is the first time it's boiled over. I'm hot and I'm angry. Why does he have to act this way? The Iraqis weren't doing anything. My own weapon is slung across my back. I walk up and get in his face. I raise my voice. "Chill out, man. They weren't doing anything. Why do you have to be so god-damn aggressive to them all the time?"

It was a mistake to confront him like this, in front of everyone. His face is flushed. He shoves me back a step.

"Why you always gotta be such a bitch, Delgado?"

"Fuck you, you don't have to threaten them, you don't have to put your gun in their faces," I say as we inch closer together.

"All right... all right... break it up you two. Get back in the con-voy, we're rolling."

A sergeant interposes himself between us. Sollugob turns away in disgust. As I climb back into the Humvee, I look around at the other MPs in the convoy and see suspicion and disdain on their faces. *They agree with him.* They think I'm a coward, or a sympa-thizer. Five minutes ago I looked around and saw friends; now I see strangers. In an instant, a huge chasm opens between the lower-enlisted MPs and myself. I never feel comfortable on missions in town again, unless I'm working directly under one of the older ser-geants. Where was all of this sentiment before? I heard the idle talk, the posturing, the usual stereotyping of Arabs, Muslims, the "bad guys," but I never thought it was this personal. Back in Florida when I told people I spoke Arabic, they had gotten these wary looks on their faces, as if I were someone not to be trusted. I didn't pay much attention then. Now I remember their sideways glances, the sudden distance. After the incident with Sollugob, it all comes back into fo-cus. Rumors filter back to me through Patterson and Shoe that people don't want to go on missions with me anymore; they don't trust me because I took a stand against one of our guys, I stood up for "them." They whisper that I'm a Muslim, that they should keep an eye on me. The revelation of these sentiments is intensely painful to me.

The Army's just like high school in a lot of ways, everyone wants to be popular. And in one afternoon, I'm out of the clubhouse.

After that trip to Nasiriyah, I begin noticing all sorts of things I had overlooked before: a whispered remark, a scowl, a casual comment about "those people." Seemingly random words and actions are coming together into a pattern; the character of the company is changing. Maybe the stress of the deployment and the growing homesickness is wearing everyone down. We're all sick of this desert, sick of this barracks, sick of being here. An ugly kind of mood is arising, or perhaps it was there all along and just bubbled to the surface now. Prejudice. You can dance around it all you like: talk about war stress, call it "dehumanization of the enemy," quote dozens of books on the history of warfare, but that doesn't change the simple truth of it: hatred. I see it in stark relief now, an undercurrent of anti-Arab and anti-Muslim sentiment.

I'm no paragon. My mind is as full of violence and prejudice as everyone else's, yet because of my background overseas, anti-Arab sentiment doesn't happen to be one of my problems. Yet ever since basic training it's been a steady diet of hatred for "the enemy." At Fort Knox, drill sergeants would often try to motivate us by reminding us of the attack on the World Trade Center and, during the war in Afghanistan, how we might someday get a chance to go over there and "kill us some towelheads." A few of our marching and running cadences had been "updated" to mention the new enemy of the United States in less than enlightened terms. It's a little shocking at first to have three hundred people chanting racist tunes, but gradually it fades into the background and you just do it because that's what everyone else is doing. You start participating automatically, singing along, forgetting about what you're actually saying. I've certainly done it, and I can say with confidence that probably every soldier since September 11 has done the same in one form or another. It's part of the training.

In our unit, the bigotry seems even more pronounced. Just before we left Fort Stewart for the Middle East our commander had given us a little "pep talk." He warned us that there would be newspapers and TV cameras at the departure site, so we should watch what we say.

"Now, there's going to be media over there, so I don't want you to go telling them how you're going to go over there and kill some ragheads and burn some turbans."

He laughed knowingly, and half the unit laughed along with him. It had shocked me when the commander said those words, only because he admitted so openly what everyone already thought: Muslims were the enemy, Arabs were the enemy, terrorists and suicide bombers all. I had stood there, stunned by the casual bigotry. Now in the middle of Iraq, looking around at my unit, I wonder how I could have been so dense for so long.

Here in Iraq, it's gone way beyond the occasional "raghead" and "terrorist" slur. In reference to Iraqis, every other word is "hajji," the current anti-Arab, anti-Muslim epithet of choice. In Arabic, a *hajji* is one who has gone on the Hajj, the pilgrimage to Mecca that is one of the five pillars of Islam. It is often used as a mild honorific, especially to describe an older man. In Army usage it means "gook" or "Charlie" or "nigger." Within a few months, I don't hear the word "Iraqi" anymore, it's always "hajji." The word becomes so deeply embedded in the Army dialect that it becomes the norm, and the words "Iraqi" and "local" and "host-country national" sound stilted and awkward. Once I start listening for it, I hear it everywhere, even in casual conversations that don't have any hostile overtones. It takes the ultimate form of subtle racism: becoming so ubiquitous that people forget it's a slur.

"Oh, it's just what we call them. They call each other that, I didn't think it meant anything racist." Really? They call *each other* that? It's a lame attempt at justification.

It's odd to find myself in this position, feeling betrayed and isolated by my company's growing hypernationalism. When I lived in Egypt I went out of my way to assert my Americanness and by extension America's superiority, because when you live overseas, your Americanness becomes magnified in your mind. America becomes the ideal, the place where all good things are. Now that I'm in the U.S. Army, listening to the trash talk of the 320th, I feel more and more like a foreigner. By the time I came to America I had lived for eighteen years in other countries: seven years in Thailand, four years in Senegal, and the last seven years in Egypt. When members of my company told me that Muslim and Islam were two different religions, or that Osama bin Laden was the "head" of Islam, I saw that I was dealing with an ignorance that was deep and fundamental. I *knew* better. Most of the guys in my company didn't; they'd never had the chance to learn. For one of the first times in my life, I'm grateful for my unusual childhood, glad to have had all those years overseas. I'm glad I can see what's really happening here.

The first sergeant is raging. We bought sodas for a company picnic and he promised the Iraqi vendor he'd return all the empty bottles. A few are missing. Where the hell are they? He threatens us with his vengeance if they're not found, promises to search the company area, promises an end to all soda purchases.

Privately, Schumacher informs me that a few of the MPs have taken to hurling bottles at Iraqis, as they drive past them in their Humvees. Shoe doesn't seem particularly bothered by this; if their sergeants don't know about it already, he seems to think, they wouldn't give a damn. Besides, we can't prove anything and they would just deny it.

At least it solves the mystery of where the missing bottles are going. Never learning the truth, the first sergeant apologizes to the vendor and gives him some extra dinar to cover the loss.

Coming back from a mission to Nasiriyah, I'm all shaken up. I collapse on my bunk without taking off my vest or coveralls. Sergeant Toro asks what's wrong. I tell him that something happened in Nasiriyah: one of the senior sergeants in our company had struck a group of Iraqi children. The kids had been crowding around him, bothering him for food, water, and candy as they always do, and the sergeant took a steel Humvee antenna from the back of the truck and beat them back with it. Half a dozen people saw it happen, but no one did anything. It all happened so quickly, and besides, he was the senior noncommissioned officer. Sergeant Toro looks at me disapprovingly, he has a three-year-old daughter at home. "That's fucked up, man," he says.

Later on, an explanation of the incident filters out, something about how the Iraqis were trying to reach for an M16 lying in the back of the truck and the sergeant had struck them in self-defense. Bullshit. Since when do we carry extra M16s with us on a mission? Even if we did, every soldier has it drilled into him since boot camp never to leave his weapon out of reach and unsecured. The official story reeks. There's no way it happened like that, absolutely no way. The incident is quickly relegated to oblivion.

Maybe it's all in my head, but it seems like the MPs are avoiding me now. They're certainly not talking to me as much as they used to. I can't really say I mind, as the last few weeks have been eye-opening. I cleave even more to my brothers in the motor pool, where I still feel welcome. Work continues, interrupted occasionally by missions into the city that feel more and more like a chore instead of a privilege. I don't feel comfortable around the MPs anymore, I feel like they only tolerate my presence because they need me as a translator.

One day an MP sergeant walks into the maintenance tent and tells me to get ready for a mission, as they might need some translation. We're not going to Nasiriyah. I'm puzzled, but I pack up my weapon and tools as usual. When the convoy gets rolling I find myself in a vehicle with Peterman, a quiet, serious MP, and a sergeant. It's immediately obvious that this mission is not routine, as Peterman appears to be charting some kind of course on the GPS unit. An hour or so outside the base, our train of vehicles leaves the road and heads off on some sidetrack. We're going solely by GPS now, Peterman occasionally calling out numbers and degrees as we head farther and farther into the desert. Just before the steady vibration of the Humvee lulls me into an afternoon nap, the lead vehicle descends down the crest of a hill and our convoy halts. Strange... the hill slopes away so subtly that you can't even see it until you're right on the edge. We find ourselves in a shallow, square depression, surrounded on one side with a long wall or sand berm. What is this place?

Gray-green Army earthmovers crawl slowly across the landscape. Experimental holes have been dug in the earth, and we see the unmistakable tread marks left behind by the steam-shovel tanks. A billowing saffron tent is visible in the middle distance; underneath it dozens of men in bright green hospital scrubs are moving and talking. The MP sergeant in charge of the mission motions us over and informs us, half-bored, that our unit has been assigned to help the Kuwaiti government excavate a mass grave site. They're sketchy on the details, but apparently during the first Gulf War, Saddam Hussein executed whole groups of Kuwaiti men and boys and buried them here in southern Iraq. The sergeant dismisses us with a warning not to wander too far and I make my way over to the large, colorful tent to talk to the men, who I assume are Kuwaiti investigators.

I hail them with a friendly *Salaam allaikhum*, and they return the greeting without really noticing me. The men are neat and professional looking, with sharply trimmed beards behind their surgical masks. Everyone is dressed in scrubs and long plastic gloves. In flawless English, one of the Kuwaitis directs us around the site and explains what they're doing. They excavated and turned up several bodies along the wall before they hit the main site and discovered a large pit with upward of thirty corpses. They're still pulling them out and counting them; he excuses himself to get back to his work. As I meander through the tent, examining various forensic tools, a flash of bright white catches my eye. I turn over the folded edge of one of several white burlap bags and find myself staring into a human skull.

Brown and shriveled and caked with dirt, it looks like it was formed out of dry mud rather than bone. The dome of the cranium has split into several large pieces, exposing the inner bowl. Long patches of hair remain on the brow, sticking up in tufts. The eye sockets stare vacantly out of the bag. Half the jaw is cracked away, exposing the roots of yellowed teeth. Beneath it, the tip of a human femur is visible, jutting out from a pile of unidentifiable decay. Pieces of fabric cling to the leg bone and trail down in tatters to the brownish mass underneath. A smell rises up from the bag: rotten meat, night soil, and powdered earth. I feel my stomach roll and I step backward, clapping my hand over my mouth.

I fight for balance as nausea overtakes me. I pause and breathe deeply at the tent entrance, taking in the hot outdoor air. All around us, rainbow-colored parasols have been stuck in the earth at intervals to provide shade for the Kuwaiti workers. The contrast of the festive umbrellas and the scene before us is utterly surreal.

Now we're standing at the edge of a pit, about eight feet deep and forty or fifty feet across. At the bottom, teams of Kuwaitis are working in rotation, digging with shovels and hands. Bones are revealed: long bones and handfuls of tiny bones, jaws and shards of skulls. Occasionally the bones are bound up like a parcel in remnants of fabric, what's left of the traditional *galabeyah* robes worn by most Kuwaitis. I see desiccated rubber sandals and scraps of red-checkered cloth that once were headscarves. The workers drop the remains into burlap bags, or pass the more intact corpses up out of the pit to be sorted on tables. As they hand up a withered bundle of fabric and bone, one of the workers stumbles and the robe attached to the corpse tears. Dry flesh and dust spills out over the pit. The bones are still there, but the flesh has dried into flakes and powder. The body breaks apart and floats gently down to the bottom of the pit, drifting like autumn leaves settling in a slow breeze. The man responsible mutters a curse and bends down to collect the bones. The work continues.

Now one of the workers has found a skull and displays it eagerly for the sergeant standing next to me, holding it up for a photo. He turns it over to point out the bullet holes in back, punched so neatly they might have been drilled. The sergeant leans in for a close-up.

"Give me one of the skulls," he says. "I want to hold one of them in my hand." The Kuwaiti gingerly passes the skull to the sergeant. The sergeant looks down at it for a moment and begins to pass it idly from hand to hand, as if it were a basketball.

"Hey, Delgado, come take my picture. I wanna get a picture of me holding the skull."

Feeling oddly disassociated, as if in a trance, I walk over to the sergeant, who is backing up into the sun to get better light. He raises the skull to chest level and holds it out for me. I snap two pictures in quick succession, the first with him showing a somber and serious expression, the second with him grinning broadly as if to say, "I got this one." He thanks me, asks me to remind him to make copies, and shuffles off.

I look down and see bodies, dry bodies and skulls with their clothes still visible. I look up and see rainbow umbrellas. Looking down into the pit I know I should feel something—horror, revulsion, pity—but I don't. I know that this is not a normal situation, that I'm supposed to feel something at times like this, but I don't feel anything at all. That's not quite true: I feel numb. I feel dead. I must be some kind of monster. I want to feel nausea; I want to feel outrage. I try to visualize what these bodies must have looked like when they were alive, try to picture the faces of Kuwaiti men, with beards like the workers here. But I didn't know these people. My image is only a fantasy; I can never know what happened here. I stand there watching as if it were the most ordinary thing in the world. My emotions are gone, as swiftly and completely as if a switch had been flicked off.

SUMMER 2003 The growing hatred in my unit has begun to weigh on me more and more, intruding into my waking thoughts. I can no longer relax in my off hours. My sleep is growing increasingly brief and fitful. One morning Shoe asks what I was yelling about and I look at him questioningly. He says I was shouting something in my sleep; woke the whole squad up. He says I do it a lot. Sergeant Wallace reminds me that I used to do the same thing back at Fort Stewart.

Even awake, I find myself consumed with self-doubt, self-loathing, about being where I am. I've started to talk to Sergeant Toro about it, either when we're lifting weights or when we're re-laxing in our room. Like a good officer, Sergeant Toro tells me to relax and be patient. He tells me I'm still just adjusting to Army life, that my feelings will change. The trouble is that it's been two years since I enlisted and my feelings haven't changed. I feel intensely hypocritical, believing in compassion, mediation, and nonviolence while simultaneously carrying a machine gun and serving in an occupation force. The conflict seems irreconcilable. Every day that I stay in the military I feel more a traitor to my beliefs. The Army that I imagined, the mythological Army that captured my imagina-tion as a boy, has proved illusory. I've come to see the Army in its worst form, a distortion of itself: violence, threats, dogma, and ha-tred. I see the way the soldiers bully each other for dominance, and then watch as those who are bullied turn and dominate the Iraqis. I feel my friends and comrades pulling apart from me, diverging from the ideals I believe in. They have changed; something in them has gone black. I have changed, too; the man I am now and the boy I was in Sarasota have grown vastly apart. Between me and the other privates, those who hate "ragheads" and long to kill the enemy, there is an unfathomable gulf. Seeing the prisoners, seeing the Iraqi civilians, fills me with profound sadness and loss. I have no bloodlust in me. I do not wish to fight.

I feel literal pain whenever I open one of my books and read the Sutras, pain at my hypocrisy and inadequacy. Although Buddhism doesn't teach sin as a concept, I feel sinful all the time. I dread the future as if a terrible judgment were hanging over my head, retribution for all my wrongdoing. Everything about this place seems wrong: what we're doing to the Iraqis, the destruction, the meaningless loss of life. It overwhelms my senses. I coast through my daily tasks as if on autopilot. On missions, I look out at the crowds of desperate people and feel impotent to help them in any way. In the motor pool, I work with dull bitterness, knowing that all my labor accomplishes nothing but to perpetuate the cycle.

One of the few books I packed in my military kit back in Sarasota was a ragged, Scotch-taped paperback of *The Bhaghavad Gita*, a gift from Amy and her parents. I have read it many times, and I find myself reading it again in these dark days, fascinated by its meaning. *The Bhaghavad Gita* is a Hindu religious text, its title roughly translated as "The Song of God," that forms one section of the much larger epic poem called *The Mahabharata*, which tells the story of the Bharata dynasty's interactions with the Hindu gods. *The Bhaghavad Gita* describes the commencement of a huge battle between two rival factions of a family, and tells the story of its protagonist, Arjuna, and his discussion with the god Krishna in human form as his charioteer. The book begins with Arjuna looking out over the ranks of his army and the enemy army and recognizing many familiar faces: friends, relatives, and teachers. Upon seeing these comrades, Arjuna is overcome with grief at the prospect of fighting and killing people he loves and respects. In his despair, he drops his bow and arrows and refuses to fight. The opening passages have always thrilled me with their passion and eloquence. Now, in the depths of a war I do not wish to fight, their stanzas take on a new meaning. I read of Arjuna's despair and the words come alive to me, thousands of years after they were written, the words of a distant soldier who had lost his will to fight.

> *Krishna, Krishna!*
> *Now as I look on,*
> *These, my kinsmen*
> *arrayed for battle,*
> *My limbs are weakening,*
> *My mouth is parching,*
> *My body trembles,*
> *My hair seems upright,*
> *My skin seems burning,*
> *The bow Gandiva*
> *Slips from my hand,*
> *My brain is whirling*
> *Round and round,*
> *I can see no longer:*
> *Krishna, I see such*
> *Omens of evil!*

Reading these words in Iraq, my own hair seems to stand on end.

> *Though they should slay me*
> *How could I harm them?*
> *I cannot wish it:*
> *Never, never,*
> *Not though it won me*
> *The throne of the three worlds;*
> *How much the less for*
> *Earthly lordship!*
> *… Evil they may be,*

Worst of the wicked,
Yet if we kill them
Our sin is greater.
How could we dare spill
The blood that unites us?
... What is this crime
I am planning, O Krishna?
Murder most hateful,
Murder of my brothers!
Am I indeed
So greedy for greatness?
Rather than this
Let the evil children
Of Dhritarashtra
Come with their weapons
Against me in battle:
I shall not struggle,
I shall not strike them.
Now let them kill me,
That will be better.

Having spoken thus, Arjuna threw aside his arrows and his bow in
the midst of the battlefield. He sat down on the seat of the chariot,
and his heart was overcome with sorrow.[3]

The plain truth is that I have no desire to fight anyone, even
those I am supposed to call my enemy. I'm not even sure they are
my enemies, those old men and teenagers trussed up in the prison
yard. How could I ever want to kill them? Were they not conscripted
to fight us? Both of us, men on both sides, have been set against each
other as pawns. They had no more choice in the matter than I. "Ain't
no point in looking pale, go to war or go to jail" is the refrain from
an Army marching cadence. We and the Iraqis have no quarrel, and

yet no choice but to fight and die. I feel despair at this intractable conflict, sensing at last that we're all trapped in something beyond our control. My heart is overcome with sorrow.

One day I dig into the depths of my B-bag and pull out a battered, cloth-covered binder, something a buddy of mine sent me a long time ago, when I was deployed to Fort Stewart. I had asked him for it in a moment of doubt and introspection, but had put it out of my mind in all the chaos of deployment, tucking it away in case I needed it later. Inside the binder is a plain brown mailing envelope. I undo the clasp and a packet of papers spills out. At the top of one of the papers, in large, bold letters, are the words "Army Regulation 600–43. Personnel–General. Conscientious Objection." I unclip the packet, set it beside me on the bunk, and begin to read.

Dakar, Senegal

1992 I'm standing on an outcropping of rock a dozen feet above the sea. The water is heaving—white-capped waves crash against the shore, spattering me with stinging saltwater. There are hundreds of Senegalese all around us, on every rock and cliff and stretch of shore; they've come with nets and hand lines and baskets and wooden clubs. A school of fish has gotten stuck between the rocks and there are thousands of them in a tight space, making them easy to catch. Black-skinned young boys are pulling up fish by the dozen in cast nets, and men with fishing lines are ripping them out of the water as soon as they throw their lines in, without any bait. Men and women are hauling fish off by the armload and cartload.

My brother and father run down to the edge of the sharp rocks and stand shoulder to shoulder with Senegalese fishermen, casting a hand line wound around an old block of wood. I stand twenty feet back, admiring some crabs caught in a tide pool. *I hate* fishing. My dad *loves* to fish, and he and my brother

The book has turned my mind to thoughts of death. I think about Amy and imagine the pain of losing her, the pain of never being able to see her again. Then I think about my own death. Mortality is a special fascination of mine, bordering on obsession. What is the experience of death? What comes afterward? These thoughts have possessed me since early adolescence. Alone in the dark, I turn my mind to the thought of my own annihilation and for the first time in months I allow myself to truly meditate on the subject of death.

No matter what I do or say, no matter how good a Buddhist I am or how much I achieve in my lifetime . . . I am going to die. There is absolutely no escape. Fear envelops me, for with death comes the terrible thought of eternity, an unknown eternity, terrible in its mystery . . . or perhaps . . . an eternity of damnation. There is nothing as terrifying as the prospect of suffering *without end,* without respite, beyond all earthly fears. Hell is the ultimate terror. I don't actually believe in hell, not intellectually, but in the dead of night the concept is emotionally real. I think back on all the books I've read on the subject of damnation. Dante conceived of hell as a series of descending rings made up of increasingly severe torments. In one segment, the wrathful dead battle eternally in the slime of the river Styx while the slothful are submerged beneath them. In a lower section, the followers of false religions are squeezed into a single, red-hot iron coffin. On the lowest levels, traitors are frozen in a lake of ice, eternally alone and separate except for the company of Lucifer. Am I a follower of a false religion? Am I a traitor? This terrible sense of eternity, the unfathomable nature of death, horrifies me. Hell isn't real, it can't be, it's too fanciful, and yet . . . why am I so afraid? Many people incorrectly assume that Buddhism does not have a concept of hell. On the contrary, Buddhist mythology has one of the largest and most intricate hell cosmologies of any world religion. I don't believe in the Buddhist hells any more than I believe in the Western hells, and yet their metaphors are so intense and so varied: the hell of being crushed between four iron mountains, the hell of being frozen and shattered into a thousand shards, the hell of being sliced apart along black lines, the hells of molten copper and molten lead, the hell of eternal battle, killing and dying and rising from the dead to be killed again, never-ending war ... All these metaphors combine and wash over me until I am in a state approaching panic. All I can see is my own imperfection and immorality. There's no way out. Eternity is coming. I feel an enormous pressure on my chest, as if someone were squeezing my heart. I try to sit up in bed, but my legs and arms are frozen. I can't breathe. In that instant, I cry out for mercy, for a message, either to tell me that my fear is justified or to comfort me.

I lay back perfectly still in my bunk, my mind completely open, listening with the innermost depths of my being for whatever the universe has to say. Rapid-fire images and sentences begin running through my head: proofs, deductions, logical assumptions. Beginning with first principles, I run through everything I can logically deduce about the nature of the moral universe. Of one thing I am certain: man is fallible. No moral system could ever demand perfection of something that is inherently imperfect. Whatever moral mechanism exists must be merciful, or at least understanding, of these frail beings called men. I think about the concept of eternity and eternal suffering, the unimaginable imbalance of it, the wild disproportion of eternal punishment for temporal misdeeds. No just system could ever demand infinite retribution for finite sins. As I imagine the surreal suffering of hell, my thoughts turn to the sufferings of the world, all the pain I see around me and read about in the paper. I think about the nightmarish existence of North Koreans in the gulag, beaten to death by guards, their bodies fed to dogs, children imprisoned for the crimes their parents committed. I think of the people just over the horizon in Nasiriyah, and in every city in Iraq, limbs severed by shrapnel, families broken apart, lovers separated, a proud culture cast down and trampled. In Afghanistan as well, countless souls have been plunged into a hell not of their own making, and I am a part of that. I have helped bring a little piece of hell to earth.

Something in my chest cracks open and I feel an explosion of mercy and sorrow and empathy. I feel limitless compassion for everyone enduring a hellish existence and forced to face the same eventuality of death. I pray, not in the sense of *praying to* someone or *praying for* something, but in the most Buddhist sense that I know: wishing for another's happiness. My thoughts linger over the forms of each of the mechanics sleeping in this room, and on each of them I focus my thought and wish for their happiness, even Spangler . . . especially Spangler. I extend my wish to everyone sleeping in the building tonight, to my whole unit, to the commander and the first sergeant and all the MPs who hate me with a passion. The Buddhist definition of love is "to wish for another's happiness," and the definition of compassion is "to wish for another to be free of suffering." My love and compassion expands and expands until I feel it cover the entire world, every suffering being. I finally say with utmost sincerity, "May every living being have a happy life. May they be free of suffering." There's no dogma here, no forms, no pretensions. For once I can say the words and mean them.

It's like waking up from a nightmare. All my suffering vanishes. I laugh to myself in bed, totally free and spontaneous. I get up and walk downstairs in a daze. According to a Zen proverb, "There is little difference between a man lying dead drunk on sake in a ditch and a man drunk on satori"—satori, a feeling of absolute balance and poise, putting your soul in a place beyond life and death. I wander past the motor pool, walking barefoot on dust beneath a starry sky, laughing and marveling at the beauty and wonder of it all. I make bold, crazy resolutions. I resolve to tell everyone how much I appreciate them. I see Sergeant Wallace alone in the motor pool working diligently by the light of a single lantern at midnight. I walk up to him and say, "What a beautiful night."

"Yes it is, Delgado, it most certainly is." He smiles that crazy, toothy grin of his and looks at me a little oddly. I continue out past the motor pool and onto the high earth barrier at the edge of our company area. A few minutes ago I was in hell, and now I have returned: reborn, newborn, awake. I feel a fading hint of something on the edge of my perception: a sense of belonging. I feel that everything around me is perfectly finished and complete; nothing, at this moment, is absent.

I ask Sergeant Wallace if he can set up a meeting for me with the battalion chaplain. I tell him and Sergeant Toro that I am thinking about filing for conscientious objector status. Neither seems very surprised, only weary and concerned.

Sergeant Wallace shakes his head slowly. "Well, you do what you gotta do, but go and see the chaplain first. See if he can help you with some of your problems."

Sergeant Toro speaks in the measured voice he adopts when counseling a subordinate, his "sergeant voice." "You know, Delgado, I remember when you were talking about the Army not being right for you back at St. Petersburg. You remember that first drill after you came back from AIT? We were sitting in the motor pool office and you told me and Sergeant Cassidy how you had changed, and I told you to wait and see about it. You've been talking like this for a long time."

"And complaining about it too!" Sergeant Wallace interjects.

I remembered how I felt after Advanced Individual Training, AIT. "I've tried to adjust to being in the Army, Sergeant Toro, but it doesn't feel like it's getting any better. I feel depressed and anxious all the time. I've got a bad attitude."

"Yeah, we know that," Sergeant Toro says with a laugh. "We see it in the motor pool. I know you've been feeling bad lately. I think it's a good idea to go and see the chaplain. Maybe he can help you."

It's late afternoon. Sergeant Wallace has released us after a long day in the motor pool. Shoe, Patterson, Spangler, and I are all soaked in transmission fluid and our hands are black with engine oil up to our elbows—except for Patterson, who is black all the way up his arms, we observe jokingly.

"Y'all just jealous," Patterson says. "You wish you was black, son."

The second we're off work Shoe vanishes without a word, perhaps off to visit his uncle and friends in the Air Force sector. Patterson slinks away too, maybe to visit one of his many "shorties." Spangler wanders off, and as I finish gathering up my tools and locking them in my toolbox, Sergeant Wallace says, "Delgado, come here, let me talk to you for a second."

His mood is serious, and we stand face to face, close enough that I have to look up to meet his gaze. Sergeant Wallace leans back against one of the support poles of the maintenance tent and puts his hand on my shoulder. He is in his green camouflage pants, and I in my brown coveralls pulled down and tied off at the waist. The sun is beginning to set behind Etemennigur. He pulls out a pack of cigarettes and lights one, taking a long slow drag before he begins to speak.

"Delgado, you know what you're going to do is going to be the hardest thing you've ever done in your life."

He continues in his quiet bass voice, surprising me with his depth and eloquence, this man of notoriously few words, now speaking fluidly and passionately. "I've talked with you. I know you're serious, I know you're a religious person, but these others, these MPs, they're going to put you through hell. They're not going to make it easy. It's going to take a long time, probably more than a year. You're gonna be home in Florida before it's done. Other people are not going to like what you're doing, and the command is going to make it real hard on you. This isn't the easy way to get out of the Army, you know, this is the hard way. I don't want to see you get in trouble. I just want to make sure you understand what you're getting yourself into."

"I know, Sergeant Wallace, I understand that. I'm not trying to get out of the deployment. I don't want out of the Army just *because*, I want out of the Army the right way. I have to do it this way. I believe the war is wrong. I can't be a Buddhist and be a part of it anymore."

A look of concern and sadness comes over Sergeant Wallace's dark, glistening face. Then his eyes twinkle with sudden inspiration. "You know, Delgado, nobody wants to kill anybody else. No soldier wants to have to kill someone. Now, I don't know anything about your religion, but I'm a Christian, as you know, and the Bible says the same things you sayin' to me. The Bible says, Thou shalt not kill. I've been in the Army for more than seventeen years now and I don't want to kill nobody. If I have to pick up my weapon to protect myself or protect one of you, I would do it and I wouldn't hesitate, but the important thing to remember is *not to pick up your weapon with hatred in your heart.*

"Some of these others, these MPs, the way they talk about the Iraqis, the way they act toward them, that's not right. You see, they have hate in their hearts. If I have to shoot an enemy soldier who's trying to kill me, I'm just defending myself, I don't hate him and I know he's just doing what he's got to do. It's your heart and what you feel inside that matters. As long as I don't enjoy it, as long as I don't do it with violence and hate in my heart, it's not a sin. You do what you have to do, but nobody *wants* to do it. That's what I believe, that's my religion."

I have never had so much respect for Sergeant Wallace as I do at this moment. His words resonate in my chest. *Nobody wants to do it.* I am moved almost to the point of tears, as all the loneliness and frustration begins to pour out of me. I know that Sergeant Wallace feels like a father to the motor pool, we joke about his attempts to teach us "character," but standing here at the edge of the motor pool as evening comes on, I'm glad he has taken on this role. His words are electric with deep, heart-felt faith. I picture the worn leather-bound Bible with gilded edges that he keeps on his bed table: often we come into his room and find him stretched out on the bed with it, reading slowly and forming each word with his lips as he reads. Whenever one of us enters the room, he closes the Bible and looks up to talk to us with a big grin on his lips. That's Sergeant Wallace, always smiling, always shouting out, "Glory! Glory!" always laughing: a gentle soul.

"You're right, Sergeant Wallace, you're absolutely right. It's your heart that matters. In Buddhism your state of mind is everything; we believe that if you perform an action with a negative mind then that action becomes negative. Nothing good can come out of a hateful mind."

"Exactly, exactly, that's exactly what I'm sayin'."

"The thing is...I don't believe I can pick up my weapon and pull the trigger without a hateful mind. Buddhism teaches that pulling the trigger itself is hatred; it's an action that is so inherently hateful that no good can come of it. I don't believe you can kill someone else without polluting your mind."

I pause, considering whether to go on. He seems receptive to my words, he's listening intently, so I continue: "There's a very old story in Buddhism. Buddha told stories of his previous incarnations, his previous lives, a lot like the parables of Jesus in the New Testament."

Sergeant Wallace's eyes light up when I say the word "Jesus."

"In one of these stories, the parable of Angry Spear, The Buddha killed someone out of compassion for him. The Buddha was a passenger on a ship that was seized by pirates. The leader of the pirates, Angry Spear, was a vicious man who was going to kill all the passengers on the ship. So The Buddha killed him preemptively, to prevent him from committing such a great sin and creating such negative karma. The idea of the story is that The Buddha killed Angry Spear out of compassion for him, because he didn't want the pirate to be reborn in a hell-existence for having murdered the passengers. There are a lot of stories like this. But you can't just go around killing people and claiming it's out of compassion. One of the main points of the story is that only a buddha has the ability to make that distinction, that it takes the wisdom of a bodhisattva to be able to make judgments like that. It takes *perfect* wisdom, and I know I don't have that wisdom."

Sergeant Wallace stares at me for a long moment. He's always joked about my "heathen ways," but he's never actually heard me talk about Buddhism. I don't like to talk about it, anyway; I hate being a preacher.

Finally he nods. "We none of us perfect, you just gotta do what you gotta do. But you do it always with love in your heart, and you're all right. I just want you to know what you're in for. Make sure you ready for it."

"Thanks, Sergeant Wallace, I really appreciate you looking out for me. I'm ready. I'm not about to change my mind."

"You're in for a hard time, Delgado, but I'll do what I can for you."

The sun's gone down by now and the horizon is purplish and bruised-looking, with a few early stars. We say our goodbyes and I walk off, drifting aimlessly in the direction of the barracks, excited but terrified. Just like that—it's official. I'm so nervous I could vomit, but my mind is already spinning frantically, thinking of the next step: what I'm going to say in my statement, what I'm going to write, arguments I'm going to have to make and arguments I'm going to have to counter. If they dredge up a Buddhist chaplain to debate my points, I might have to confront the question of the Buddhist "mercy killing" like that described in the parable of Angry Spear; I'm already thinking of a few passages to frame my interpretation. I have so much to say. I'm looking forward to the chance to get it all down on paper, to make my case, but that doesn't mean the prospect isn't terrifying. After all the theorizing and agonizing, the moment is finally here: I will finally get to say my piece.

I know I'm ready. No matter what they try to say or do to me, I can handle it. I may not know much about mechanics, but I know Buddhism; months of study have taught me well. My Buddhist bible is tattered and held together with tape from a thousand readings; I know every word of it inside and out. For countless hours I've studied, read, meditated, gone over the arguments in my head. I've pondered this decision for so long, there's no way they could ask me anything I haven't already asked myself a dozen times lying awake in my bunk at night. My guys in the motor pool are with me, Sergeant Toro and Sergeant Wallace are with me; fuck everything else. Honestly, there's no name that anyone could call me that I haven't already called myself, in the darkest recesses of my heart: coward, traitor, weakling, dreamer, fanatic. What must I do to be the man I want to be? I know there will be anger, hatred, isolation. I've already seen it on the faces of my fellows when I start to talk about Palestine, or Egypt, or the Iraqis, or a dozen other subjects on which my views don't conform to their narrow view of the world. Living the life I've lived, being where I've been, has torn my eyelids off... and I can never go back to the tiny little world of St. Petersburg, believing it's the only place on earth. Nothing could possibly be worse than sitting up every night staring at the ceiling. I breathe out. I feel calm, collected: satori. I feel unstoppable, as if my fate were an immeasurable wave driving me forward toward an unknown end. At this moment the outcome seems unimportant. Everything—Thailand, Sarasota, the Army, Buddhism, Iraq—has been leading up to this moment in my life. I think of the words of the famed samurai Miyamoto Musashi:

> Under the sword lifted high,
> There is Hell making you tremble;
> But go ahead,
> And you have the land of bliss.

My internal conflict is over. I feel powerful and free, as if I were alone between heaven and earth. Whatever happens tomorrow or the next day, they can't ignore me any longer. I will object.

Part Three
THE OBJECTOR

TALLIL AIRBASE, SOUTHERN IRAQ

AUGUST 2003 Chaplain Ellis folds his hands across his chest and leans back in his chair. Every so often he nods reflexively as I tell him my life story. At a few key points he interrupts to ask whether my father was Buddhist, how long I've felt this way, and other questions about my religious development. He is fascinated by my account of growing up overseas and visiting so many different countries. His wrinkled face bespeaks kindness and empathy, and as I look up at him throughout my narration, I feel more and more comfortable. When I finish describing how I was exposed to Buddhism in Thailand and how I had come to study Buddhism as a college student in Sarasota, Chaplain Ellis begins to speak. He is a soft-spoken, deliberate man who chooses each word with care, and I must force myself to be patient as I listen. He is a Protestant; I don't remember now what denomination. He tells me that he is not familiar with Buddhism as a theologian but that he understands that it is one of the great world religions and that its teachings are explicitly pacifist. Gesturing to his side, he points out that he himself does not carry a weapon although he is allowed to if he chooses.

"I'm a hunter. Back home I go hunting, and of course I carry a rifle then. But over here my job is to save lives, not take them. I know a couple of chaplains who carry their own personal pistols, but I never have. I don't have any desire to take another human being's life."

I smile. Chaplain Ellis seems genuinely interested in helping me follow my conscience. I ask him what I should do. He says that he doesn't have a problem counseling me if I decide to file for conscientious objection, but he would feel better about it if I spoke to someone who was a little more knowledgeable about Buddhism. He points out that the Republic of Korea forces stationed at Tallil probably have a Buddhist chaplain, and that I should arrange a meeting. I nod my assent. As I stand up to leave he asks whether I brought any Buddhist books with me, he'd like to look them over, understand where I'm coming from. I tell him I am happy to lend him my books, but that he'll have to forgive their tattered condition.

"Oh, don't worry about that." He smiles knowingly. "All my Bibles are the same way."

A few days later, having been unsuccessful in contacting the Korean Army chaplain, I tell Chaplain Ellis that I think I have exhausted my counseling options. Well, no one can say I didn't try. It would have been nice to speak with a Buddhist chaplain. I wonder what he would have told me? I'll never know. I want to move forward with conscientious objection. Chaplain Ellis pats me on the shoulder in a fatherly way and says he'll be happy to make out a report. He gives me back my books.

The initial request for conscientious objector status is absurdly simple: a standard 4187 Personnel Action Form with "conscientious objection" written under "requested action." I sign the form and drop it off at the clerical section that day. There. No clouds, no thunderbolts; the first part is done. I inform Sergeant Wallace that I would like to turn in my weapon; I won't be needing it anymore. He instructs me to clean it one last time. Damn, I was hoping to get out of that. That evening I attack the barrel of the SAW with a stiff brush, scratching off every possible atom of carbon or sand. Even though I haven't fired it since training at Fort Stewart, I scour the inside of the barrel with a copper-bristled rod and oil every mechanism. I even polish the stock and run a soft cloth over the wire shoulder-stop. This one time, I'll be able to say that I cleaned my weapon thoroughly.

With the weapon polished to glistening, I lug it, my three drums of ammo, and the spare barrel downstairs to the armory, a metal shipping container with an impressive lock. Sergeant Motes, the weapons fanatic, is standing by the door as usual, looking over each piece as it is turned in for storage. I offer up my weapon and barrel for inspection. He scans them critically, but finally lets them pass. He doesn't know that I'm bidding farewell to the weapon forever.

A long time ago, when it was first assigned to me, I named my weapon, as many soldiers do. Mine was Squad Automatic Weapon Number 128, I believe. The name I chose for it was *Rta:* the "rhythm of the universe" in Vedic thought, the cosmic mechanism that creates order out of chaos. Back when I still thought having a gun was cool, something about a "divine ordering principle" had appealed to me. The name was also a pun on my friend Rita, who, like my machine gun, could chatter at an impressive rate. Rta was an old-style SAW, with a longer barrel. She had bright blue numbering painted on her stock and a new makeshift sling of braided 550 cord, as I had lost the original. She was a heavy old bitch, but she fired straight.

As I stood there at the armory, I felt a sudden poignant sadness. I would never use the weapon again, never fire it, but we had a long history together. I felt almost disloyal to it, heavy, unwieldy, and uncomfortable as it was. It would be a pleasure never to have to carry it again. Still, I was sad to see it go. When Sergeant Motes closed the steel collar of the weapons rack over its barrel, I turned away. Sometimes even *things* can become a part of you, and when you have to let go of them it feels as if a limb has been sliced off. My parting with Rta marked a turning point for me, as final and immutable as if I *had* lost an arm.

I'm beginning to think that no one has noticed my application, that maybe I should file another copy or talk to the commander myself, when one day as I am finishing loading my equipment into the back of a Humvee for a mission to Nasiriyah, the ominous figure of the first sergeant appears, preceded as always by his sharp voice: "Delgado. Put your stuff away, you're not going."

I freeze, stunned. *They know.*

"You know what this is about, right, Delgado?" he says.

"Yes, First Sergeant."

"Come see me in my room. Master Sergeant Carlson and I want to have a talk with you."

"Yes, First Sergeant."

I put my gear away, then trudge back upstairs to the first sergeant's room. My knees feel like water. When I step inside, the three senior noncommissioned officers of the company are standing around me in a semicircle: the first sergeant, Master Sergeant Carlson, and Sergeant First Class Baird. No one looks amused. It is Master Sergeant Carlson, the oldest member of our company, platoon sergeant of Headquarters, who speaks first. "We hear you don't want to go on missions anymore, Delgado."

"No, Master Sergeant, it's not that I don't want to go on missions."

"Well, that's what happens when you turn in the paperwork that you did."

"I can still translate. I want to help out," I say.

"You see, Delgado, we can't let you go off base without a weapon," says the first sergeant. "If you can't defend yourself, you would be a liability. What am I supposed to tell your mom and dad if you get killed on a mission without a weapon?"

"I don't really think it makes much of a difference, First Sergeant. Even if I had my weapon I wouldn't use it."

The three of them bombard me with questions. Why I want to do this, why I want out of the missions. I tell them again that it's not about getting out of the missions, it's about the war, the Army, the big picture. Their tones are friendly but stern, as if they were concerned fathers trying to talk their teenage son out of getting a tattoo. I get the sense that they're trying to pressure me into taking my CO application back.

"You know they're never going to let you out of the Army with this, right Delgado?"

"I'm not trying to get out of the deployment, First Sergeant."

"So you're telling me if you're on patrol in Nasiriyah and some terrorist points a weapon at you or one of your buddies, you're not going to return fire?"

"I don't know, First Sergeant. I don't think anybody knows until they're in that situation."

"So you're saying you wouldn't defend yourself or the members of your team?"

"I don't know...I might point my weapon at them...or fire shots to try and frighten them off. I don't know if I could deliberately try to kill someone."

Saying these words is a mistake; by not being clear, I give him an opening to infer that I might be capable of killing. Several months later, the first sergeant will draft a statement opposing my CO status that comes back to these words, which in my opinion are radically misquoted. I shouldn't even go down the "hypothetical" road with him. Maybe I'd fire shots in the air, maybe I'd try to kneecap the enemy, maybe I'd just try to get out of the area as fast as possible, or maybe, in that half second, all my training and instincts would take over and I'd fire, aiming center-mass...I don't know. Anyone who says they know for certain what they would do in that kind of situation is lying. What I do know is that I never want to put myself in a position where I might be called upon to take another's life. That's not the attitude I perceive in the rest of the company, however. The way I see it, a lot of the soldiers try to start trouble where there isn't any, constantly bragging about wanting "some action" and not wanting to go home without at least one kill. I'm not like that.

The sergeants don't seem to like my answers. They tell me that if they go out on missions they want to know for sure that I'm covering their backs just like they're covering mine. I'm offended by this. The last thing I want to be is disloyal. I'm not a traitor and I'm not a coward. I tell them that I would watch their backs, that I would do everything to protect them, that I'm just not sure that I could kill someone when the time came. They look at me with extreme distaste. Although they don't say it, I can feel the accusations: coward, quitter, wimp, traitor.

"I want to help the unit, First Sergeant," I say again. "I'll go on missions, I'll be a mechanic, I'll translate. I can still be an asset to the company."

"With the paperwork you filed, we can't let you go out, Delgado. You'll stay on base where it's safe and work in the motor pool."

I can see that this decision is final. I'm grounded. I probably should have seen it coming, but I didn't expect to feel so diminished. So childish. Clearly I've lost the respect of the senior NCOs. Not that that's going to make me back down from my beliefs. I feel ashamed but also liberated, as if a burden has been lifted off my soul. Every day that I step outside this base and into the streets of Iraq, I'm putting myself in a situation where I might be forced to kill. The code of Buddhism is to respect all life. I will miss going out on missions, but now my conscience is lighter. The MPs are going to despise me. That I can live with: the way they treat the Iraqis is wrong, and it's only going to get worse. I don't want to be a part of that. It's too bad that the first sergeant and the others think I'm a "bad soldier," but that too I can live with. I've already taken a lot of flak for thinking and speaking the way I do. I can take more.

I don't tell anyone in the unit about my application for CO, except for the guys in the motor pool. Somehow, though, within a week of the first sergeant pulling me off missions, *everyone* knows. In a "section leader" meeting, it's put on the agenda that Delgado is trying to get out of the Army as a conscientious objector, a pacifist, no less. The section and squad leaders quickly make sure their soldiers know what I'm doing and what they think of it. They figure that the easiest way to make my ugly little "problem" go away is to embarrass me in front of the other soldiers. They're not stupid; they know how a fraternal organization like the Army works. The best way to make my application disappear is by making sure that everyone knows about it and gives me a hard time until I withdraw it. Word gets back to me through Shoe and Patterson that a lot of the guys are talking, calling me a terrorist sympathizer, talking about how they're going to give me a "wall to wall counseling," Army slang for dealing with a troublemaker by kicking the shit out of him. I look over my shoulder at every MP that passes by me, wondering—are they the ones talking about me? The MPs don't trust me now, and they let me know it as often as possible. To their enormous credit, the members of the motor pool stick by me no matter how bad my status gets. Even as I become a pariah, no one in the motor pool budges an inch except for Spangler, who seems to disagree with my decision. Patterson and Shoe even stick up for me to the MPs, at the risk of being called sympathizers themselves.

"You don't know Delgado," Shoe tells them. "He just doesn't wanna kill anybody, all right? So why don't you quit running your mouth?"

Schumacher . . . piss-and-wind Schumacher who's friends with all the MPs and gung ho as they come, sticking up for me even though there's nothing in it for him. Even though he'll be given a shitload of grief for it. Patterson, too, telling people they haven't heard my side of the story, telling them to give me a break. That's love, that's brotherhood.

As for me, I try to keep my head down and do my work, interacting with as few people outside the motor pool as possible. My mind is on my CO packet, and the statement I now have to write to explain my beliefs.

"Conscientious objector" is something I've heard about vaguely in the context of the Vietnam War but have never encountered personally. In the last month I've learned from the folder sent to me that conscientious objection has a long history, dating back to the years before the American Revolution. In fact, one of the original drafts of the Second Amendment included an exemption for conscientious objectors—that "no person religiously scrupulous of bearing arms shall be compelled to render military service in person"—but the proposal was narrowly voted down and reworded. Thus, conscientious objection was just a few votes shy of becoming one of our fundamental freedoms, along with the freedom of speech, the freedom of religion, and the freedom to bear arms: the freedom *not* to bear arms. Reading that makes me feel a little better, a little less of a religious freak. Apparently the founding fathers, especially James Madison, thought that "religious scruples" against military service was important enough to merit mention in the Bill of Rights.

Most of the information sheets I've read discuss cases from the distant past: World War II, the Civil War, and pre-Revolution colonial militias; they are short on current information. And then I come across the codex that I need: a complete CO application filed in the mid-1990s by a sailor whose name has been blacked out. It's an unusual case: the sailor filed on purely ethical grounds, citing his moral opposition to the drug enforcement and border control responsibilities of the Navy. He won. Better than that, he published his entire packet online, with a detailed walk-through for anyone else interested in applying for CO status. I want to thank him, as his experience gives me the tools, his packet tells me everything I need to know, step by step. His name and personal details have been redacted, but I hope someday to be able to tell him what this information has meant to me.

The modern process of conscientious objection involves three stages: the written statement of the applicant, a series of interviews with a chaplain, a psychologist, and an investigating officer, and the recommendations of each officer in an individual's chain of command. There are two types of CO application; 1-0 status and 1-A-0 status. Applying for 1-0 status means that you seek to be discharged from the military entirely, while 1-A-0 signifies that you will continue to serve in the military in a noncombatant role. I am applying for discharge, and that is very important, because there are no "switches." If you apply for discharge you are either accepted or denied. You can't be given the other type as a compromise. The military compiles your written statement, the statements of the investigators, and any recommendations for or against in your chain of command and forwards all the material to the Department of the Army Conscientious Objector Review Board (DACORB) in Washington, which is the final authority. Based upon the contents of the packet and the relevant recommendations, the department approves or denies your request. Officially, all this is supposed to be decided within ninety days, but in practice the process usually takes about a year. Mine will end up taking more than nine months.

From the beginning, I have no expectation that this will happen quickly. I know that applying for CO won't shorten my deployment by even a single day. That's not important. I'm not trying to duck my responsibilities. I am a Buddhist and an ethical person and I will comport myself as such. I'm not looking for the easy way out . . . I want out the right way, for the right reasons. When I sit down to compile my application, I know that determining my status may take upward of a year.

I shift my weight on the overturned ice-chest, where I sit leaning over the keyboard of a laptop I've borrowed from Patterson. For the next few hours I focus completely on the CO application, letting the room, the Army, and everything else drop away. After a halting start, I gain in speed and confidence as I lay out the broad structure of my objection. A central part of the application asks for "a description of the nature of the belief that requires the person to seek separation from the military service or assignment to noncombatant training and duty for reasons of conscience." At this section I pause for almost a half hour, reflecting on how I am going to summarize Buddhist theology to an audience that may be totally unfamiliar with Eastern religions. I decide to go with a straightforward historical approach, as if I were writing an encyclopedia entry.

> The belief that requires me to seek separation from military service is my adherence to the Buddhist religion and the ethical and moral beliefs arising from my devotion to that religion. Buddhism is a major world religion on which information is widely available, so I will only summarize its principles in brief and in relation to my request for separation.
>
> Buddhism is a religion that arose from the philosophy and teaching of Siddhartha Gautama (also known as The Buddha), who lived in northern India from 563 to 483 BCE. The most basic principle of the religion is that life is full of suffering and the way to escape suffering is through control of the mind, correct moral behavior (the Eightfold Path), and the elimination of selfish desires. Although Buddha is revered in the tradition as the ultimate teacher and moral guide, there is no deity or external power at the center of Buddhism. Buddhism strongly emphasizes the individual's search for truth, the sanctity of all life (human and animal), and compassion for all living beings. Buddhism is absolutely opposed to all forms of violence, oppression, and warfare. Buddhism is widely known as an explicitly pacifist religion of which one of the fundamental values is nonviolence.

Having laid the groundwork, I find my voice. This section on the "nature of the belief" is the largest and weightiest of the application, comprising five main points that compel me to seek conscientious objection:

> (1) Buddhist scripture prohibits participation in war and violence. (2) I personally believe warfare to be morally wrong.

(3) I believe that membership in the Armed Forces, in any capacity, contributes to a mission of violence. To remain a member would be the same as giving my moral assent to the use of violence. (4) I do not believe I can kill another human being; therefore, I would place my comrades at increased risk. (5) The military requires me to perform other actions that are counter to my conscience, such as servicing weapons and exterminating wildlife.

The exposition of these ideas takes pages. I record the last two years of my life, explaining how I became a Buddhist and what drove me to seek conscientious objection. Patterson and Sergeant Toro look over my shoulder in amazement as my statement grows into a stack of densely typed computer pages. "What? You writing a book, Delgado?" they demand jokingly. I smile absent-mindedly and nod, my thoughts already on the next questions.

In truth, the depth and force of the statement surprises me. I've gone on for almost ten single-spaced pages so far, and I'm not sure how much they're going to be willing to read. It's time to make an end to it. Although the sun is beginning to set, I blaze on. I want all this to be done by tonight. I despair of ever being able to explain to some official two thousand miles away what it feels like to be me, here in the desolation of a war-torn country. How can I tell some Army brass about all the sleepless nights I've spent in Tallil, staring up at a crumbling, whitewashed ceiling? How can I tell a general how much it hurts to be called a traitor when all your life you've dreamed of finally feeling like a real American? How can I tell someone who's never heard of Buddhism about the ocean of compassion? I have to make them understand. The "nature of the belief" section of the application takes me longer to write than any of the others. How do you explain who you are in a handful of pages?

I slump over the keyboard in exhaustion. It's not the clearest or the most eloquent statement I've ever written, but it will have to do. The sun has set and Patterson wants his laptop back. I save everything on a disk and sneak off down the hallway to print it on the administration section's computers. As the document spools out, I smile inwardly at the irony of using the Army's computers to file for conscientious objection. I feel simultaneously giddy and nauseous. If my application is denied, I'll have to stay in the Army until 2009, the end of my contract.

I return to my room holding several crisp copies of the application. Everyone else is asleep, or getting there. My body is exhausted but my mind is racing. I lie awake for hours, doubts and fears drifting over me like the fine currents of dust settling on my bunk.

Over the next few days, I file the remaining components of my CO application and wait for the other shoe to drop. I work in distracted anxiety, as I know that the command is reading and digesting my essays.

It doesn't take long. I receive word that the commander wants to see me in his room. I shudder at the thought of being in close proximity to the man, never mind having to endure whatever inspirational rant he has planned. Still wearing my stained and matted motor pool uniform, I knock gently on his door, wishing I could somehow avoid this.

The commander is half stretched out on his bunk in his PT uniform. Glancing over at the corner, he motions for me to sit down on the bunk across from him. It's unnerving to be sitting so close to the man I constantly mock and deride; I wonder if he can smell my insubordination. He tries to be friendly, addressing me cheerfully and bantering about the desert heat or some such thing. I mumble in agreement and he launches forth on his discourse. The commander is a man who will not look you in the eyes while speaking to you. Throughout our conversation—or should I say the commander's monologue—his eyes remain fixed on that same spot in the corner, just over my left shoulder.

"Well, I've looked over your application, Delgado," he begins. "I know you're an intelligent and well-educated person, I know that you come from a good family, I know what your father does. I've seen you working with your unit, and I've known you since St. Petersburg and I really do believe that you're trying to become a Buddhist."

My hands clench at my sides.

"Look, you wouldn't be the first Buddhist or the last Buddhist to ever have served in the military. There are lots of them in the Army. I'm a Roman Catholic, so that's the background I'm coming out of, but I know that Buddhism doesn't preach against self-defense."

I try and interject something but he overrides me. I am forced to sit there in meek silence while he tells me what I believe.

"I understand that you're trying to go through some sort of religious conversion, Delgado. But the fact remains that you can be a Buddhist and still serve the Army. You can still serve in the motor pool. I'd be happy to have you as a noncombatant in my motor pool. Sergeant Wallace and Sergeant Toro tell me that you do good work. You understand that they're never going to let you out of the Army with this, right? It's not going to happen. All they're going to do is read your application and say that you're already a noncombatant, since all you do is turn wrenches. They're just going to reassign you as a noncombatant. You're not going to get out of fulfilling your contract."

He doesn't know what he's talking about. Either he hasn't read my application or he hasn't read the regulations. I know that they cannot give me noncombatant status as a compromise for my application. It's all or nothing. But I'm not about to tell the commander that.

"Besides, Delgado, I've seen the books you read. I know you're not *that* opposed to violence. I see you reading those violent fantasy novels."

"What novels are those, sir?" I ask.

"You know . . . all those fantasy and science-fiction books. They have plenty of violence in them and you don't seem opposed to that."

"Are you referring to *The Lord of the Rings,* sir? Is that what you mean by a violent fantasy, sir?"

"Okay, Delgado, tell me: what's the last book you read?"

"*Heretics of Dune,* by Frank Herbert. Considered a classic of American science fiction, sir."

"Okay, before that what did you read?"

"*God Emperor of Dune.*"

"And before that?

"*Children of Dune.*"

Inside I am bursting with mirth; I'd just worked my way through most of the *Dune* series, and I'd love to recite each and every volume to him in backward progression.

"Well, anyway, you read violent fantasies."

"Sir, even if I did, there's a difference between violence in novels and violence in real life. I don't see how reading novels—classics—has anything to do with my religious beliefs."

"All I'm saying, Delgado, is that you're *not* totally opposed to violence."

"I am, sir."

"Well, you signed a contract with the Army and it's your duty to fulfill that contract. You are still able to serve the military. I've read your statement about sleep disturbances and depression. If you're under so much stress then how come you're not going to see the battalion chaplain every day? If you're really so depressed, how come you haven't asked to see a psychiatrist to put you on prescription antidepressants? If you were really in as much 'moral turmoil' as you claim, you'd be going to see the psychiatrist every day."

"Sir . . . with all due respect . . . everyone handles stress in different ways. Just because I'm not on prescription drugs doesn't mean I'm not depressed." I pause for a moment and add quietly, "I think that I'm a better judge of my own mental state than you are, sir."

"If you were in so much mental distress there would have been signs of it before now," he says.

"There have been signs, Captain. I've been talking to Sergeant Toro about conscientious objection since I got back from AIT, and the sleep disturbances since Fort Stewart. Ask Sergeants Toro and Wallace."

"Well, this is the first I've heard of any of this."

"You don't work with me every day, sir."

"Well, I like to think I know my soldiers pretty well. I know you guys in the motor pool, I know that your morale is high."

When I recount this remark to Sergeant Toro and the guys that evening, we all double over in laughter. He has absolutely no idea what we are thinking, or how much we disrespect him, and he has the audacity to tell me to my face that my "morale is high." I can barely tolerate being in the same room with the man.

The commander's talk continues to the tune of: you're wasting your time, you'll never get out of the Army, I know you don't really believe this stuff. I sit there, nodding and smiling. He tells me to my face that I'm not sincere, that I'm just trying to get out of the deployment; he makes broad aspersions against my character, and not once does he turn to look me in the eye. Throughout the long lecture, I repeat five words to myself, like a mantra: We'll see about that, Captain.

One night, on my way back to the barracks, I'm passing the large metal shipping container that is the supply connex when one of the unit clerks hails me.

"Hey, Delgado, I'm going to need your ballistic plates back."

I stop dead in my tracks. Ballistic plates are the rigid part of our body armor, two ceramic shields that fit into the flak vest to provide protection against high-velocity rounds. Without them, our vests are not rated to stop anything above a pistol round. The ballistic plates are essential to survival in a combat zone; some members of our unit had even had family members purchase them on the Internet and ship them over so they wouldn't have to go without them. Cold fear seeps through me at the thought of turning in the only part of my body armor that is worth a damn. I know what this is about.

He explains to me that he's heard I'm not going on missions anymore, that I've filed for CO status. He says that the unit is short on body armor inserts, so his superiors told him to take my ballistic plates. He seems genuinely apologetic about it.

"Don't worry, Delgado, you're going to be on base from now on anyway. You won't be needing them. Can you run up and get them for me before I close up here?"

I return with the plates and hand them over. What can I do? It's a legitimate order from the chain of command. I am overcome with bitterness. I can feel the hand of the commander or the first sergeant behind this little scene; they're trying to intimidate me. The clerk numbers my plates and packs them away. Wild thoughts fly through my head: they're trying to get me killed! They certainly want to put the fear of God in me.

The clerk's prediction that I won't need my armor proves to be false. Much later, at Abu Ghraib, when our unit is under continual mortar bombardment, I will in fact need those plates, but I won't get them back.

The next few weeks pass as if in a dream. I get out of work early one day to go see an Air Force psychologist for the "psychiatric review" portion of my CO application. An Air Force doctor in perfectly starched desert camouflage conducts the interview. He's a nondescript older man who asks me if I've ever heard voices or if there is a history of brain tumors in my family. I go back to work in the motor pool. My application for CO doesn't stop Sergeant Wallace from assigning me a pile of leaking half-shafts and upper ball joints to replace.

After work, walking down the long corridor from the maintenance room toward the stairs, I spot Nick Sollugob in the distance and shudder internally. He seems to hate me more than anyone else does, and every time we meet I can feel trouble brewing. Shoe tells me that Sollugob sometimes talks shit about me, calling me a coward and a sympathizer. On the rare occasions when I see him, he gives me a death stare and brushes by me threateningly. He's one of the youngest members of our company, about my height and build with a fresh high-and-tight haircut, a narrow, angular face, and steel-rimmed glasses. We actually look pretty similar, but we couldn't be more different: I'm quiet and bookish, he's boisterous and athletic. He loves being an MP. This is a narrow hallway, and there's no way we're going to be able to pass without incident. My body braces in anticipation.

This rivalry is a recent development. Seeing Sollugob always makes me feel sad, because we used to be friends. Back in Sarasota, before either of us had ever thought about being deployed, we used to hang out together and joke around, and he would make deadpan remarks in his half–New York, half-Jersey accent. He was funny. The two of us had enlisted around the same time with the same recruiter; that had made us something of a "class." I remember him calling me once to hang out on a weekend when we didn't have Army duty. We were friendly on all our monthly drills, and I thought of him as one of my buddies in the unit.

When we got deployed, things started to change.

It was gradual, imperceptible, but I noticed that we seemed to be pulling away from each other. There were inevitable debates and arguments in the barracks, with everyone throwing in their two cents about the coming war, politics, terrorism, and everything else, and I think that's when Sollugob first began to dislike me; I always seemed to be siding with the Palestinians, with the Iraqis, with "them." I think he perceived in me (correctly) a strong distaste for President Bush, war in general, and this war in particular. In Iraq, the situation only got worse. We became strangers, then petty rivals, and finally open enemies.

Now that we were fighting a real war on the same side, it seemed more important than ever to be onboard with whatever the Army and the captain had in mind. Yet I found that the more I experienced wartime life and the vagaries of the Army, the more misgivings I had about what our sacred "mission" really was in Iraq. The day Sollugob and I clashed in Nasiriyah over pointing a weapon at civilians, I knew that something had gone irrevocably wrong between us. At that moment, I think we both knew we weren't "pals" anymore. Once word got around that I was applying for conscientious objector status, or rather once the captain and first sergeant *made sure* that word got around, I felt that Sollugob dropped all pretense of civility. Our rooms were right next door to each other, so conflicts were inevitable. He now seemed to view me with contempt, and I became curt and hostile to him as well.

Of course, this was precisely what the command had intended: to make me a pariah, to strip me of my friendships and social status until I became so lonely and desperate that I would recant my CO packet and beg to be let back into the club. "Peer counseling" is what I believe they call it. The result was that every young soldier who was still onboard with the Army and the unit felt it was their personal mission to make me feel unwelcome.

We're only a few feet apart now, and both looking at the wall. Okay, okay, all good, everything's going to be fine, we're not going to have an incident...and then SLAM! He checks my shoulder with such force that I literally spin where I'm standing and land with my back against the concrete wall. For a moment I'm stunned, not physically but emotionally, as I try and process what has just transpired. Then I feel it: In one instant, rage floods into my soul. I cannot believe the affront, the blatant injustice, the audacity. I'm confused and hurt, but from that confusion and hurt come rage, hatred, and bloodthirsty darkness swimming up into my heart from some deep, dank pit. I step forward from the wall and turn to face him. I am not myself. On any other day, I would have absorbed the shoulder check and walked on, not wanting to "make a scene." For some reason, today is different. Maybe it's the blatant nature of today's insult, maybe it's the cumulative effect of a dozen little "shoulder checks" and whispered remarks, maybe it's the fact that the command has been so effective in its little scheme to make me a nobody, but today I don't walk away. I turn, and in my mind I am ready to do violence.

Sollugub meets my gaze with one of equal defiance. We don't say anything; each of us knows the message being sent. Our posture and faces are communicating something as old as the first human beings with rocks and sticks; older, even, back to the apes. This challenge is purely animal, subvocal, and we both know what happens from here. Violence is imminent. I mumble something inarticulate and reach out and push him hard, forcing him a half pace back. This is all part of the ritual: insult, stare down, push forward, push back, blow to the shoulder escalating to a blow to the face . . . it's rote. It would be another typical shoving match except that this is the culmination of a long, slow boil. This is going to end with someone shedding blood.

He responds to my challenge by shoving me back. Everything has slowed down. I'm actually going to do it, I think, I'm actually gonna hit this guy. We both step in, our faces only inches apart.

Just before I throw a punch, Shoe and Patterson round the corner of the corridor and they're instantly between us. Shoe holds Sollugob back and Patterson stands in front of me, mumbling soothing words: "Hey, hey, hey, c'mon now, settle down."

They separate us by force. I feel Patterson's hands on my shoulders and arms, but I don't struggle. As quickly as it came on, the rage has left me. I don't really want to fight. Shoe hustles Sollugob off to his room and Patterson leads me down the hallway away from them. I can feel the anger leaving my body as a physical sensation. I feel hot and flushed all over, pumped up. I can't believe that a second earlier I was ready to hit Sollugob over his bumping me in the hallway; the last minute seems absurdly distant and dreamlike. So much for my enlightened mind . . . when it came down to it, I flew off the handle like every other young guy with testosterone pumping in his veins. Some Buddhist I turned out to be. I feel momentarily elated, relieved because the situation was defused but also because I had the balls to turn around. Yeah, it sounds funny but I actually feel proud that I *didn't* let it go—something needed to be said. I feel like I forced him to respect me. I swagger down to the motor pool, puffed up for about ninety seconds.

Then it's gone: the elation, the euphoria, the pride, all gone. I didn't solve anything today, all I did was put one more notch on Sollugob's list of grievances and maybe escalate the feud a little. It won't make one damn bit of difference to the way anyone treats me. Five minutes after it happened, I feel depressed. When I met Sollugob two years ago, he was a kid who had just graduated from high school, smiled a lot, laughed a lot, and was excited to be going off to Military Police School, a funny guy who would make a good college student. A couple weeks ago he pointed his assault rifle at a kid's face and motioned like he was going to blow his head off.

Every day he seems harder, more calloused. I got angry with him that time because I was afraid his macho posturing and yelling would go too far and he might accidentally (or purposefully) pull the trigger. I felt that he, like so many others, had grown careless of Iraqi lives, of any life. Something is going out of him, or maybe something that was always there is coming to the surface; it's hard to tell. Who is the real Sollugob, the young guy I knew or the hardened soul I saw in the corridor? Or maybe I'm the one who's changed.

Maybe it would be better if I just went to the command and told them that I changed my mind, that I don't want to be a conscientious objector anymore. Maybe it would be easier to just wait out my time and not have to deal with all this friction and all this bullshit day in and day out. No. I stop myself, cut short that train of thought. I've already made my declaration and there's no going back. If I recanted now, I would be doubly scorned for caving in under pressure. I'd still be the outcast, the lily-livered bookworm who tried to get out of the Army and failed. No, I will walk the walk, but

God, how I want to belong. One of the things that had most attracted me to the military was the legendary esprit de corps, that unbreakable bond conveyed in the black-and-white war movies. These last weeks have shown me just how shallow that "brotherhood" can be. You're one of us as long as you don't disagree with us or dare to question us. The "team," the "unit,"—it's all been a sales pitch. I'll never be part of this group now, no matter what I do. The incident with Sollugob only solidifies this in my mind, and I realize with cold, hard finality that there's no turning back now: either they will break or I will. I just wish it didn't have to be Sollugob.

I'm outside hammering stakes into the ground with a wooden sledgehammer. It's hot and dusty and I'm in a foul mood: Sergeant Wallace has ordered us to stake down the maintenance tent because of the high wind and dust. The ground is hard-packed, making it extremely difficult to drive in each dull wooden stake, and the maintenance tent is positioned in direct sunlight. My mood gets darker with every swing of the enormous, clumsy hammer. I'm muttering obscenities and moving deliberately slowly. After forty-five minutes I'm nearly finished, and I lean forward onto the hammer to catch my breath and wipe the stinging, acrid sweat from my brow. My brown T-shirt and cinched-up coveralls are dripping with perspiration. It feels great to be almost done and have a chance to grab some water. I'm looking down at the dirt and breathing heavily when suddenly I feel a hand slip around my neck and a forearm lock tight around my throat. I am heaved upward and bent back into an arch. The hammer slips from my fingers as an arm tightens around my neck. Someone has me in a chokehold. I smell sickly-sweet breath and sweat. Then there's Wilson's voice whispering only a few inches from my ear: "Whatcha gonna do now, Delgado?"

At first I'm only annoyed that Wilson is hassling me, interfering with my work. It's a joke, he's horsing around, he's messing with me. He's a cocky, rude specialist from Jamaica with jet-black skin and a pair of effete round glasses. College-educated, he makes pretensions of suavity and sophistication but he's frequently crude and con-frontational. His sergeants are always riding his ass for being dis-respectful and insolent. He loves to come up to people who are minding their own business and fuck with them, for a laugh or just for the hell of it.

I put my hand on his forearm and pull down to relieve some of the pressure and that's when I notice them: a group of soldiers standing around us, maybe twenty feet away in the shadow of the barracks building, just watching. They're the younger guys, MPs. I spot a few of the ringleaders, the guys who really have it in for me and have gone out of their way to let me know they despise me. They're laughing, pointing, egging Wilson on. They've gathered to see the spectacle, to see what the infamous pacifist Buddhist is go-ing to do. Wilson bats my hand away and tightens his grip around my trachea. I look back to the crowd and see expressions of pure malice; they're enjoying this. Heck, they probably put him up to it. He begins to squeeze now, really squeeze, and my air is cut off. In an instant I realize that Wilson isn't horsing around anymore; he's really trying to hurt me. This isn't about fun, this is about pecking order, getting back at some smart-ass, college-boy conscientious objector. He's not going to kill me, but he is going to hurt and em-barrass me in front of everyone, make me a running joke, prove to everyone that I'm just as much of a bitch as they say I am. Here on this dirt patch behind our barracks building they're going to show me something ugly and teach me what happens when you go against the pack. They're going to make me pay.

An old instinct kicks in. Throughout high school I was on the varsity wrestling team, with a coach who lived and breathed grap-pling. I was Eastern Mediterranean Champion in my junior year. When I came to America I no longer had the option of wrestling at my small college so I took up Brazilian jujitsu at a local dojo that proved to be home to all kinds of tough and canny fighters. The rear naked choke that Wilson has me in is the foundation of jujitsu, the first and most basic submission technique. A tough Brazilian master drilled me in it over and over again in his barely articulate Portuguese drawl: "Lift your hiippss . . . hand on dee ellbbowww . . . make submeeeesion." Having been endlessly choked and squeezed and even knocked unconscious in training, I have a deeply honed instinct to protect my throat.

I work the four fingers of my right hand up under my chin and form a blade with my hand against the side of my face. This takes all the power out of Wilson's choke. He can't knock me out as long as I have that hand between the bones of his forearm and the veins in my neck. As soon as I counter the choke, I realize I have him: he doesn't have any technique, he's just bullying me with the one basic move he was taught in Army combative training. I'm hot and uncomfortable and annoyed, but I'm fine.

I do a rapid series of calculations. Wilson is slim. He's just grabbed from behind an opponent who is taller and outweighs him by thirty pounds. I feel confident that he doesn't know as much about grappling as I do and doesn't think I'm much of a threat. My arm is twice the size of his, honed by months of lifting hundred-pound Humvee tires every day. He's caught me on a bad day and in a bad mood. I'm certain that I can crush him utterly if I choose to.

Now the moral equation kicks in. Although I had wrestled in sport and sporadically trained in martial arts, I had never truly fought: not in the schoolyard, not a bully, not a drunken brawl, nothing. It had been deeply embedded in me by polite society that the one thing you must never do is fight. I was always a "good boy," bookish, not the type who would ever get in a fight. A chubby kid with long hair and glasses in middle school, I would rather be pushed and knocked down than stand up for myself. All these memories flash through my mind as Wilson and I struggle in the yard.

The first rule of Buddhism is not to hurt living beings. I hold that the deepest spiritual value is to be at peace with yourself and through that inner peace to be in harmony with others and the outside world: never to do harm, never to fight, to submit to injustice rather than violate your own peaceful nature. I am loath to break that code. Hurting Wilson won't make me feel good, it will only make me feel guilty and angry. I don't want to fight. I don't want to be a hypocrite. I don't want these thugs to drag me down to their level and prove that my commitment is not as deep as I know it is. I want to be a good Buddhist, and good Buddhists don't hurt other people just to prove a point. Then I look out and see the faces of the other soldiers, leering in delight, waiting to see me get my ass kicked. Patterson and Schumacher have appeared and are staring in confusion at the scene in front of them, not knowing what to do, waiting to see if Wilson is going to get what he richly deserves. I hate the whole goddamn scene—I hate being a spectacle for these people who want to see blood—yet I can't escape the realization that this is a battle I'm going to have to face sooner or later. All the nasty words, all the shoving and hallway shoulder checks, have been leading up to this point.

Wilson's not a leader; he didn't come to this by himself. The pack instinct is driving him. If I don't put an end to this and stomp him here and now, everyone will see that I'm an easy target and I'll be fighting these bullies for the rest of the tour. All my pacifism won't mean a thing when every young tough in the company decides that he's going to earn brownie points by hassling the traitor. If I don't fight now, I'll only face more violence. Damn them for putting me in this situation . . . damn them for forcing me to make this choice . . . damn Wilson for making me sink to the level of his "pals."

My mind is made up. I will do the terrible thing. I will shut this encounter down so quickly and so hard that no one will challenge me again. It's the only way to survive in this soldiers' world, where the weakest guy gets picked on until he cracks. May Wilson forgive me.

I step back on my right foot and shift my weight forward, then with a quick shimmy step I get my left foot between his legs and now I'm behind him. He still has my neck, but in a sloppy kind of headlock rather than a real choke. I pop my head up and back and the hold is broken. Now I lock my hands around his waist, tight and low, and prepare to take him down. At this moment, just before I drive him into the ground, I pause. He has no idea what's coming. I could easily lift him into the air right now. I squeeze his ribs and feel their flexibility and delicacy, the difference in our sizes. I have him in the perfect position for a classic wrestling takedown: a front trip. I put my right foot in front of his to block him, and then I lean down on him with all my weight and drive my elbow into the meat of his left thigh. We slam into the ground together, and I drive him forward so he lands on his face. His body compresses under me and I can hear the wind leaving his lungs. His glasses fly off and he eats a mouthful of dust. A collective "ooohhhh" escapes from the onlookers as they see the situation suddenly reversed.

While he's still stunned from the impact, I work my hands free and switch grips, locking my arms around his neck in the same choke he had me in a moment ago. Unlike Wilson, I know how to execute this choke properly. I don't apply it gently; I scissor his neck between my forearm and biceps and place the sharpest part of my forearm against his jugular. I clamp down on his throat with a vengeance, with all the accumulated pain and misery of being laughed at, picked on, hit, and threatened. I tighten my grip around his throat with every ounce of my strength, collapsing the veins in his neck, until his eyes bulge out of his head. I can feel him struggling beneath me, trying to pry my hand loose, but the choke is solid and tight—he will be unconscious in about six seconds. I am crushing him now, my 190 pounds concentrated on the small of his back and my arms and shoulders pulling back on his head like I'm going to wrench it off. I feel his hand on my forearm: tap, tap, tap, frantically. He's tapping out, the grappling signal that he's giving up, he's had enough. I hold the choke for just a second longer, to let him know that I could really knock him out, and then I release it and roll off his back. It's over. In less than ten seconds, Wilson is lying facedown in the dirt, gurgling and gasping for air.

"You got lucky, Delgado. Lucky shot," he rasps, pawing around for his glasses.

"Yeah, right."

I stand up and brush myself off. Patterson and Shoe are whooping and laughing. "Goddamn, Delgado, you choked his ass out!"

The rest of the crowd just stares at me sullenly. Nobody can believe that I actually know how to fight, that I just terminated Wilson. Their fun is over; they've been disappointed. Almost instantly they disperse and drift away. They won't be bothering me again.

Shoe and Patterson spread the word about what happened, telling everyone how I choked Wilson out in five seconds after he grabbed me. Sergeant Toro and Sergeant Wallace congratulate me, telling me I did exactly the right thing in that situation. I feel regret for having hurt someone, but also a grim satisfaction. When I walk into the smoking area that night to relax, some of the older sergeants are sitting around and laughing about it, obviously enjoying the fact that the noisome Wilson has been publicly shamed. "Heard you choked out Wilson, Delgado."

Word gets around in the company, but the command takes no official notice of the incident. Suddenly, all the pushing and checking in the hallway ceases. Nobody else steps forward to lay a hand on me or get in my face; even the guys who hate me keep a respectful distance. After this incident, everyone knows that though I may be a conscientious objector, a Buddhist and a pacifist, I am not to be fucked with. I'm not an easy target. I never have to fight again, and for that I'm thankful.

SEPTEMBER 2003 I'm crouched inside the wooden box that serves as a phone booth on the second floor of our barracks. Four large sheets of plywood give the illusion of privacy around the green military phone that has become the lifeline of our company. If you wait until after midnight, you can often use the phone for an hour or more, so that becomes my habit. I call Amy every chance I get, just to hear her voice and be reminded of home, where I have friends and someone I love waiting for me. Florida is six or seven hours behind, so it's early evening where she is. I'm waiting for the military operator to connect me. It's so hot and stuffy inside the box that I leave the door open, hoping that the clerks working outside can't hear my conversation. But really I don't care if anyone's listening. Something wonderful has happened.

Amy picks up after several rings. God, it's good to hear her voice.

I tell her about the rumors in the company that we might be going home soon, that our six months are up; some other unit is coming to take our place. Even Sergeant Wallace tells us in our evening briefings to be ready in case we're told to pack up for home. I'm so ecstatic I can barely contain myself, and Amy is excited too, happy and relieved.

"I can't believe this is happening," I tell her. "I can't believe I'm going to be home soon. I miss you so much."

Six months gone... it seems like an eternity, one never-ending day. But it's over now, I'll be home soon, away from all this hate and scorn.

We talk long into the night, giddy with anticipation, until someone knocks on the door and demands to use the phone.

Afternoon is fading; the sun is going down. The unit is standing in formation in front of the barracks, a rare occurrence, so something serious must have happened. We're called to attention and go through all the formalities. The first sergeant does the ceremony of exchanging command and the commander strolls out in front of the unit. Horror. I feel a terrible sense of déjà vu. It's just like St. Petersburg, when he told us we were going to war, just like Fort Stewart, when he told us we were going to Iraq. The commander is puffing himself up with gravitas; I can feel a speech coming. This will not be good news.

"I know that most of you are expecting to be redeployed to the States soon..." My hands begin trembling at my sides and I can feel my eyes stinging and watering. We're not going home. It's been revoked. The commander explains that he also expected us to be going home after six months, but things have changed. The government has declared that every soldier in Iraq will do a full 365 days, "boots on the ground," so we have another six months in Iraq. Three months of deployment and Fort Stewart don't count.

The commander continues: we're going to stay until the job's done, we're going to continue doing our duty, you're the best unit a captain could ever wish for; and so on. The speech goes on, but I'm lost in a haze of despair and can't really hear it: Something about an order from the Department of the Army, something else about a unit that was supposed to relieve us but isn't going to, something about doing whatever is asked of us. It's too terrible to comprehend.

The formation ends, but almost no one leaves. Dumbstruck, people congregate in clusters, and angry words fly back and forth. Shoe and Patterson and I proceed to curse God, the commander, Donald Rumsfeld, anyone we can think of who might be connected to our extension. Shoe seems on the verge of murder; he stalks off to smoke by himself. I curse the captain and President Bush in the most horrid terms I can imagine, and that still doesn't begin to express the magnitude of my hate. Six more months in this hellhole, as if we were starting from scratch. Amy is going to be devastated, but I'm too full of rage to be sad. I wander off to the rear of the barracks, near the sand berm that separates us from the Black Diamonds, the unit stationed to our rear. I try not to cry. I swing my fists impotently at nothing.

"FFFFFUUUUUUUCCK!" I roar at the empty air just before dark. I don't feel any better. "FFFFFUUUUUUCK!" I'm almost as loud the second time, but not quite.

I stay outside until well into evening, pacing around the smoking area, muttering curses under my breath. "I know it sucks, Delgado, but you can't do anything about it," Sergeant Toro says when he joins me there, putting his hand on my shoulder. "You know what you need to do? You need to smoke one of these with me." He reaches into his hip pocket and withdraws a package of Black and Milds, cheap aromatic cigars with a white plastic tip. I shake my head. He knows I don't smoke.

"Delgado, I'm telling you, it'll make you feel better, calm you down."

What the hell. He passes me a cigar and lights it, then lights one for himself. I draw in and choke.

Sergeant Toro laughs. "No, no, man. You don't inhale it."

I draw again, this time just holding the smoke in the back of my throat. I blow out curls of smoke through my nose. The smoke is rich and vaguely sweet; I can taste it on the front of my lips.

"There, now. You've got it."

In a few moments the pungent smoke has saturated my nose and mouth, every breath tastes of spice, cinders, leaves. When the small cigar has burned down to the last half inch before the plastic tip, I decide that Sergeant Toro was right—I do feel better. It's dark now, the stars are out, and I sit on the bench of wooden crates and smoke the cigar with exaggerated motions as if I'd been doing it all my life. In the dark I can't see the face of Sergeant Toro or anyone else sitting there, only the disembodied red glow of their lit cigars, like a family of wisps. The day's news seems manageable now. Tomorrow I'll get up and go to the motor pool just as I do every other day. That night, I smoke most of Sergeant Toro's pack.

"You know, I think I like these. I could get used to this."

He laughs. "I told you it would make you feel better."

To this day I smoke cigars—not often, but when I feel particularly upset and unfocused. Every time I light one I remember this moment: six months in Nasiriyah, a wreath of foul smoke, and those tiny red lights floating around me in the dark.

In all of this drama, I have nearly forgotten about my pending CO application. In fact, it's been so long since I've heard anything about it that I'm beginning to fear it's been lost in some bureaucratic snafu. What the hell is taking so long?

Then, after weeks of silence, a flurry of activity begins. All at once, my statement has been processed through the battalion and I'm scheduled to meet with an investigating officer in the next week. This is the key moment: I'll have to defend my position and confront his counterarguments directly. I'm dying for it, and I know I'm well prepared. I hear that a certain Captain Ferguson has been appointed my investigating officer, someone from the 744th battalion.

I run into Captain Ferguson one day while filling out some more paperwork for my CO application. He is a tall blond man in his mid-thirties, with an informal, friendly demeanor. My spirits rise. He talks comfortably about his college days and seems not at all antagonistic. Wow, it could have been much worse. I was expecting a rampant ideologue in the mold of the commander. What I get is a pleasant, calm, Nordic-looking officer who shakes my hand and says he looks forward to interviewing me. I walk out of the battalion headquarters with a new optimism. Indeed, with a sympathetic officer and my two-week home leave coming up soon, I dare to feel a twinge of hope.

Over the next two weeks, my anticipation of leave grows to ridiculous proportions. I'll actually be home soon, get to see the real world, relax and decompress. Work seems easier now, and time falls away toward that all-important date.

I believe it's the first sergeant who first informs me at a platoon meeting that there is a problem with my leave. I am ushered into another closed conference with the commander, who informs me that I will not be allowed to go home, because I am a "flight risk"—he fears that I will not return from leave. Unnaturally calm, I ask him what would make him assume that.

"Well, the application you submitted. You've admitted that you don't want to be in the Army anymore. I can't just send you home; what if you don't come back?"

I drop the "sir" and the civility. "Oh, I see. Since I don't want to kill anybody, I must be a traitor, huh? Because I don't believe in war then I must not have any honor or loyalty?"

"Delgado, no one's calling you a traitor. We just can't take the risk that you won't come back. We've already lost one mechanic from the motor pool;[4] we can't afford to lose another."

"I am not a flight risk. I've made it clear from the beginning that I want to leave the Army in the right way. I don't think you're allowed to take negative personnel actions just because someone files for CO status. Since my objection is based on Buddhism, what you're doing amounts to religious discrimination: because I adhere to the principles of Buddhism, I can't be trusted. You're accusing me of being a deserter simply because of my religious beliefs."

"No, Delgado, this has nothing to do with your religious beliefs. This is because of your CO application."

"Sir, my CO application is based solely on my religious beliefs. I'm going to take this up with an Equal Opportunity representative."

This is a bluff on my part. I have no idea who the company EO representative is, and even if I did, I suspect there's little they could do against the captain himself. I'm just hoping the threat of professional embarrassment will be enough to sway him.

"Delgado, this doesn't come from me. My hands are tied. This order comes from Battalion Headquarters, from the lieutenant colonel of the 744th. You'll have to take it up with him. This isn't my decision; I can't do anything about it."

"Well, then I want to speak with the colonel."

"You'll have to set up an appointment through your chain of command."

"I'll do that, sir."

Our meeting ends. I'm not angry; I know exactly what I'm going to do. I'm not going to take this lying down. Strangely, this sudden blow only fires my resolve to attain CO status. Losing my home leave is just the latest in a long string of indignities, from the insults to the confrontations to the seizure of my body armor. I'm going to tell Captain Ferguson exactly what's been going on with my unit and my command since I filed for CO status. I'm not going to let these bastards get away with this. Now I can't wait for the CO interview. I'm going to become a thorn in their side.

SEPTEMBER 29, 2003 The fateful day arrives. I shave and put on my specially set-aside uniform, the one I bothered to fold and flatten out, and my less-worn pair of boots.

I get to the battalion headquarters almost half an hour early. A little past the appointed hour, Captain Ferguson arrives and directs me to a back room illuminated by a large window. A desk has been pushed into the corner, and in the center of the room, two molded plastic chairs sit facing each other.

"Now, I don't want you to be nervous," Captain Ferguson says as he takes the seat opposite me, holding a clipboard. "This is not an antagonistic proceeding."

Not an antagonistic proceeding. I recognize those words. He's quoting directly from the Conscientious Objector regulations. A good start. He explains that the conversation will not be recorded, so I have the right to read his report of the meeting and issue a rebuttal if I choose. I nod. My stomach is a churning mass. In an empty room with two plastic chairs in the middle of a desert, our conversation will decide *everything.*

Captain Ferguson stares at me. His ice-blue eyes are intense and unreadable. His hand hovers over the notebook.

"Why don't you start by telling me a little bit about *when* you became a Buddhist."

I sit opposite Captain Ferguson for well on three hours. The interview results in this written report of our meeting, the transcript that became the centerpiece of my CO application. It is unedited.

The undersigned met with SPC Aidan Delgado on 29 September 2003 concerning his Conscientious Objector application. Following are the details of our conversation together.

I initially asked SPC Delgado when he became a Buddhist. His reply was around 25 September 2002, when he stopped eating meat, was approximately the time he became more serious about his Buddhist faith. This date corresponds with the date mentioned in his Conscientious Objector application.

I then discussed his commitment to the Army, asking him when his commitment expired and how his discharge would affect his future employment opportunities. SPC Delgado's commitment to the U.S. Army Reserve as a drilling member expires on 18 September 2007 and his inactive commitment expires on 18 September 2009. SPC Delgado believes he will be discharged under honorable conditions if his classification is approved and will lose his GI benefits, cash bonus, and VA benefits. He also understands that he will have to repay his $3,000 cash bonus of which he has received half as well as his GI bill money (he has received 3 months of $168 per month plus a bonus kicker of $150 per month.)

I asked SPC Delgado what the teachings of Buddha had to say about fulfilling one's commitments. He responded that he didn't feel he had a right to change but that the Army has provided an opportunity to eliminate his commitment based upon its desire to allow service members to practice their religion. He felt that given this opportunity, his proceeding is neither shameful nor dishonorable. Regarding commitment, Buddhists believe that the person is the ultimate moral compass. SPC Delgado states that he has been doing something that is wrong, supporting an organization that uses violence to achieve an end state. In SPC Delgado's view breaking his commitment to the Army is of less importance than rectifying the issue of active participation in an organization that uses violence. SPC Delgado further related that Buddha himself left his family to go into the wilderness and contemplate an end of human suffering and pursue religious awakening between the ages of 20 and 40, abandoning his wife and family as well as turning his back on responsibilities as a prince. In light of Buddha's experience, an annulment of SPC Delgado's commitment to the Army Reserve as a result of his belief would not be uncharacteristic of Buddhism. Further, SPC Delgado stated that it would be "in fact, a type and shadow of Buddhist renunciation."

I then asked SPC Delgado about how he believed an honorable discharge as a conscientious objector would affect him in the future. He stated that he would not want to be a member of an organization that wouldn't allow conscientious objectors to be members or employees. Therefore he sees no long-term ramifications from following the course he believes to be right at this time. Furthermore, he believes that there would be long-term moral ramifications in not taking this course of action.

I then posed the question, why not complete your current commitment to the Army Reserve and not re-enlist? He stated that a six-year commitment is not short-term. He stated that it is not a preference but rather an imperative that he leaves because military service places him in a moral quandary. SPC Delgado also believes it is religiously important for him to make a public statement. He believes a religious sentiment is not something you can put off, he works every day to support an organization that is not congruent with his beliefs.

I then mentioned that we are not actively fighting a war in Iraq at present. In fact, the U.S. Army is attempting to build the country and the majority of the engagements we enter are due to self-defense. We must defend ourselves against a minority that is trying to prevent us from improving life for the majority. SPC Delgado replied that in Buddhism "an end doesn't justify a means." By force the U.S. Army placed itself in a position to build the country of Iraq. He believes that we are here against popular will and we remain by force. And furthermore believes that he actively supports the machinery of a machine that is here to oppress.

I asked him to define his unit's mission. He replied "not to build Iraq's infrastructure," the main mission is to incarcerate criminals and enemy prisoners of war as well as provide security. He does not believe the U.S. Army is here solely to rebuild the country but here for other reasons.

I then asked him how, as a mechanic, he saw himself as oppressing or killing other people. He replied that it is sheer membership in an organization that a person doesn't agree with. No matter what role he fulfills, by being an active member he gives his silent assent to what the Army is about: "using violence to achieve an end."

We then discussed what Buddhism teaches about self-defense. "Buddhism teaches to turn the other cheek but doesn't mean you are a doormat."[5] He said he would use a minimum level of force to put down a threat. Part of self-defense is to avoid situations that may call on you to use self-defense. When queried about a situation where you can only meet the threat by killing the other person, he stated that he was unsure he could kill another person but would like to believe he would die for his beliefs.

I then asked him if he felt he would ever change his mind about being a Buddhist. He stated it was the only religion he ever practiced. He believes Buddhism is what he always believed innately. As he studied Buddhism he felt like he held most of its beliefs previously and finally found a religion that is compatible with those beliefs. SPC Delgado stated his belief is not a fad and that he does not feel he is in some sort of phase.

I asked him if he held those beliefs, why did he join the Army? SPC Delgado indicated he was an atheist when he joined the military. Even then, he really didn't want to ever have to kill people and thought of it as a last resort. Later he became a practitioner of Buddhism as he studied it. Furthermore, he joined the military on 18 September 2001, not in a wave of patriotism surrounding September 11, he had been discussing joining for some time prior, rather because he felt that he was stagnating in life and wanted change and a challenge. He did relate that his father never liked the military and currently works for the State Department. SPC Delgado says that although he didn't join in a wave of patriotism, he still loves his country. He became a mechanic because he felt he could acquire some good job-skills and develop himself. He stated he wasn't a very mechanical person and wanted to develop that side of his skill set. He also stated he wanted to avoid any situation in which he could end up having to kill someone.

I asked him about the potential that his Buddhism, conscientious objector desires would pass. He stated it was not something that will pass. He is a religion major in college and has examined many of the religions of the world. After such study he doesn't feel he will change his belief in Buddhism and they are in synchronization with his beliefs, therefore there is no reason to change.

I then asked him if this is his way to get out of Iraq. SPC Delgado discussed living in Cairo, Egypt for 7.5 years from fifth grade to high school and having seen the squalor of the Cairo slums. He mentioned that he doesn't mind serving through the deployment if he has to but doesn't feel long-term like he can stay with the Army. He has also lived in Senegal, Philippines,[6] and Bangkok and speaks Arabic. Because of his experience he says that the living standards here in Iraq have not surprised him.

I asked him if it would be satisfactory for him to complete the deployment and then be separated from the Army Reserve. He stated that he would like the process to proceed at a normal pace and be separated as soon as that process is complete. However, if he doesn't get separated until after the deployment, so be it.

SPC Delgado has also expressed his concern that the battalion commander has revoked his ability to take leave because he is believed to be a flight risk solely on the basis of his conscientious objector application, as relayed to him by his first sergeant. He has also requested, through his first sergeant, the opportunity to discuss this issue with the battalion commander.

Signed,
George T. Ferguson, IV

FALL 2003 Over the next few days, Captain Ferguson calls Sergeant Toro and Sergeant Wallace in for interviews. Sergeant Wallace jokingly shakes a fist at me for getting him involved, but their interviews are over in less than an hour. They return to the motor pool and tell me that everything went fine, that I'm going to be fine, but I can't help wondering what Captain Ferguson thought of my interview. He was polite, but did he believe me? The first half of October crawls by as I wait for some feedback.

Two weeks after the interview, Captain Ferguson calls me back to Headquarters to look over his statement and sign it. It seems a fair enough record of our conversation. I glance through the rest of the papers in front of me and see Sergeant Wallace and Sergeant Toro's statements, both apparently supportive. Chaplain Ellis has also written a strong supporting statement, even though he is technically not supposed to submit an opinion. Beneath his statement is one from the commander, voting against me—no surprise there —and beneath that is a statement from the battalion commander, also voting against me. This surprises me, as I've never met the man. It doesn't bode well for regaining my home leave.

When I finish signing the statement, Captain Ferguson shakes

my hand again and wishes me good luck. I tell him that I'm still trying to see the 744th commander about getting my leave back, but
his face, as always, is inscrutable. The handshake must be a good
sign, I think desperately. I wonder if he's even allowed, under the
CO regulations, to wish me good luck. I don't know if he sympa-
thizes with me or not, but everything I've seen and heard of him
thus far lead me to believe that he will give me a fair hearing.

I pass the next two months doing intensive exercise. Sergeant Toro
and I have been lifting weights together for a long time, but now I
begin to ratchet up the pace. I have also begun to wake up before
drawn and go for long runs on the winding service roads that encircle the base. Soon I'm up to five miles before breakfast, then six.
I hear of a base-wide race, a ten-miler pitting all the countries stationed at Tallil against each other, so training becomes my sole fixa-
tion. I run and run and run until my mind shuts down and is lost
in the steady rhythm of my feet on the blacktop. I run past missile
casings and the burnt-out hulls of jets. I run out past the hills and
dunes, where the borders of the base vanish into a thin line of posts.
Running becomes a kind of meditation. I find that my day goes
more smoothly with the rough peaks of my feelings ground down
by the morning's exertion. I learn to cope with the uncertainty of
my fate.

One day there is something waiting for me at the company
clerk's office. It's a copy of my completed CO application for me to
look over, sign, and rebut, if I choose, before sending it up the chain
of command. I glance through it without interest; it's all stuff I've
written or statements I've already seen. Then I notice a single piece
of paper attached to the front with a paper clip, and scanning down
the header I see the name of Captain Ferguson. It's his recommendation, the decision of the investigating officer, that makes or breaks
the whole application. My heart stops. The first three parts of the
statement are just summaries of his investigations. Then the first

sentence of the fourth paragraph leaps out from the page, as if written in flames.

I have found SPC Delgado to be sincere in his beliefs...

Triumph! I emit a guttural cry of victory and pump my arm in the air. I have been vindicated. A long paragraph follows this statement, explaining why Captain Ferguson found me sincere and why he came to that conclusion. I breeze over it quickly, too excited and joyous to read it in its entirety. He ends his official statement with the verdict:

I recommend approval of SPC Aidan Delgado's application as a Conscientious Objector 1-0 and his classification as such.

Nothing can touch me now. All the bullying, all the scorn, all the grief from the commander has been rendered meaningless by these words. I've got a chance now, a hell of a chance. In truth, Captain Ferguson is the most fair and decent officer I've ever met. The Army will place the most weight on the opinion of the investigating officer, hopefully enough to cancel out the opinion of the captain and the battalion commander.

I do nothing but smile the rest of the day. Sergeant Toro asks what's gotten into me and I tell him the good news, hugging him and Sergeant Wallace and thanking them profusely for all their help. Sergeant Wallace smiles his big old grin and says, "Glory be." That night I weep with relief and gratitude.

Strangely, all the equipment we packed up getting ready to go home stays packed. We spent nearly two weeks boxing and labeling it, and now it just sits there. It's odd, as though we're getting ready to go somewhere else. No one in the motor pool likes the thought of that; for all the dull misery of Tallil, things are stable here. There's no telling what will happen with this unit and this captain—perhaps Tallil is no longer exciting enough for them. As the commander has told us, he's not going to tell his grandkids he was a gate guard in the Iraq war, and I know that many of the MPs feel the same way. They want a more badass mission. From what we read in *Stars and Stripes,* every other part of the country has it worse than we do: Umm Qasr, the big prison camp in the south, Samarra, a nasty little village on the way north, and Baghdad, the eye of the storm. I'd be perfectly happy to wait out the rest of the war right here. If we do have to go somewhere, let it be some godforsaken outpost.

Sergeant Wallace keeps his face in his notebook as he says it. "Just wanted to let everyone know...we movin' to Baghdad."

Shoe is overjoyed. He pumps his fist at the prospect of getting into the action. "Hell, yeah! Fuck, yeah! We goin' to BAGHDAD! BAGHDAD, baby!" He's yelling and whooping down the hall now. Sergeant Toro looks concerned. Spangler and Patterson seem annoyed. Moving north means a lot of work for us, and a whole lot more danger.

"Wanted to give all of y'all a heads-up: we've been tasked to run the prison up there, Baghdad Correctional Facility, called, uh... Abu...Abu Ghraa-yaa-ab, Abu Ghr—Delgado, how do you say that?"

"Abu Ghraib."

"Yeah, that."

"That's the place where Saddam had some kind of death camp, right? It's notorious."

Sergeant Wallace nods. "Yeah, yeah. Something like that. It was a big prison under Saddam. Well, we goin' there now. You all be ready for the move."

He leaves us to digest the news. Sergeant Toro starts in with how dangerous Baghdad—and the entire Sunni Triangle—is. Spangler joins him, saying his wife is worried to death already. Everybody is worked up about the move. Shoe is now running up and down with his rifle, shouting "Baghdad!" in my face every time I start to point out how much this sucks. The rest of us begin exchanging the little snatches of rumors we get from the MPs' patrols: almost every convoy moving north through that area has gotten hit. Our worst fear remains unspoken, as it goes without saying: Baghdad is where all the combat is.

Overnight, the 320th has Baghdad on the brain. People keep saying how different things are going to be, how we're going to have to get serious. Dinner conversation turns to RPGs and IEDs, sniper fire, and convoy missions. Shoe and his friends position the saltshakers and ketchup bottles to illustrate tactics and maneuvers.

I feel a dark detachment from all this. With no weapon, I won't be participating in any battles, and with no armor, I'm dead anyway if a bullet or a fragment hits me. I'm more concerned with the enormous burden of packing away the maintenance tent and all of the associated machinery. God, what a task that will be.

A morning in November; it's time to leave. Our vehicles are lined up outside the barracks, snaking all the way up the service road. I'm riding in one of the cargo trucks with Sergeant Lewis, the hilarious, foulmouthed cook who was once on the Marine Corps wrestling team, and I couldn't be happier to have him for company. We stand around for the convoy briefing. The MP sergeant in charge of the briefing looks at the front of my vest, then jabs me in the chest with his fingers.

"Delgado, what the hell are you doing? Where's your ballistic plate?"

"I don't have one, Sergeant. They took it back."

"Well, you better tell them to get you one. That's your life there, man."

I smile helplessly and throw up my hands. The convoy briefing is over. I climb up into the cab opposite Sergeant Lewis. We start our engines in unison and wait for clearance from the base command. Just as our truck is inching up the line, I spot a figure moving down the convoy line, speaking with each soldier in turn: Chaplain Ellis. As he reaches my side, he climbs onto the cab and embraces me through the window.

"I don't know how to thank you for everything you've done for me, sir," I say. "I won't forget you."

"Good luck, my son. You be careful on the ride north and try to stay safe. I hope everything works out for you. I'll be praying for you."

He hugs me one last time. As the convoy rolls off, I watch the chaplain's stooped figure getting smaller and smaller in the distance. He waves and waves until he and the barracks are completely out of sight. I feel a sudden, poignant nostalgia for Tallil and the ragged building that has been my home these last months. I snap half a dozen photos of ordinary things, so that I won't forget. As we move down the road, I wave to everyone we pass. The other soldiers seem to know, from the length of our convoy, that we're moving out for good.

The ziggurat rises in the distance, looming over our train of vehicles like some monstrous gatekeeper. We crawl out from beneath its shadow. Before us lies the blank vastness of the open desert, white on white as far as the eye can see, but my eye lingers on the ziggurat, the Babylonian monument whose foundation creates terror.

Eteminnugur sits sullenly atop the high ground, unmoved by our passing.

Part Four
FATHER OF THE BANISHED: ABU GHRAIB

ABU GHRAIB PRISON

NOVEMBER 18, 2003 We arrive at our destination on my twenty-second birthday. The journey north was all dust and vibration and the rumble of the engine. Somewhere between Nasiriyah and Baghdad, I have the distinct sensation of crossing an invisible line: one moment we're getting smiles and waves from friendly villagers and the next, only sullen stares of contempt. I hadn't realized just how privileged we'd been to be accepted in southern Iraq. Now we're in enemy territory.

The north gradually changes from desert to marshy lands with palm trees. For the first time in months, we see patches of natural greenery and pools of standing water trailing into canals. The air is cooler here, and moist. It could be a different country.

In the distance, we can make out a low gray wall, rimmed in razor wire and punctuated by overhanging towers. It's our first glimpse of Abu Ghraib.[7] As we turn off the main road, we negotiate a maze of roadblocks and hairpin turns through several guarded checkpoints and rows of makeshift barriers. Every few hundred feet there is a cluster of soldiers and an armed Humvee, all trying to contain a huge mob of Iraqis that has gathered outside the prison walls. Men in formal coats and black-shrouded women wave scraps of paper, clamoring for entry. These people must be here to visit relatives; almost all are holding bags of food or clothing. The guards seem overwhelmed, with the crowd just barely contained behind a barbed wire cordon. The soldiers wave us through and we enter the prison through a side gate, really just a ragged hole in the perimeter wall.

The prison complex is enormous, divided into sectors by roads and inner walls. Much of the interior is rough open ground, some of it littered with rubble. Only a small portion of the base seems to have been repaired and occupied. After several wrong turns, we finally pull into a sort of courtyard on the western edge of the base. We do our best to line up the vehicles in a patch of dust adjacent to the inner wall, and the commotion churns up a suffocating cloud. When we dismount, the first sergeant calls us to formation and we stand there powdered from head to foot, breathing in dust. The first sergeant lays out the basics: which buildings will be our living quarters, where the showers and latrines are, where each platoon should park its vehicles.

As night falls, we unload the bare minimum of supplies from our vehicles. The dust is unbearable. Hustling inside the large buildings, I enter a cellblock two stories high, with a narrow stairwell at one end and a single door to the main hallway. Bright blue bars and latches contrast sharply with the white walls. I follow Patterson into the last cell on the left, our temporary quarters. The cell door slams shut behind me with an ominous clang. This is my first time inside a prison cell, which is about two-thirds the size of a motel room, and at the moment the four of us mechanics, Sergeant Toro, and Sergeant Wallace are crowded into it. We unfold our canvas-frame cots and drop our bags in exhaustion. I'm too tired to find the showers, so I change into my PT uniform and rinse the dust from my face with a handful of water from the water trailer. All six of us are in bed by early evening, but none of us can fall asleep. For one thing, it's damned cold in here. It's the first time I'm uncomfortably cold in Iraq. And the prison interior is pitch-black: not a single pinpoint of light filters into our little room and I cannot see the faces of Shoe or Patterson, less than two feet from mine. A low whistling sound comes in from a gap in the boarded-up windows. The air itself seems damp and musty, like the interior of a natural cavern. That's what it feels like: a cave…a deep, dank cave. Patterson is the first one to verbalize what we're all thinking.

"Yo, this place is spooky as hell," he remarks. "What'd you say about it, Delgado? Saddam killed a bunch of people here?"

"Yeah, I read somewhere that he used this place as, like, a death camp. Thousands of people were executed here."

"I heard some of the MPs who came up here first said that there's, like, torture chambers and an execution room and shit," adds Shoe.

"Apparently he crowded tens of thousands of prisoners in here till they starved to death," I continue. "Dozens in a single cell like this one."

We all pause for a moment, listening to the eerie winds. A shudder passes over me.

Patterson's voice rises out of the darkness, clear and dead serious: "You know there's got to be some ghosts in this place."

"Like all the people who died here are still haunting the place," says Shoe.

"If there ever was a place for lost souls, this would be it," I say after a moment.

The conversation goes dead after that. The darkness is so thick, it's like smoke in the room—I can feel it swirling and coiling around me. I can't see my hands when I hold them in front of my eyes. The only sounds are the moan of the wind and the distant sound of trickling water. I don't believe in ghosts. I try to imagine a few dozen people in this room, think what it must have felt like to be confined and starving in the darkness. I don't believe in ghosts. Fear seeps into my being. Wrapped in a thick sleeping bag, I shiver convulsively. In my imagination, I see pale, immaterial hands and fingers reaching up and touching me, white fish-faces staring at me from the corners of the cell. I shut my eyes in horror and don't dare to move. My mind is playing tricks on me; this is silly, a child's fear.

But I swear in that moment I feel a press of lost, anguished spirits crowding around me. I feel their horror, pain, sorrow, and anger. I feel intensely that I'm being watched by these forms, their shadows pointing and whispering: unwelcome. This *is* a haunted place. The air is thick with death.

The night's dread dissolves with the shock of a cold morning. The dining room near our barracks is all stone—stone benches, stone walls, stone tables—creating the startling effect that the room is a single continuous rock. Water leaks from the roof. I can't shake the feeling of being inside a cave, sitting on a carven stalagmite.

Outside, there's an icy dampness in the air. Yesterday's dust has turned to a thick mud; it must have rained last night. Sergeant Wallace points us to the trucks to begin unloading, and in fifteen minutes my boots are caked in three inches of earth. It's slow going. The plan is to organize a new motor pool so that work can resume. Almost all the MPs have been assigned duty as prison guards and their rotations begin right away, so the barracks is left to us, as headquarters. Facing out from our barracks courtyard is half a football field's worth of churned mud, bordered on the far side by the perimeter wall. To our left, an interior wall divides us from the prison camp. The field is too soft for working on vehicles, so we'll have to use the driveway and a rear court on the other side of the barracks.

The first couple of days are slow; our supplies haven't arrived from the south yet. Eventually members of headquarters join the rotation on prison guard duty. There's little else for them to do. All except me, of course, since I am unarmed. The mechanics have a relaxing change of pace from the clamor of Tallil. We do a few leisurely repairs with the tools we've brought and have a lot of time to wander around and explore the new environs.

We quickly discover that there's nothing to see or do. Our part of the base has only recently been occupied, so there are huge piles of concrete debris blocking access to most of the base. The areas we can see are a twisting complex of buildings painted the same drab blue on white. No sense walking around. There are no generators in our sector, either, so the inside of the barracks is as dark as a tomb and as cold as the open air, colder even. Without electricity there are no phones, no TV, no light to read by, and no warm place to sit and talk. By our second day at Abu, I am bored to death.

We briefly amuse ourselves by exploring a section of the perimeter wall, climbing up into an abandoned guard tower, and looking out over the city. Baghdad is a rifle shot away. Neither the tower nor the wall is in good repair, and gaping holes leave the perimeter open in places. Sergeant Wallace says we'll have to get around to fixing that, but by late afternoon each day there's nothing to do but break out the canvas chairs and sit around an old barrel on the edge of the barracks. Shoe picks out some old scrap wood from one of the piles of debris and sets it ablaze with his lighter, and soon we have a little fire going. It's only mildly warmer than the air inside, but at least it's something to do. I listen to Shoe and another soldier talk about hunting, cars, places in Tampa, and it's nice to feel accepted. These are things I wouldn't otherwise hear about, and people I might not otherwise have met: auto mechanics from Tampa, highway patrolmen from St. Petersburg, line cooks from Clearwater. They come from a world as different from mine as Cairo is from theirs. I can't say that I add much to the conversation, but I relish it: I feel acutely American, sitting around a fire on a lounge chair, rubbing my hands together and hearing about Ford versus Chevy. We spend the greater part of the next few days sitting around that barrel.

NOVEMBER 21, 2003 Nighttime. No light, no heat. We hear the sounds of chanting and yelling coming from the prison yard, just over the dividing wall. I wander outside to see what all the commotion is, and hear a steady chant of "Allahu Akbar! Allahu Akbar!" The prisoners sound angry. I hear stirring and commotion in our own barracks, and a group of MPs rushes past me.

"What's going on?" I ask one of them.

"The hajjis are freaking out, chanting and throwing stones and shit. Come on, we're going up on the roof to check it out."

I feel honored that they're inviting me to accompany them. It's a rare event that the young guys invite me to do anything, given my CO application. I fall in behind them and then notice Wilson among them. He's actually been pretty cool since our last encounter, almost chummy. Every now and then he stops by our room to chat with Patterson, a fellow Jamaican, and he's distinctly courteous to me. Thank God. The last thing I want is a feud.

"C'mon, you can climb up here." One of the MPs springs up the wall along the halls that divide each wing of the barracks building. The hall is designed to let air pass freely through it—every other brick has been left out, and these gaps make decent handholds. I climb the ten or twelve feet in a few seconds and swing myself up onto the outside roof of the corridors, marveling at how easy it is. A few yards down, MPs are helping each other climb up onto the actual roof of the building, another ten feet above us. With a little grunting and fumbling I manage to do likewise, and now I'm twenty or thirty feet above the ground. From here I can see over the dividing wall into one of the prison camps, and even over the perimeter wall into the surrounding countryside.

The view is fantastic. I can now make out the shape of the base, and even see the lights of Baghdad twinkling in the distance. Over to our left, in the prison camp, we see off-white tents and thick coils of razor wire studded with fence posts.

The shouting from the camp is louder and clearer from up here, and we can now distinguish a mass of prisoners in their long robes marching in a circle around their enclosure. As they pass the point closest to us, we see they're holding up banners made of torn-up tent material. Their chants seem to be reaching a crescendo of rage and emotion.

"What are they saying, Delgado?" one of the MPs asks me.

"God is the greatest. Over and over again," I reply.

"That's it?"

"Do any of you guys know why they're so pissed off?" I ask.

"They've been complaining about their living conditions for, like, the last week," one of the MPs volunteers. "Each of the camps elected one guy as their spokesman and he's, like, their representative to the guards. They've been complaining about the cold, and the food, and having their cigarettes taken away.

"The guys from the other companies who've been here a while said they do it all the time . . . I heard that before we came they had this really big riot where they were chanting and throwing stones and shit. This is the loudest it's been since we got here, but the other guards say that this ain't shit compared to a while ago."

The wind is sharp up here. I bury my face and hands into my field jacket. The prisoners keep screaming: "God is the greatest! God is the greatest!" as though they'll never tire of it. Where do they get the strength? I'm in thermals and a thick coat and I'm freezing, but they just keep marching and yelling. "Allahu Akbar!"

Most of our little group gets bored after half an hour and climbs down, but a few of us stay on. We move to the edge of the building closest to the motor pool and sit with our boots dangling over the side. Our yard is a pool of shadows.

Far in the distance, the edge of Baghdad is visible as a collection of spires and towers and domed mosques. The lights of the city blink on and off as people go to bed or close their shops for the night. Arcs of orange and red light crisscross the city from one building to the next: tracer rounds, bullets with an incendiary tip that glows red-hot so you can see what you're shooting at night. Every night there is a gun battle in Baghdad and the tracer arcs go back and forth for hours, hundreds of little orange flashes, sometimes till dawn.

There's a firefight going on right now, just on the horizon. I am mesmerized by the splotches of light.

"You see those tracers?" one of the MPs asks me. "Those are the Iraqis shooting at each other. You know every shopkeeper has his own AK and when two of them get in an argument they just open up on each other."

"You sure those aren't ours? It looks like there's both red and orange tracers."

"Naw, man, it's the Iraqis, shooting at each other." He seems pretty sure, and he's been to Baghdad so maybe he would know, but I don't buy it. The tracers travel in high arcs over the city, as though the combatants were shooting at each other from far apart; this is not two shopkeepers having an "argument." I swear I can make out two colors of tracers, theirs orange and ours reddish. I think we're fighting someone again. It looks like a hell of a battle—there are tracers flying everywhere, with some popping straight up into the sky like Roman candles. When we fired tracer rounds in basic training, we saw that some bullets ricocheted straight up into the air when they hit something solid, and others jumped over the horizon like skipping stones. It was eerily beautiful to stand in the foxhole at Fort Knox and watch hundreds of tracer rounds pouring over the targets in a steady stream like a fireworks display, the rounds leaping and spinning for our entertainment.

But these are not being fired at pop-up targets. Each one of these bullets is being aimed at another human being, and for every round that we can see there are three that we can't. Every fourth bullet is tipped with strontium or barium to make it burn as it travels, tracing its path in the night. It's strange, but from this distance, the battle looks serene and beautiful: dancing orange lights leap back and forth, yellow house lights blink off and on, spirals of red skitter up into the sky and come crashing down. It's a stunning display. In that moment it seems like it's all being done for my benefit, for sheer enjoyment, people rattling off .762 rounds just to create a pleasing pattern for me, sitting on a rooftop at Abu Ghraib. For a brief moment

I allow myself to forget that these bullets are slamming into concrete and plaster, tearing chunks out of walls, windows, doors, flesh. That the hands holding these worn triggers are filthy and dripping with sweat as they aim their little arcs of color at the distant shapes of enemies: us and them, trying earnestly to kill each other. That those incandescent tips that light up the sky so beautifully burn red-hot when they strike skin, muscle, and bone. From here it's all so abstract, and I sit watching long after everyone else has climbed down.

NOVEMBER 24, 2003 We're sitting around the barrel, laughing, when Master Sergeant Carlson runs out of the building. "Everyone get your shit on, grab your weapons, and report to the TOC. There's some sort of riot going on; they've called out the QRF. They need everyone down at the prison yard."

The Quick Reaction Force; it must be serious. Sergeant Toro, Spangler, and Schumacher scatter to get their equipment, and Shoe's eyes are gleaming with joy at the prospect of action. He's practically tripping over himself.

I turn to Master Sergeant Carlson and ask him what I should do.

"Delgado, you just stand fast. Tell anyone who comes by here to get their shit and report to the company headquarters."

"Yes, Master Sergeant."

So, just like that, I'm left standing alone in the courtyard. I pull my chair to the center of the yard and sit down. Every few minutes, someone passes by on their way into the barracks and I tell them to report to the TOC.

"Yeah, yeah, we heard."

I've never felt so superfluous, but this is what you get for declaring yourself a conscientious objector: left out of everything. Oh well. I occupy my post for about forty-five minutes, consumed with curiosity. What the hell is going on over there? The guys have been gone a long time. Eventually I go upstairs for something to read. I find a copy of *Rifleman* magazine, and try to take my mind off whatever crisis is going on. After an eternity, Sergeant Toro and Shoe waddle into view through the barracks door, weighted down under their vests and jangling accessories.

"You guys, what the hell happened down there?" I ask.

"The prisoners were throwing stones at the guards," Sergeant Toro tells me. "They were afraid they were going to rush the wire, so they had all of us stand by with our weapons in case. They ended up taking care of it, though. They didn't need us."

Shoe seems disappointed. "Goddamn, I thought I was going to get the chance to shoot somebody finally," he says.

With that, they turn and head inside to put up their gear. Before long, Sergeant Wallace appears and sets me on some trivial tasks around the barracks, so I can't ask any more questions.

That evening, we all gather around the fire barrel again. Shoe pulls out a packet of popcorn and goes in search of something to use as a skillet.

Several MPs stroll over and join us beside the fire. Among them is a boyish-looking sergeant named McCullough, a squad leader from one of the MP platoons. He has a flat-top haircut and round, apple cheeks that make him look half his age. He has got to be the nicest sergeant in the company. He's one of those guys who always has a smile and a joke for any situation, walks up to everybody and slaps them on the back like they were best friends. It's always a pleasure to help out Sergeant McCullough. He sits down.

"Did y'all hear about the riot?"

This is how I learn what happened on the other side of the camp during the prisoner demonstration. Sergeant McCullough tells the story with quiet enthusiasm, nodding and gesturing for emphasis. Just after one o'clock, the prisoners in the Ganci compounds—the eight razor-wire enclosures outside the prison wall, where most of the detainees are held—began to riot, or at least that's what the Army called it, though I learn later that they were mostly just marching and chanting. In essence, the prisoners were upset about their living conditions: cold weather and the lack of blankets, jackets, and warm clothing. They were also complaining about the food, which they claimed was often served spoiled or infested with vermin, and was generally inadequate. On top of this, the representatives protested the confiscation of the prisoners' tobacco and not being able to smoke. They had been marching and demonstrating for several days in a row. The demonstration got out of control and turned violent. The prisoners started throwing stones and pieces of wood from the tent floor. The MPs on duty responded with nonlethal rounds: rubber bullets, beanbags, and tear gas. In Sergeant McCullough's telling, one of the prisoners threw a rock and hit a soldier in our company, Specialist Pitts, in the face.

Sergeant McCullough expresses his anger at seeing one of his soldiers' faces bloodied. At some point during the demonstration, he can't say exactly when, they get the order to use lethal force. He tells us that he knelt down behind a barrier, loaded his weapon, said a prayer, then stood up and fired. He says he thinks he hit three prisoners and he knows he killed one. In total, twelve prisoners are shot and three of those die of their wounds. He says one of the prisoners was shot in the head and his face split open like in the movie *Terminator 2*. Another prisoner had been hit in the groin, and according to this account, the guards left him on the ground and he bled to death. He says they took pictures of the bodies after the shooting. They got copies in the TOC.

Those are the facts of the story, but what I remember most about it is the way that Sergeant McCullough told it. He is perfectly calm; recounting the fatal shot as if it were a hunting expedition. Throughout the story, he looks down and shrugs modestly as if to say, "It was nothing special." The other soldiers are all pressing him for details; clearly they are proud of him and envious of his accomplishment: killing an Iraqi. As always Sergeant McCullough is modest and polite, saying he didn't do anything anyone else wouldn't have done and that he was scared to death the whole time. The way he smiles when he says this makes me think he's a little proud of himself too.

At first I don't know what to think or say. I only know that I am bothered. It takes a few minutes to process. Then I think, This is a little fucked-up. He shot an unarmed prisoner on the other side of a barbed-wire fence for throwing a stone. Four people are dead for throwing stones in protest of their living conditions. Don't judge, I remind myself, you weren't there, you didn't see it. Maybe the action was necessary. They were probably afraid for their lives. Then I look to my left and right and see the young guys in my unit: laughing, smiling, talking about how much they wished they had "got one" too. I reconsider. This is fucked-up.

"So, Sergeant McCullough...you shot an unarmed man, behind barbed wire, for throwing stones at you?" I ask.

I try to make it sound as nonconfrontational as possible. First, he's a sergeant and I'm a specialist. Second, he's a hell of a nice guy and I don't want to call him out. I expect him to be angry. He isn't. He responds calmly. Look, they bloodied Pitts's face, they were throwing stones, big stones that could have hurt or killed someone if they'd hit him right. There were hundreds of them and just a few of us. We tried to use nonlethal rounds.

He's explaining the situation to me; he's not mad. I fall silent. It's not my place to push it anymore. After all, I wasn't there. But a thought lodges itself firmly in the back of my head: These were unarmed men, prisoners under our care, and we just shot twelve of them for protesting against the prison conditions. All the ugly rumors at Tallil, all the "hajjis" and all the nasty racial humor comes flooding back to me. This is the blossoming of it all: the "shoot first and ask questions later" mentality. And three men are dead because of it.

I feel the last ounce of my attachment to the 320th wither and disappear. I'm not one of these people. I'm not one of *them* anymore. What happened today was wrong: shortsighted and trigger-happy at best and downright vicious at worst. From here on out, I don't want any part of what we're doing at Abu Ghraib.

Later, months later, I read official accounts of what happened on November 24. I read through the investigations of various generals: the Taguba Report, the Jones/Fay Report. I read the International Committee of the Red Cross (ICRC) report, piecing together bits of each with Sergeant McCullough's account.

The Taguba Report:

> Several detainees allegedly began to riot at about 1300 in all of the compounds at the Ganci encampments. This resulted in the shooting deaths of 3 detainees, 9 wounded detainees, and 9 injured U.S. Soldiers... concluded that the detainees rioted in protest of their living conditions, that the riot turned violent, the use of nonlethal force was ineffective... the use of deadly force was authorized.[8]

In an annex to the Taguba Report, the commander has written: "There was a riot in late November where my unit had to respond to. One of my soldiers killed an Iraqi rioter after expending his nonlethal rounds. There were a total of four rioters killed that day in order to calm the riot, but that was only after using up all the nonlethal rounds. There were a number of my soldiers injured that day."[9]

The Jones/Fay Report:

> A milestone event at Abu Ghraib was the shooting incident that occurred in Tier 1A on 24 November 2003 (see paragraph 5e.) ... LTC Jordan displayed personal bravery by his direct involvement in the shoot-out, but also extremely poor judgment. Instead of ordering the MPs present to halt their actions and

isolate the tier until the 320 MP BN Commander and COL Pappas could be notified, he became directly involved. As the senior officer present, LTC Jordan became responsible for what happened...the situation after the shooting which came to be known as the IP Roundup...The Iraqi Police, hence the name "IP," became detainees and were subjected to strip searching... were kept in various stages of dress, including nakedness, for prolonged periods as they were interrogated. This constitutes humiliation, which is detainee abuse. Military working dogs were being used not only to search the cells, but also to intimidate the IPs during interrogation without authorization...LTC Jordan should have controlled the situation and should have taken steps to reinforce proper standards at a time when emotions were likely high given the circumstances. The tone and the environment that occurred that night, with the tacit approval of LTC Jordan, can be pointed to as the causative factor that set the stage for the abuses that followed for days afterward.[10]

So the shootings had led to the strip searching of the Iraqi guards, forced nudity, humiliation, threats by military dogs, an "environment" that led to days of abuse. The report itself admitted that what the guards had done in the aftermath of the shooting was "detainee abuse." Needless to say, it was a shadow of things to come.

November 24 turned a page for the Army at Abu Ghraib prison, just as surely as it had turned a page for my own feelings about the mission.

The ICRC report:

24 November 2003: During a riot four detainees were killed by U.S. MP guards. [The Taguba Report states three killed; I heard that one of the injured prisoners later died of his injuries.] The killing took place after unrest erupted in one of the compounds (no. 4). The detainees claimed to be unhappy with the situation of detention. Specifically, lack of food, clothing, but more im-

portantly the lack of judicial guarantees and, especially important during the time of Eid al-Fitr [the holiday that marks the
end of Ramadan], lack of family visits or lack of contacts all
together. The detainees alleged to have gathered near the gate
whereupon the guards panicked and started shooting... The
narrative report furnished by the CF [Coalition Forces] does
not address the reason for the riot in any way and does not give
any recommendation as to how a similar incident could be
avoided.[11]

The report substantiates the accounts I heard of why the prisoners rioted. With these three documents, and the account of
Sergeant McCullough, a clear picture of what happened on November 24 emerges in my mind. This is the way I see it:

The prisoners are demonstrating against the poor living conditions. It's cold and they're hungry. They elect representatives in each
camp to speak for them. They're angry and confrontational. The
guards on duty don't speak any Arabic; they can tell that the prisoners are upset but they can't understand what they want. The
prisoners congregate at the front of the yard, nearest the gate, just
like the Red Cross said, because that's the point closest to the guards
who will hear their grievances. They're angry, they're frustrated.
Someone throws a rock. The mob mentality takes over. Lots of people start throwing things, venting their anger at the cold and the
food and the lack of family visits. The guards are terrified. All they
see is a crowd of hundreds of prisoners near the gate; they think
they're trying to force it open. The Red Cross says the guards
"panic" and start shooting. They try to drive the detainees back
with nonlethal rounds, they run out of ammunition, and the order
comes down: Use lethal force. They lock and load just the way they
were trained to. The first shots ring out and the prisoners panic and
run. The guards keep shooting. When the dust settles, twelve men
are lying on the ground. Three die right there, another dies later
from his wounds. The Army writes up the whole incident as a "riot"

or "attempted escape." The report gets buried until other events force the authorities to go back over the account of that afternoon.

Within a week of arriving at Abu Ghraib, I see the veneer peel away from something ugly. Here and now, in this dismal place, I understand that what was set in motion in Nasiriyah is about to gain a terrible momentum. All the violence and hate that's been building will be unleashed, now that the guards have the Iraqis under their thumbs. The November "riot" is not the start of violence but the fulfillment of it, a culmination of the dark promise of Nasiriyah. In a way, it's the blossoming of the seeds of 9/11, of all the partisan speeches and sideways glances at Muslims in the airport. I begin to see the dark and shameful flipside of the occupation: brutality, racism, killing. I take some solace in the fact that I have already stated my opposition to this, that I have already set myself apart. In the days and months to come I will only set myself apart further. After listening to Sergeant McCullough's story, I feel a vast and terrible karma set itself in motion: a hateful and destructive wheel at last coming full circle. The four killings in November aren't the end . . . they're only a portent of what is to come.

One evening, Schumacher walks into our room with a glittering CD clenched in his fist. He asks to borrow Patterson's computer, and the three of us sit down to see what he's got. He loads the CD, pulling up an image of two soldiers in our company carrying a long black bag. I look closer. A body bag.

"Remember that transport mission I went on a while back?" Shoe says. "Where we took the bodies of those Iraqis killed in the riot to the morgue? The guards took a bunch of pictures."

He clicks through several more images: the same soldiers hefting the body bag, and then another loading it into the back of a cargo truck. The third image is of a pair of bags lying in the back of an Army truck, with no soldiers in the frame.

"Before we rolled out at the gate, the MPs pulled the truck over in the waiting area and opened up the bags. Took a bunch of photos of the dead guys, you know . . . kinda like trophies."

Shoe reaches over and clicks the touch pad. A photograph of a man's face appears. He's young, maybe late twenties, with long sideburns and a wispy mustache. I am looking down on him from a three-quarter angle. His teeth are yellowed and several are missing, but aside from that he looks healthy and handsome. His eyes are half-open, as if he had been awakened suddenly from sleep. A reddish stain is just barely visible running down the bridge of his nose and onto his lip. A pair of gloved hands is frozen in midair: unzipping the body bag and holding it open. On the edge of the right glove the word "Hellstorm" is clearly visible. This is one of the men killed on November 24 at Abu Ghraib, killed for throwing a stone or being in the company of those who did. Shoe lingers on the picture for a moment, letting us take it all in, then flips to the next.

Bright reds and pinks leap out at me. I'm looking at another man who's been shot in the face. The upper-right quarter of his head has been torn away. The outline of the wound is framed in splotches of fresh blood. This must be the one that Sergeant McCullough described as having his "head split open"; I wonder who it was who shot him. I never find out. Above the ruined mass of the man's right eye, I can see clearly into his skull. The contents are moist and pink, the wrinkled texture of the brain clearly visible. Blood has splattered across the outside of the body bag and drips down to form a pool beneath it. This man's eyes are open as well, or at least the one eye that remains. His eye is wide, his mouth half-open in an expression of shock or terror. Patterson and I turn away . . . but then turn back. War pornography. Graphic. Arresting. I feel nauseated, but I keep looking. We stare at that image for over a minute in silence. One of us says something crude to break the tension; the others laugh half-heartedly and try to come up with some retort of their own. We're afraid to see what might come next. Shoe taps the keyboard.

The frame jumps backward: now we see the whole truck and two soldiers in the back of it, leaning over the man's corpse. On the right side of the screen, a third soldier's head and arms are visible, snapping a picture. The soldier in the truck, on the left side, is bent over the corpse's head with a plastic MRE spoon, as if to scoop out a bite. His pink face is smiling ghoulishly, his tongue moist and visible. A wedding ring glistens on the hand that holds the spoon. The other soldier is seated on the right, wearing a neutral expression and holding his helmet in both hands. His left shoulder is turned to the camera and proudly displays our unit symbol and the letters "MP" on his brassard. Above these initials, in tiny lettering, are the Arabic words for "military police"—*il-shuurta askari*—that the company had local tailors embroider on the jackets of the MPs when they arrived in Iraq, so that everyone would recognize their authority.

I know both of these men. The one on the left is a specialist, a bit of a blowhard and a stickler for cleaning weapons. The one on the right is a serious and businesslike staff sergeant, who is well liked by his soldiers. I can't believe that either of them has posed for such a damning photograph, particularly one involving the desecration of a corpse. If only the folks back home could see us now, I say to myself. Is this the Army I idolized as a little boy? Is this the Army that's so brave and true and wonderful? I stare down at this image of two of our soldiers posing over the brains of a prisoner who was shot for demonstrating: shot in the face, for throwing stones in protest of his living conditions. *For throwing stones.* This photograph becomes my image of the whole "glorious mission" in Iraq: two soldiers posing like ghouls over the shattered corpse of an Iraqi. The description is apt—"ghoul" is derived from the Arabic word *ghul*, meaning demon. In Arabian folklore a *ghul* is a monster that inhabits graveyards and other desolate places and eats the flesh of corpses. I have to preserve this image, to show people what went on here. I ask Shoe if I can get a copy of the pictures. Yeah, no problem, he says. When we get back to the States, he places a copy of the disk in my hand.

One day Sergeant Toro returns from a prisoner-transport mission visibly shaken. His usual cheerful disposition is gone, and his words are grim and deliberate as he tells me and Patterson his story.

He was tasked with transporting a load of prisoners from Abu Ghraib to the hospital in Baghdad. He and Schumacher went together, Sergeant Toro to drive the truck and Shoe to guard the prisoners. A group of MPs would be leading the mission. When Sergeant Toro arrived at the mission site, they had him back the truck up to the entrance of the Hard Site, the unit inside Abu where detainees with "intelligence value" and dangerous prisoners are held. One of the prisoners to be transported was from this segregated part of the prison, and he was of special interest to the guards. It seems that in the course of the last week, this prisoner had somehow smuggled in a handgun and shot one of the MP guards in the chest. The guard, a massive man, had taken the bullet across the front of his armored vest, and the bullet didn't penetrate, only knocked him down, injuring and enraging him. The other guards then subdued the prisoner with physical force and, rumor had it, a blast from a shotgun into the prisoner's legs. This prisoner was now to be transported to the hospital to receive treatment for his wounds. Two MP guards dragged the man from his cell and hauled him out into the daylight to be loaded onto the truck. He was naked except for his underwear and a bag over his head.

"He was fucked up, man," Sergeant Toro tells us. "His legs were covered in little holes, maybe from shotgun pellets. It looked like someone had just beaten the shit out of him. His legs were so messed up, there was no way he could stand on his own." Sergeant Toro couldn't say for sure how the prisoner had gotten his injuries; later I will see photos of the man's cell, which looked like someone had mopped the floor with his blood. The MPs manhandle the injured man, toss him up into the bed of the truck where his hands are bound with plastic ties to the wooden bench. Sergeant Toro explains that the morning was so cold, he was freezing in his thermal underwear, uniform, field jacket, and liner. The prisoner is in his underwear.

It is a forty-five-minute trip to the Baghdad hospital. As Sergeant Toro and Schumacher prepare to get under way, Sergeant Toro expresses misgivings. "This is fucked-up, man," he tells Shoe. "It's freezing cold outside and that guy is wounded and naked. He could get hypothermia. He's going to die before we get to the hospital."

Shoe is unmoved. "Fuck him. That's what he gets for trying to shoot one of our guys."

The convoy sets off. The road is rutted, and the prisoner is bouncing up and down in the back of the truck. An obese man, he is wailing and crying out as the vehicle lurches over the bumps in the road, jostling his shattered legs. His weight and the jarring motion causes the wooden bench he is sitting on to break. Coming down on his injured legs with the full weight of his body, he screams. Schumacher, riding in the back with his SAW, later tells me that he was amused by this, not concerned, seeing as how this man had tried to kill one of our soldiers. Sergeant Toro, however, is horrified. He fears the prisoner will go into shock.

Just outside the entrance to the Baghdad facilities, the MPs pull over to the side of the road and cover some of the prisoners with blankets. Sergeant Toro says they don't want the military authorities to see that they transported the detainees naked in freezing weather; they know they're not supposed to do that. One of the MP sergeants, in an uncommon act of kindness, strips off his own field jacket and lays it over the prisoner with the injured legs, as no one else seems ready to help him.

Inside the base, the guards open the back of the truck and motion for the prisoners to get out. They gesture to the prisoner with the injured legs to jump out on his own or they'll pick him up and throw him out. His legs are so badly damaged that he can't even stand. The prisoner, a man in his late thirties, begins to weep hysterically and beg for mercy in Arabic. The MPs appear poised to heave him out of the truck bodily. Sergeant Toro steps in. He and another soldier grab the prisoner under his arms and slowly lower him to the ground, supporting his body on their soldiers. They load him into a wheelchair to be taken to the hospital.

After this mission, Sergeant Toro refuses to go on any more prisoner escorts. He doesn't ever want to be a part of something like that again. As he recounts the story, his face goes dark and sorrowful. He says he wishes he had done more, taken a stronger stand. He says he should have refused to move the truck until they put a blanket over the prisoner, should have refused to let them subject an injured man to such treatment. He says he knew that what they were doing was wrong but that he couldn't do anything about it, after all he is only an E-5 sergeant and like everyone else has to follow the chain of command.

Sergeant Toro and I still talk about this incident, even two years after it happened. The prisoner was hostile, no question. He shot a guard, and there was no doubt that he needed to be controlled and isolated. He was dangerous—but not at that moment, with both legs shattered and his hands tied. At that moment, he was just a wounded man on his way to the hospital. The guards made it personal. Sergeant Toro says he didn't feel that the man was an enemy and deserved to be punished, he only felt sorry for all the pain they were putting him through. To this day, when we talk about that man in the back of the truck, a pallor comes over Sergeant Toro's face and he repeats over and over again, "That was fucked up. It was wrong."

Since the beginning of the deployment I have known Sergeant Toro to be a good man, a just man, a fair officer and a moral one. Now I know him to be a merciful man, one who feels the way I do about what's happening here.

So much petty, day-to-day cruelty goes on inside the wire, and the guards seem to think it's normal. No one talks much about the way we treat prisoners, but it makes my stomach turn every time I think about it. I have a nagging feeling that many of the men inside Abu aren't terrorists at all, they were just in the wrong place at the wrong time. That only makes the brutality seem even more un-justified. Since it seems to be getting worse, I'm relieved to know that I'm not the only one who sees that something terribly wrong is happening at Abu Ghraib.

DECEMBER 2003 Sometimes we hear distant crashing noises. We know that these sounds are falling mortar rounds, but they're not real to us yet. As we begin to settle in to life in the prison camp, we mingle with the other units who've been stationed here longer, and they tell us stories. The unit that's clearing out, the one we're taking over for, tells us to expect a heavy bombardment soon. As we help them move their stuff out of the rooms we'll be occupying on a permanent basis, they give us their combat resume: the number of bombardments they've taken, how close the mortars fell to them, the closest calls in the unit. It's both bragging and warning. I'm skeptical. We've been here more than a week already and we haven't had anything serious. They tell us to wait and see—that we'll get ours soon enough.

The other privates and I move into a new upstairs room on the corner of the barracks. Every evening we hear rumblings and dis-tant echoes, but nothing ever comes near. What exactly does it feel like to be shelled? Is this what they're talking about—a couple of odd rounds on the other side of the base? We quickly get used to the shelling as no more than background noise. It's no worse than an average thunderstorm. We start to settle in like hermit crabs occu-pying an old, cast-off shell: the walls of our room are covered in the playful graffiti of its previous occupants as well as a detailed calen-dar marking off the days until they are sent home. The handwritten calendar has been drawn across an entire wall of the room, and each day meticulously records Coalition deaths, mortar fire, and enemy contacts. Judging from the calendar, the last occupants had an eventful tour of duty: every week records either a mortar barrage, an IED attack, or rifle fire. In enormous letters across the calendar someone has written, "I CAN'T BREATHE! STOP SMOKING (AND SPRAYING LYSOL)," and below that are a few tattered cuttings from men's magazines, the last occupants' favorite girls. The place feels nicely lived in. All we do is shove all their things off the shelves and into the garbage and replace them with our own. I tape Amy's photo to the wall, along with one of my father and brother. Just like that, their room becomes ours: Schumacher and Patterson and I, away from the oversight of the sergeants for the first time in a year. The only downside is that Sergeant Wallace stuck Spangler in here too. Thankfully, Spangler immediately walls himself off in a corner of the room by constructing an absurd giant box out of plywood so that he can "have his privacy."

Eventually our equipment is shipped up from the South, and Sergeant Wallace puts us all back to the grindstone. He transfers the routine of Nasiriyah seamlessly to Abu Ghraib; the only difference is that now we have to clean dried mud out of our tools rather than picking out sand, and we wear two shirts and a set of thermal underwear under our coveralls. At the end of every workday, Sergeant Wallace lumbers up to our room to give us the evening briefing: what the platoon leaders have decided, who's assigned where, and any special tasks. One evening we're joking around in our room after a briefing, listening to the sounds of falling mortar rounds. I'm reminded of Mark Twain's description of thunder as sounding like "someone rolling empty barrels down the stairs." Someone comments on a particularly loud crash.

Then the room wobbles, and all speech is lost in a sudden roar of sound. A mortar round has struck just outside the wall of our building. It's followed by several more. Dust and fumes billow into the air as Sergeant Wallace begins to shout his orders.

The events of the bombardment pass as if in a dream—the plaster floating from the ceiling, the panicked rush to get to ground, my absurd attempts to shield my unarmored body, Shoe's crazy grin as we huddle together in the doorway, the first sergeant's ridiculous cry, "They're coming over the walls!"

What I will remember most about this night, though, is the fear I felt of dying. My utter lack of samurai indifference. The emotion left in the wake of the attack is more real than the event itself.

Over the next few months, Shoe and I become connoisseurs of mortar attacks. Distant or isolated rounds don't count; they have to fall close enough and thick enough to put the fear of God in you. After a while it's only the exceptional ones that stick out in your memory at all, as the routine of bombardment and taking shelter becomes an ordinary part of every day. Abu Ghraib is located between two parallel highways leading to Baghdad. This position makes it an ideal target for mortar crews, who can easily pull off the side of the road, fire a small mortar from the back of a pickup truck, and drive off before the base even knows it's under attack. They fire a couple of rounds blindly, lobbing them over the high wall without being able to see what they're hitting. Most of the rounds land in the unoccupied sectors of the base, but a few always manage to find a barracks or a populated area. The chance of sudden mortar fire is simply a fact of life at Abu Ghraib. It is strikingly consistent. The attacks almost always happen at dusk, just after the sun sets, and almost never two days in a row. Usually they fire a quick salvo, change location, fire a few more, and then retreat while the base command is trying to triangulate their position. Some of the MPs stationed in the perimeter towers tell us that they can often spot the mortar crews setting up or relocating: generally a trio of men who either drive off or fade into the furrowed fields and countryside surrounding the base.

In the aftermath of these attacks, at least those that happen near our company area, Shoe and I go out to survey the damage. Like tourists or bird-watchers, we creep through the impact zones, snapping photos of debris and blast craters. We point out to each other spray patterns of flak that ripped through the plastic Porta-Jons and perfectly punched holes in the water tank, as clean as rifle rounds. I snap a photo of Schumacher's stained pant legs as he stands at the rim of a crater, the churned earth pockmarked with crevices and tiny fragments of the mortar casing. These will be cool photos to show everyone back home, prove to them that we really were in the war. I waste more photos than I should on holes in the ground and unidentifiable pieces of metal. They won't be impressive to anyone but me. Then we turn and gaze in disgust at the damage to the vehicles, despair rising in our hearts as we take in the shattered windshields and deflated tires. Goddamn, rebuilding a single tire takes almost two hours. Every mortar round that falls flattens every tire in a ten-meter radius and shatters every bit of glass to boot. I come to hate the mortar rounds with a personal vengeance, as every one extends my already unbearable workday. I come to think of the bombardments in terms of vehicles, for that is really what they are to me: so many vehicles damaged, so many repairs to do, so many new windshields and turn signals and so on. I never think of them in human terms.

There's a strong inclination not to think of the people at all. Death by mortar strikes me as somehow more horrifying and ignoble than death in battle, so indirect, so impersonal, like being felled by a lightning bolt or a meteor. There is a terrifying randomness and arbitrariness to it. The other units tell a story from the week before we got here, about how these two Military Intelligence guys were resting in a tent when a mortar round came down through the roof of the tent and hit one of the guys in the chest. At least that's the way they tell it. Getting struck by a falling mortar, hit in the chest no less, in a couple of square kilometers of open space? Maybe it's not true, but the fact stands that two soldiers were killed by mortars the week before we got here. Totally arbitrary. What can you say of a mortar flying through the roof into your bedroom? There's no precaution you can take, no chance for courage or resourcefulness. Your ticket just gets punched. The hand of fate comes down from the sky and crushes you into oblivion, there's no other way of processing it. Mortar bombardment is like Russian roulette, both horrifying and liberating, since usually there's little you can do to save yourself. If your number comes up, that's all she wrote. Earlier I described the Iraqis as living in resignation to the hand of fate; now we are the fatalistic ones.

Our company seems to have an almost charmed status. We come as close as you can to being killed without ever being injured. After one shelling, Specialist Lyons shows us a black cloth CD case that she had been holding in the crook of her arm. A jagged hole has been torn through the center of the case, perforating all the CDs, the fragment missing Lyons's arm by inches. A likable old cook called Pollard recounts how he had been sitting in one of the Porta-Jons when a mortar round exploded not twenty feet behind him. A cluster of metal fragments blew through the toilet, outlining him in flak but missing his body entirely. We all laugh as he pantomimes leaping out of the Porta-Jon with his pants around his ankles and trying to run. These stories remind us all how truly random our fate is: an inch to the left, half a foot closer, and they would have been dead. I begin to understand what the old veterans were talking about in all those memoirs of World War II, when they mention how the people who survived the war weren't braver or tougher or smarter than anyone else, they were just lucky. Unconscionably lucky. The 320th is lucky. We go through I don't know how many bombardments, people get fragments through their clothing, fragments nicking their helmets, people are on the other side of a low wall when a round strikes it, just barely shielding them. Mortars fall within twenty feet of me and I don't catch a single piece of shell. With every strike, the mood gets more serious, this fortune can't last forever. We're all waiting for the day when our luck runs out . . . but it never comes. Not once does a mortar round break the skin and draw blood from any soldier in our company. Lucky. Damn lucky. We joke about the 320th guardian angel, who makes up for our having been cursed with the commander. Making light of the constant bombardments, we go about our daily routines, pretending not to care.

Weeks pass. Sergeant Wallace informs me that I will no longer be working in the motor pool, that he has been given a special assignment for me. My heart sinks in anticipation of some new harassment for the conscientious objector. What will it be this time? Guarding a trash pile? Cleaning the latrines? Counting piles of Iraqi dinar at the detention center? Worse: from now on I will be working as a radio operator at the brigade headquarters. Sergeant Wallace says that the commander and his second in command chose this duty for me because I have a college education, and they need someone with a "head on their shoulders" who can do math and work a radio.

I sense bullshit. There must be some terrible catch, and there is: shifts at the brigade TOC are twenty-four on, twenty-four off, and when I'm not at the brigade I'll still have to work in the motor pool. I could throttle the captain, both captains. I'll be surrounded by nothing but officers all day, plus I'll be working in a different unit so there won't be any sergeants I know to look out for me. They have the nerve to make it seem like some kind of honor to be loaned out to another unit for extra work. I sense an impending "detail from hell."

I am not disappointed. When I arrive at the brigade, I find that I will be working under some of the most senior officers at the base: Lieutenant Colonel Phillabaum, Major Dinenna, and some captain who speaks to me as if I were five years old. All are demanding and particular. While I am there, I am to man the battalion radio and relay their commands as well as take reports from all the field units assigned to the base. In essence, I become the voice of the brigade over the radio, using the headquarters call sign "Shadow Main." Every hour, I take the prisoner counts from each section of the Ganci compounds, recording how many prisoners are sick, absent, or have been moved. I update the counts on a dry erase board and relay any information between the officers at headquarters and the gates and guard towers. A relaxed staff sergeant shows me the ropes and assures me that he will be nearby if I have any questions. The first few days I get everything wrong: from radio procedure to inaccurate counts to not cleaning off Major Dinenna's whiteboard. As the weeks pass and I learn each of the officers' eccentricities, I develop a strong picture of how Abu Ghraib operates. All the paperwork on the prison operations passes through my desk on the way to the senior commanders and I am always in the room when the officers are discussing policy. In my new capacity, I learn more about Abu Ghraib prison and its detainee operations than even the guards working the cellblocks.

Both my hourly prisoner counts and the officers' discussions confirm my initial suspicions: the prison is critically short-staffed. We routinely have between four and six thousand detainees and only a handful of companies to manage them. Much of the officers' chatter concerns manpower shortages and how to accommodate the rapidly increasing prison population. Under the guise of being a simpleton, I ask the captain how the prison runs, and he is only too happy to take me "under his wing" and explain it all to me.

Abu Ghraib is the repository of the Iraqi justice system, or what's left of it, as well as a clearinghouse for everyone taken into U.S. custody in the whole northern half of Iraq. Across Iraq, there is a network of prison camps and outposts designed to funnel all captured personnel to a few large complexes: Abu Ghraib in the north, Umm Qasr in the south, and a few others. The problem is that prisoners are constantly being shuffled between all these outposts and getting lost in the bureaucracy. We have a notorious problem with "phantom prisoners," who the books say are in Abu Ghraib but are nowhere to be found. Often the translators are forced to tell family members that their loved one may have been transported to the other side of the country, or that we don't have any idea where he is. The constant transfer and retransfer of prisoners soon becomes inordinately complex, to the point where we can't say for certain which prisoners are where. Compounding this burden is the fact that we have to rely on hired contractors for all translation and interaction with the Iraqi justice system. To my knowledge, there are no Arabic linguists working for the Army in the Ganci compounds at Abu Ghraib. All the interactions with prisoners, their families, and the local magistrates are done through third-country nationals: Kuwaitis or Saudis hired out for this purpose. Most of the ones I interact with on a daily basis seem to belong to some firm called Titan Corp., and they are responsible for all the daily responsibilities at the prison camp.

The operations are a mess. Inside the wire, we have U.S. soldiers as guards working alongside Iraqi police who are absolutely untrustworthy. On one occasion, the Iraqi police smuggled in a pistol to one of the prisoners, and on another they helped a prisoner escape by giving him a police uniform. Tensions inside the prison camp are always high. Every so often the guards perform a "shakedown" and rummage through the prisoners' living area, always turning up an abundance of sharpened stakes and other improvised weapons, which are sorted and logged in the headquarters. The prisoners are hostile and restless, largely because of the conditions in which they are forced to live. Detainees live in canvas tents set on wooden platforms on the ground, each cluster of tents hemmed in by a razor-wire barrier. It's freezing cold outside and they never have enough blankets and coats. They're packed sixty or so people to a tent, in cramped quarters, so sickness spreads rapidly throughout the camp. One day when I'm working the radio, a frantic voice crackles through the line: it's a guard at the prison camp, telling me to send for a medevac. While I'm waiting for the request to go through, the voice of the guard grows increasingly hostile and panicked.

"What the hell is going on, Shadow Main? This guy is turning blue. He's going to die."

I'm in a terror. I tell him that the medical team is on its way, it's already been dispatched. I call again to the emergency medical section, yelling for them to hurry over to the Ganci compounds. But it's too late: the prisoner dies right there in the yard, while I'm on the radio trying to get him help. This absolutely crushes me. I feel responsible. I called for a medic the second they reported it, I did, but it wasn't fast enough. A man died on my watch, died while waiting for treatment.

A lot of other prisoners are sick, too. Sometimes they die; that man is not the first or the last. When we are finally sent home from Abu Ghraib, more than a dozen members of my unit test positive for TB, including Sergeant Toro. It's clearly from working in close proximity with the prisoners, even though the Army states in its reports that there was no TB at the prison. I begin to get the feeling that the Army is covering up a lot of what's going on inside Abu Ghraib.

"Filth" and "squalor" are just words. It's easy to read that "Abu Ghraib was a filthy pit" and just shunt that fact into a back corner of your mind. It's something else to look out over the wire and see pools of offal and piles of garbage in the midst of a "professional" U.S. military prison. When you smell the reek of prisoners' cramped canvas tents, or see them bundled in layers of filthy clothing, the words take on a visceral truth. Abu Ghraib is nothing like any prison I've ever seen or even read about. From what I can see of the Ganci compounds, the majority of the prison area is a patch of thick mud punctuated by tents and trenches of sewage. It is so filthy that, if you saw it, there's no way you would believe it was the product of U.S. ingenuity. It reminds me of the worst slums in West Africa, or the pits of human misery in the underbelly of Bangkok. There is nothing military or professional about it.

Pictures of the Abu Ghraib cellblocks don't tell the whole stoy. When I serve in Abu, there are less than two hundred prisoners living indoors in the infamous Hard Site. The rest of the four thousand live in the outdoor tent city, exposed to the elements. Major

Dinenna is always gathering his subordinates to discuss the food situation: there seems to be a problem with the food at Abu Ghraib, which is supplied not by the Army but by local contractors. When the food arrives, it is often rotting already, or rife with rats and other vermin. The prisoners are up in arms about it, as many of them get chronically ill with diarrhea and food poisoning. Major Dinenna is always in a bad mood about this, threatening to flay the contractors limb from limb if the meal service doesn't improve. The whole prison camp is a wretched hellhole: disease, unsanitary conditions, inedible food, and cruel weather. I shudder when I pass the prisoners and see the conditions that are forced upon them. Every time I see them standing out there in the cold, I pull my field jacket a little tighter around me.

To be honest, before I spent much time at Abu Ghraib, before the November 24 riot, I had thought, Well, this place is pretty rough, but these are some of the most dangerous people in Iraq. These are the people who are fighting and killing us every day. As I pass the days and weeks at battalion headquarters, however, the very nerve center of the prison, I come to learn differently. One day I'm flipping through a stack of papers on my desk, one of the many documents lying around. It's a manifest of a group of prisoners, a few hundred new arrivals to the prison camp. I flip idly through it just to see what these people are in here for. What I find astounds me: page after page of rap sheets with crimes such as "petty theft," "public drunkenness," "forged Coalition documents," and the ubiquitous "suspicious activity." The realization hits me with the force of a physical blow: these men are not insurgents at all. They're petty civilian criminals. They aren't even the "enemy" we claim to be fighting.

Worse, a substantial percentage of the detainees appear not to have committed any crime at all. The authorities of Abu Ghraib have a policy of "sweeps," meaning that every time we take fire from the outside or there is some kind of insurgent activity, the base sends out teams to sweep up every Iraqi male in the area and bring them inside Abu Ghraib for questioning. The International Committee of the Red Cross report summarized this policy well:

> Certain CF military intelligence officers told the ICRC that in their estimate between 70% and 90% of the persons deprived of their liberty in Iraq had been arrested by mistake.[12]

Between 70 and 90 percent *arrested by mistake.* The ICRC went on to describe the operating procedure of a sweep:

> Sometimes they arrested all adult males present in a house, including elderly, handicapped or sick people. Treatment often included pushing people around, insulting, taking aim with rifles, punching and kicking and striking with rifles...they rarely informed the arrestee or his family where he was being taken and for how long, resulting in the de facto "disappearance" of the arrestee for weeks or even months until contact was made.[13]

I see the results of this policy every day on my whiteboard as I compute the number of prisoners in each compound. The prison is becoming vastly overcrowded and we hardly ever release anyone; when we do release detainees, every few weeks maybe, it's a few dozen out of more than four thousand. The MPs complain more and more often that they are understaffed, guarding more prisoners than they can handle.

Once I learn who the prisoners are and what they're in for, I turn my back absolutely on Abu Ghraib and everything we're doing here. I feel a physical revulsion for the prison, and for the duties I'm forced to perform in relation to it: I am an agent of injustice. We're holding innocent men and petty criminals inside a hellish prison camp for months at a time, completely hidden from the outside world, months in which they are dying of disease, being killed by mortar bombardment, and even shot by guards. This prison is responsible for the death of many innocent men, and I work here. The living conditions at Abu Ghraib are appalling, both for the prisoners and the soldiers, but beyond the misery of life inside is a deeper and more disturbing failure: a failure of policy. Every aspect of the prison camp is in shambles, from the chaotic shuffling of prisoners to the rotting food to the murderous tensions between the detainees and guards. General Taguba himself deserves the last word:

> In addition to being severely undermanned, the quality of life for Soldiers assigned to Abu Ghraib (BCCF) was extremely poor. There was no DFAC, PX, barbershop, or MWR facilities. There were numerous mortar attacks, random rifle and RPG attacks, and a serious threat to Soldiers and detainees in the facility. The prison complex was severely over-crowded and the Brigade lacked adequate resources and personnel to resolve serious logistical problems.[14]

It doesn't take a lot of research and documentation (although there is plenty of that to be found) to know that what we are doing at Abu Ghraib is morally wrong.

I watch and listen, absorbing all the details I can. I have to tell people what really went on here, I think to myself; no one would ever believe that the mighty U.S. Army would be running a place like this. I lose all emotional investment in the mission and come to see Abu Ghraib for what it is: a leviathan of oppression, negligence, and monstrous cruelty. I take some small measure of peace knowing that I have already publicly declared my opposition to all this, but that doesn't change the fact that I show up for work here every day, fetch the officers' coffee, and clean Major Dinenna's desk. I am culpable, too. Every night, I go back to my cell and stare at the flickering television until Sergeant Toro comes to remind me to hit the gym.

Here at Abu Ghraib, I become a prisoner as well, in spirit if not in fact. The cell door clangs shut after me just as soundly as if I were an inmate within these blue and white walls. More than ever before, daily life is a punishment: waking up to fix vehicles, going over to headquarters to shuffle numbers on a whiteboard and make notations every half hour in a little book that no one will ever read. I thought that the endless repetition of working on vehicles had brought my morale as low as it could go, but I was wrong. Mundane as it was, fixing vehicles still gave me a momentary glimpse of satisfaction, a stir of pride and excitement when I revved the engine and it roared to life. Now even that feeling is tainted, marred by the knowledge that every vehicle I work on is used to perpetuate a system that I despise.

I had once told Sergeant Toro that I enjoyed working on the trucks of soldiers I liked and respected, knowing that it was making their lives easier. With the knowledge that I've gained working in the headquarters, I begin to fit the 320th Company and our narrow purpose into a larger scheme. We are one of many companies, not really responsible for anything on our own, but taken together we form a mechanism that keeps the entire prison running: from the guards who stand along the wire to the cooks who feed them to the mechanics who service their equipment. I begin to see my tiny fragment of war service as part of an enormous glittering structure, comprising thousands of individual soldiers, each secure in the knowledge that what they are *personally* doing isn't wrong. I look at the truth of the prisoners' experience and then I look at my stated life, and it feels false, right to the core. The truth that I believe is that prisoners are being terribly abused inside Abu Ghraib, degraded, falsely imprisoned, even killed, as happened in the November riot. But it's not *my* fault, I'm just a mechanic fixing the vehicles of the guys who run the prison. It's not really *their* fault either, they're just standing around guarding the prisoners as they were ordered to do by those higher up the chain of command. Well, who the hell *is* responsible for all this, then? All of us ... the generals ... I don't know, me personally? That's what it feels like. Lying on the ground underneath a Humvee with mud caked in its tires, I finally look up and perceive my place in the web: I can call myself a conscientious objector and denounce war all I like, but I'm still here, still playing my part like a good soldier. The dark cloud that had lifted from me in Tallil returns and settles over me, bringing with it a terrible longing for home.

My unbending routine saves me, or at least gives me a frame to cling to on a daily basis. Around seven each morning I get up and grab a carton of skim milk to mix my protein shake. Then I purloin a cup of hot water from the company TOC to make a cup of green tea, which Sergeant Wallace usually shares. Tugging on my coveralls over three layers of clothing, I make my gradual way down to the motor pool when I'm not working at the brigade. I try to do as little as possible all morning, until it's time for my second protein shake, and then a long lunch to avoid even more work. I go back to the yard and fix a few more things until early evening, when we finally wear down Sergeant Wallace's resistance and he excuses us for the night. Every evening without fail, Sergeant Toro and I go down the hall to the makeshift gym that the units have constructed. We lift weights like there's no tomorrow: our main recreation apart from watching DVDs of *The Sopranos* and *Deep Space Nine*. Every night I burn up the day's frustration and emptiness under an iron bar, until everything else fades out of focus. After the gym, I make my way to the back of the barracks building, where the ever-ingenious MPs have rigged a shower system to an outside water tank. I stand on a wooden crate and gasp for breath under a torrent of icy water. Frozen and breathing steam, I make my way upstairs to hang out with Shoe and Sergeant Toro.

My mood follows a daily routine, too. I begin every morning quiet and calm, still cruising on the high of my morning meditation. By midmorning I'm bored. Then by lunchtime, I sink into a pit of despair. I can't tell you why, but every afternoon I can feel the hope go out of me like the air out of a balloon. My life seems utterly meaningless. As the sun rises highest in the sky, I feel so depressed that I'm nauseous. For about a month I dry heave on my way to lunch, ducking behind the maintenance connex so the other guys won't think I'm sick. Pain and emptiness manifest themselves in the pit of my stomach. That's how life in Abu Ghraib as a conscientious objector feels: you want to throw up, but you can't. I barely eat lunch, not that a double scoop of canned corn is so appetizing anyway. Only during our nightly DVD sessions am I truly happy. In the company of my friends I feel free, removed from the dull reality of Abu. It lasts until I sleep.

March is our one-year mark; I just have to keep my mind focused on March. March…March…then everything will be all right again. This too shall pass.

DECEMBER 31, 2003 Another cold, windy, jet-black night inside a base with nothing to do. Light filters over the wall from the prison camp, where the generators are running all night as usual. I'm sitting outside in our little courtyard around an empty half-barrel with some broken-up crates and ammo boxes providing a pitiful little glow. Everyone always congregates outside, despite the bitter winds. Sometimes at night you get the feeling that you just can't be inside anymore, you can't spend another minute in a *prison cell* staring at those endless blue and white walls, that you have to be out in the open, in unlimited space under the night sky. The prison walls seem to be closing in around you, looming over you, crushing you in narrow stone halls and endless lines of painted blue bars. You start to feel like *you* are the prisoner instead of *them*. You want to breathe again. So almost every night there's a fire outside, even on the coldest nights when no fire could possibly keep you warm. No matter how many times you sit around the same fire you find you still *have* to go, to see the dancing orange flames and hear the crackle of the wood splitting and popping. There's something cheery and homelike about a fire, a fire makes a hearth, and here we have need of warmth, some semblance of home.

A few guys are sitting with me: Shoe, Kosinski maybe, I don't remember who else. As usual, everyone has pushed their chairs up as close to the fire as possible, so we're all hunched over, elbow to elbow, trying to suck up the warmth. Gloveless, filthy hands are stretched out and rotated over the fire to take out the chill. God, we look like hoboes gathered around a fire-barrel. "Hey guys, tonight is New Year's Eve!" someone says. We all blink in surprise for a moment; up to this point, the holiday hadn't crossed our minds. One day was pretty much like the next inside Abu, and special days never really seemed to be all that special; they certainly didn't mean a change in the routine. Christmas had been a nonevent, except for having the day off and the grotesque mechanical snowman that stood perpetually waving outside the medical clinic down the hall. The cold, the damp hallways, the blue and white walls, nothing had changed. But here it was tonight, New Year's at Abu Ghraib. How depressing.

I've never been one for holidays, nor have we ever had much of a holiday tradition in my family. For the last few years in Cairo, my parents hung a lightbulb on a houseplant for Christmas, and we dropped the gift exchange entirely. No holiday spirit, as you might say. That never bothered me though. Christmas never really meant anything to me. I didn't buy into the religious origins and I just couldn't get into it like the rest of the world seemed to, hated red and green. While everyone else was recounting huge feasts, and cookies, and warm family memories, I would sit back pensively and think about that lightbulb, buzzing dimly in the corner. So, no Christmas. But New Year's . . . well, New Year's is about as close as I come to giving a damn about any holiday. Not for any particular reason, no great memories, no family reunions, no drunken debauchery. I guess I just loved the *idea* of the holiday: beginning again, starting over, wiping the slate clean. As silly as it was to pick a particular day to start over on, every year I would find myself getting happier and happier from the day after Christmas till the end of the year.

There is something about those magical six hours or so, from evening till midnight on New Year's Eve, that seems so fresh and alive with possibility. You could do anything, go anywhere, dance and make merry and die, to be reborn as a new person when the clock strikes twelve. At least you could in my mind. That's what it had always felt like to me: saying goodbye to the old year and your old self, becoming someone different. New Year's was a time to let the old person in you die, and celebrate this by making resolutions for the next year, making palpable statements of how you will change. Of course, no one really believes in such transformation, not really. No one believes that you can become someone different just by believing and trying hard enough; they always say you can't teach an old dog new tricks, and people are quick to knock you back into old habits, into the person they know. But one night of every year, one night, people scribble their dreams on little yellow Post-it notes and make promises to their loved ones. Quit smoking. Lose ten pounds. Be a more loving husband. Take that trip to the Bahamas. Learn to swing dance. On that night, it's all real, and I love that. One night to take charge of your life. Take charge of your life ... it seems like a bitter joke in my surroundings. Being here at Abu Ghraib, under the blankness of the desert sky, I think about a very different New Year's I spent in the desert ... the Big One, the Millennium.

Cairo, Egypt

December 31, 1999 It was the end of the world, everyone had said, but I feel great. My three closest friends and I make the last-minute decision to take a taxi out to the Great Pyramids around 10:30, and try to see if we can get tickets to the laser light show supposedly happening there. The streets of our neighborhood near school are deserted. I lean into a black-and-white cab window: "Giza, al-ahram, min fadlak. Eiyshreen guineyah bes"— "Giza [District], the pyramids, if you please. Twenty [Egyptian] pounds only." Our cab races along the banks of the Nile, shimmery under a bright moon, blaring Arabic dance music and ignoring the rules of the road. We stop every few minutes, at all the clubs and hotels on the route, asking around for tickets to the pyramids show. Too late, "sold out," they all say. The Cairo traffic is horrible as usual, our cab comes to a halt just outside Giza, and we just barely don't make it by midnight. We ring in the New Year in the back of a broken-down Egyptian cab, just out of sight of the pyramids. My friends are disappointed that we didn't make it to the pyramids by midnight, but I'm not, for some reason I'm happy to be right here, stuck in traffic. My digital watch beeps twice, and we lean out the window and howl like madmen, our taxi driver too, all lost in the moment: the millennium, the end of the world. Honk! Honk! A cacophony of car horns explodes into the night, the banks of the valley resonate with the sound.

We spend the next few hours on foot, running around like drunks, trying to sneak into the show and avoid the battalions of Egyptian police trying to keep us out. It is cold and none of us has proper jackets, and there is no way we are getting into the show, but I will remember this night as one of the happiest of my life. We don't *do* anything, except get shooed away from a concert by Egyptian soldiers, but it feels like we *could* do anything. I point up to the shadow of the Great Pyramid and scream to my friends, "How many people can say that they were here tonight? How many? How many people can say they rang in the new millennium at the base of the Great Pyramid? I wouldn't want to be anywhere else on earth right now!" The night is ours, we can run as far as we want in any direction and stay out till dawn if we choose to: parents, school, impending college, the concerns of the real world, all fade into obscurity in those hours. For one night before we have to pack up and go our separate ways, for these three hours, we are completely on our own.

This year is so different, only four years removed but an eternity away from 1999. There is none of the joy of that New Year's Eve, no magic, no mystery. Just me outside in the cold again, in the desert again, thinking of happier times. I am overwhelmed with nostalgia. The sadness rolls over me suddenly; the feelings of loss, of inertia, as strong as I've ever felt them. I miss home, my home. I feel my distance from it, my immense separation, as if it were a hand shoving me away. I look up into the air and it's dark, I feel like a pinpoint. I remember how I used to look up at the moon in basic training and try to imagine my friends looking up at it too, how I used to trace an invisible angle through the moon, between where I'm standing and where they are. It used to help me not feel so lonely, like no matter where we were we could look up and see the same sky. Now the sky makes me feel isolated, alone, and unseen. Abu Ghraib really is the far side of the world. I'm as separate as I'll ever be, even with dozens of soldiers within a hundred feet of me. I didn't care about spending my birthday in Iraq, but this is the holiday I had hoped to be home for.

I'm done for the night. My head is swimming with pain and fatigue; the present has nothing to offer me, it's dead. Years from now I'll look back on this and say it was the worst New Year's of my life, I think to myself. Remember it: the worst New Year's of your life. I say my goodnights and stand up awkwardly, pulling my field jacket close around my body. I want this night to be over, the memories are too sharp, too contrasting. I can't bear to ring in the New Year here, of all places. You can't change here, you can't become someone new here. Abu Ghraib is stasis. Abu Ghraib is sameness. Abu Ghraib is the opposite of change. Once tonight is over, it will be easier. Tomorrow will be another workday with another list of petty things to do; my mind will return to autopilot. The grind will be easier than this. I just need to sleep, and close the curtain on this entire year.

On my way back from using the latrine, I pause in the middle of the roadway to fumble with the hood of my jacket. My digital watch beeps twice, and I look down. 12:00. That's it: it's 2004. I look at my watch as the numbers tick past, trying to feel something. I don't; the moment is wholly unremarkable. Then I hear a sound: a long, piercing whistle, and then the building, the road, the courtyard is illuminated in unbearable, sudden light. Night becomes day. Someone shouts from the yard and I look up, shielding my eyes from the painful brightness. Directly above us, a trio of flares explodes and then drifts gently downward, trailing fire. It's only my second time seeing flares in use, the first since that long-ago skirmish at Tallil, and I've never seen them so close. These are falling right over our heads, landing in the courtyard. It's true what they say, the flares light us up as bright as day, a noonday sun at midnight. Right after the first salvo comes another, then a third: multicolored lights now, red and green in quick succession. People in the courtyard start to cheer and I realize: it's our artillery. The artillery sections inside the base have sent up these flares to celebrate the New Year, our own version of fireworks. Somebody is going to get chewed for this, I think, some brilliant, wonderful human being is going to get in deep trouble for firing these flares and I want to tell him: it was worth it.

I stand in the courtyard for several minutes as the flares rain down on us, belching torrents of sparks as they drift on their little parachutes. The drab buildings come alive with light, the night is obliterated. For about ten minutes, the first ten minutes of 2004, Abu Ghraib is at full daylight, bathed in a sea of colors. It wasn't a moment ago, but it's New Year's now. I smell it in the gunpowder fumes, I see it in the lights, it's New Year's, it really is. I don't hear *Auld Lang Syne*, but I feel it: gratitude, humility, bidding farewell to the year that is dying. I feel thankful for the year, thankful for my friends and for Amy and for everything that's happened to me. My heart is full. I don't feel alone anymore. The sky is too bright to look up and I shield my face from the glare. Covering my face with my gloved hand, I close my eyes on Abu Ghraib, on 2003, close my eyes on Iraq...and someone else opens them. My eyes open to a world filled with light and color, a world raining fire, and the sound of men shouting in triumph. Mud and concrete and stone walls are alight. If you were to turn your eye there, looking down from a high enough vantage point, you would see the tiny figures of soldiers running and dancing and spinning with their arms out in the false dawn. You would see bursts of green and red exploding overhead in defiance of all military regulations, showering sparks on the field below. You would see one soldier a little apart from the rest, standing halfway between the latrine and the line of buildings, staring up at the sky with his mouth moving but no sound coming out. His face is blazing with orange and red, his eyes glistening. Thank you ...thank you...thank you, he whispers to the sky.

JANUARY 2004 They finally get a phone center and Internet service set up on the other side of the base. Instantly a trip to the center becomes a part of our evening ritual: just after dinner and before lifting weights. I call Amy every few nights, but often when I'm talking on the phone my mind wanders or I find myself griping about all the daily annoyances of Abu Ghraib until I know she's tired of listening to me. It feels good just to know there's someone on the other side, even though it's only an ethereal voice on the telephone. It helps to remember that I have another life. My sense of time melts even further.

One day Shoe wanders into the motor pool laughing. He says he's been talking to the MPs who work in the prison: there's some big scandal brewing, somebody's about to get into some deep shit. I set down my wrench and turn to hear the details. We mechanics love any development that embarrasses the military police. Shoe says the guards over at the Hard Site have been filming and photographing the prisoners naked and forcing them to do things to each other.[15] According to the rumors, one of the MPs in that unit saw the pictures, got angry, and sent copies to CNN.

If this is true, then the military police are about to open one hell of a can of worms. The American media would die if they ever saw half the things that are going on here. Shoe and I laugh, both because it's so absurd and because it sounds just like the MPs: taking dirty pictures of the prisoners. I ask whether it was any of our guys and Shoe says no, they just heard about it from the unit that did it. It's daily life at Abu Ghraib: the guards messing with the prisoners, doing God knows what to make their lives a little more miserable. Neither of us have any idea of what those pictures actually contain, or what is really going on over in the Hard Site.

I laugh it off and shake my head. "There's no way the Army's going to let that stuff get out. They'll censor it or something. I doubt CNN would even run it, it's too racy for television and it makes the Army look bad. I don't think those pictures will ever be seen again." Besides, you can't believe everything you hear, I think.

"Yeah," Shoe says, "but if they ever did get out, those MPs would be in a world of shit."

We go back to work. Later we tell Sergeant Toro the rumor. In short order, it's all over the company. Everyone's heard the talk. But with all the shit going on here, I think, who's going to care about some pictures? Nothing will come of it.

The next week, something odd happens. An officer from another unit, a captain, I believe, stops by the motor pool to talk to us. This is unprecedented. He stops us in the middle of work and asks us to come and speak with him for a moment. He asks if we've heard any rumors about what's going on in the prison. We tell him we have. He nods, and says he and other officers have been going around to inform the troops not to talk about this anymore. He says that the rumor is all over the prison and has even leaked back to the States via e-mail and phone. He tells us that we have to do our part to stop the spread of this rumor, that the military is handling the situation and they don't want this to blow up into something bigger than it is. Stop talking about it, he tells us, and tell any of your buddies to stop talking about it.

He leaves. Shoe, Sergeant Toro, and I turn to each other and smile knowingly. Apparently, everything we've heard must be true, or the Army wouldn't be going to this kind of trouble trying to stifle it. Last week it was just unfounded rumor, typical soldier talk, but today it's something else. Something really is going on over there in the prison.

A few days later we receive word that our unit is having a formation in the main hall. This, too, is extremely odd. We all assemble in the hall that doubles as our unit gym. The first sergeant calls us to attention and then turns the formation over to the commander. The captain dispenses with military formality and begins to rant at us immediately.

"I just came back from Brigade Headquarters with all the other company commanders, where General Karpinski chewed our asses about all these goddamn rumors going around! You all need to stamp this talk out! Immediately. Apparently there's word going around that some MPs were doing some things they weren't supposed to be doing and somebody took pictures of it all. You don't need to be writing about this to your families, you don't need to be telling them on the phone, and you don't need to be talking about it to each other. You better stop spreading these goddamn rumors!"

The commander pauses for a moment and then switches tactics, becoming suddenly congenial and chummy. "Look, we're all a family here. We don't air our dirty laundry in public. If we have a problem within the military, then we'll handle it internally. We don't need to let the media and the civilians into our business. If you have photos that you're not supposed to have, get rid of them. Don't talk about this to anyone, don't write about it to anyone back home.

We're a family and we're going to handle this like a family. I don't want to hear any more of this kind of talk in my unit. You all just focus on going home in March, hoo-ah?"

Hoo-ah, we respond. The commander rambles on for a bit and then dismisses us. As I leave, I wonder what could have possibly gotten the entire base command so worked up. There's no doubt now that everything we've heard about is true, and it must be even worse than we thought, for the commander himself to get on our backs about it. All a family? I laugh. We're only a family when the captain wants us to do his bidding or conceal some wrongdoing. The Army has tried that rhetoric before, talking about family and Army pride and everything else to try to get you to buy into what they do. When the Army talks about "handling something internally," it's only because they've done something so obviously wrong, they can't allow the rest of the country to see it. This doesn't surprise me. After all, if Americans back home saw Iraqi prisoners shot dead for throwing stones, saw the wretched conditions inside Abu, or saw the way the MPs dealt with the prisoners, what would they think of our glorious and righteous invasion? The truth about Abu Ghraib has to be concealed, has to be "kept in the family," because if the average citizen saw what we're doing to the people here, they would know in their guts that it's un-American.

Personally, I'm glad the photos might get out. Something has to blow the lid off this place, and people will never believe it if you just tell them. They have to see it for themselves. Maybe these photos will open a crack in the facade, and then someone will shine a light onto the whole prison system. When this thing blows up, it's going to be a nightmare for the Army and the government, and one thing's for sure: whoever exposed those photos must have some brass balls.[16] I can only imagine what his unit must be doing to him, even worse than being a conscientious objector. He was right, though. Whatever it costs him personally, whatever it costs the Army, he was right, and I admire him for taking a stand against all the evil and horror that is becoming routine in this prison. This kind of thing, this misery that exists in Abu Ghraib, is what rots and weakens an institution like the Army. If people are allowed to get away with it, all the petty cruelty and injustice, then they come to accept it, to justify it, to make it a part of the institution itself.

The one thing I know about the Army from my brief three years in it is that the military is a vast, lumbering, bureaucratic machine that is virtually a government unto itself. Most soldiers gripe about this on a routine basis: they see so much corruption, waste, and stupidity in the military, but it's impossible to change anything because the system's not set up for it. Complaints vanish into the bureaucratic ether, never to be seen again. Anyone who rocks the boat or speaks out is quickly punished and isolated; the chain of command seems designed to make sure that any problems never reach a level where someone can do something about them. The sad truth is that often the only way to make changes is go outside the Army system and take grievances to the media, to Congress, or to the American public. The body-armor shortages didn't get fixed until soldiers started writing home about it, writing to their congressmen, writing to the media, asking Donald Rumsfeld about it, putting him on the spot. It was the same with the armored vehicles and the long deployments and the stop-loss policy—the involuntary retention of soldiers beyond the terms of their enlistment contracts—and every other thing that soldiers should have been able to voice with the Army. The system is designed to keep things quiet, to avoid dealing with soldiers' concerns, to filter them through so many levels of officers and intermediaries that they get lost until they disappear. The Army won't change unless you force it to, unless you apply so much pressure from the outside and create such a public outcry that it has no choice but to clean up its act.

I see now that these pictures and videos, whatever they are, will be a turning point. Perhaps the people back home will finally see a small part of the truth. Something here has got to give, for no sin this large and this great can be concealed forever. The law of karma, of action and reaction, is inescapable. Whatever the Army has sown here through its own policies and its own culture, it will reap in equal measure.

Days after the captain's speech, Sergeant Wallace and our platoon sergeant give us word that everyone in the company will be searched: our rooms, bags, lockers, everything. The Army is determined to find any incriminating evidence and seize it. With a wink and a nod, they tell us that they'll be required to seize anything technically against the rules, so if we have any "personal material" we should stash it in a safe place during the search. It would certainly be embarrassing for the unit if they did a search and came up with a pile of *Hustlers*, bootleg porn movies, and copies of graphic photos from the November riots and elsewhere in Iraq. They know damn well that 95 percent of the company has one of the above in his bag or locker. To ensure that the procedure is fair, everyone will be searched by an NCO from another platoon. Sergeant Wallace tells us to be ready for it when they call us.

Schumacher, Patterson, and I are called together and are marched upstairs by a trio of MP sergeants from one of the other platoons. They joke with us as they tell us to empty our bags, half-apologizing for having to rifle through all our stuff. They laugh about having to take some poor sap's girlie magazines because he didn't have the sense to hide them. After a few minutes of pawing through our old clothes and surplus uniforms, they are satisfied and tell us to put everything back. The searches continue down the hall. The three of us turn to each other and laugh at this latest development: the Army is foolish to think they're going to find anything, especially when they told us days in advance that we would be searched. If they want to find all the evidence, this is not the way to go about it.

Still, it seems to indicate a kind of desperation on the part of the military brass. Things must be getting bad if they've ordered a search of every soldier's personal effects, that or they *really* don't want this stuff to get out. My curiosity about the photos continues to rise. Just what could be so bad that the Army would take these measures? Of course, although I don't realize it at the time, not until months later, I am witnessing the first shockwaves of the infamous Abu Ghraib prison abuse scandal. The photos and videos in question were the notorious images that have now been plastered on every news channel and Internet site across America; the iconic images of the hooded prisoner dangling electrical wires and the contorted bodies of detainees bound in various poses of shame and degradation.

Months later, when I am back in the States and the scandal breaks, I am amazed to see the depravity and variety of the abuse but I am not surprised at all that it happened. In my experience, the event had been long foreshadowed in Iraq, since my days in Nasiriyah when soldiers would hurl abuse and bottles at Iraqi bystanders. At Abu Ghraib, I had seen photos or heard tell of a dozen incidents that fit the pattern of what we later saw. The shootings in November had confirmed that the guards had no special regard for the prisoners' lives. Afterward they had opened the body bags and made sport of the Iraqis' shattered bodies; obviously something beyond simple machismo was at work inside Abu Ghraib. Some dark and obscene atmosphere had built inside the prison camp, so much so that it had turned ordinary, decent men into ghoulish caricatures. Sergeant Toro's prisoner-transport story had reinforced my impressions of the harsh and repressive environment. It was common knowledge that guards would threaten and manhandle the prisoners—such conduct was almost a badge of manhood. Being tough with the detainees was just part of being a "good soldier" and a team player. The way the younger MPs referred to the prisoners and to the Iraqis in general made this no secret. I had heard about the sexual nature of the photographs: the forcible nudity, the simulated homosexual acts, the videotaped sex between guards and prisoners, but I was taken aback by the particular intensity and sadism of the photographs. Somewhere along the way, in the midst of all the hardship, the mortars and attacks, *we* had become op-pressors. We had become sadists. We had become torturers. Not all of us, certainly, not even a majority, but enough. Enough to call it more than a "few bad apples," enough to make it an Army-wide problem. Enough to call into question the whole culture of Abu Ghraib and of the Army occupation of Iraq.

By now, the reports, the pundits, the generals, and the bloggers have all analyzed this to death. There's nothing substantial I can say about it that hasn't already become public discourse: yes, the prison was undermanned, yes, the command climate was negligent, yes, the soldiers were left unsupervised, yes, there was widespread anti-Arab racism. All these things have been said and said again until they've lost all meaning. All I can add to that is to talk about the daily reality inside Abu Ghraib: a reality so bleak and joyless it could drive men to the edge of madness, and did. Picture a cold, wind-swept wasteland of rubble and ruined buildings. Picture living there with a thousand other people guarding four or five thousand pris-oners, some of whom want to kill you. Picture no light and no heat for a month. Picture no phones, no Internet, no contact with home for several months. Picture getting shelled every day by an invisible enemy and never being able to do anything about it. Imagine what that would do to your mind. Picture people around you getting killed or maimed by random explosions. Picture having to fix vehi-cles in three inches of freezing mud for a captain you despise. Picture having to work with and handle prisoners who are filthy, diseased, and angry. Picture not understanding a word they say. Pic-ture going home to a prison cell. Imagine sitting in those cells, stew-ing in your own frustration and impotence. Imagine getting paid about $1,200 a month to sleep on a cot, eat rations, and get shot at in a cold, lonely prison camp. That's a reality that could drive any-one to acts of violence. That's an environment that breaks people, and some people have lower breaking points than others.

That's part of it, that's the universal part, something we could all understand: how stress and fear could turn ordinary people into monsters. Yet I'm not satisfied with that as the whole truth. There's something deeper to it, something that hasn't been talked about yet openly. The fact is that there were thousands of soldiers rotated through Abu Ghraib and not all of them turned abusive, not all of them hurt and degraded the Iraqis, some of them even said no, some of them even did something about it. What separates us? What divides those who turn hateful and those who stay human? The answer is complex and nontrivial. It can't be summed up in a sound bite. Over these last few years I have meditated long and often on this topic, trying to see into the sometime-abyss of the human heart. I believe that through reliving these times, I have found pieces of my own truth. I believe that Abu Ghraib holds many teachings, many sutras, about the way that men live. I'm still trying to unravel them.

Why does one soldier become cruel and the other hold fast to his humanity? One element is their upbringing. A man who has never seen the world, never lived as a stranger among foreigners, who has never known a life and a culture other than his own is in some way limited. He cannot help but feel his own way of life to be superior, to be the *only* way. This was one of the poisons I saw seeping into my company from the beginning: parochialism, ignorance, knowing nothing about Islam, or the Middle East, or any other society outside American cities like Tampa and St. Petersburg. My own life was an unearned blessing, because of who my father was and the family I was born into I never had those blinders. My whole life I lived as a white boy among Thais, among Africans, among Arabs. I had lived in Cairo and come to call it home. Once you've lived among *the other*, once you've had your eyelids torn off by seeing the grand spectacle of all the nations and peoples, you can never go back to the narrow little world of Tampa Bay and believe it to be the center of the universe. My life abroad taught me that, and that was an advantage of my father's profession and my birth, something that most Americans don't have. It's no special quality in me. Anyone who lived a life among foreigners would never be able to hate them with that special intensity of someone who's never left America.

Certainly there is also the individual sadism of particular soldiers. That is beyond question. Yet in any sizable population there are those who are prone to violence—that is a statistical reality. The real concern for me is what causes that number to increase? What brings forth that dark side of people? What are the policies and broad causes that led to Abu Ghraib? Another part of the problem is moral and religious, and by that I mean to say that at its root Abu Ghraib is a spiritual problem. Many people believe in good and evil. Just that, that simple: good on one side, evil on the other. By default, we are always on the good side. This means that any who oppose us must logically be evil. Buddhism tends to take a circumspect view of good and evil, avoiding that distinction entirely and instead speaking of "positive" and "negative" actions as measured by their effect in the world. It is never as final and absolute as good and evil. Yet duality invades every level of society, from religious sermons to the political rhetoric that drove us into this war. The absoluteness of good and evil is an incredibly dangerous doctrine, dangerous in the wrong hands and without proper restraint. I believe that experience demonstrates that never in life is anything wholly good or wholly evil. Good and evil are metaphors, signposts to guide us in the right direction. To render good and evil as actual physical truth is to render an infinitely complex moral world into absurd black and white. Further still, to hold that truth out to the mass of humanity and invite them to act upon it is to invite disaster and fanaticism.

Abu Ghraib is rooted in the belief of good and evil, as are many wars and atrocities. Only when we believe in the absolute evil and moral corruption of another can we justify torture and atrocity, and by extension we must therefore believe unshakably in our own righteousness and justness. I believe that much of the violence and horror in Iraq springs directly from this polarization of real life: President Bush says that we are the good guys, the injured, the victims, and that we are engaged against an "evil ideology," against evil itself. When one is fighting evil itself, one tends to lose sight of the individual humans involved. An Iraqi man is no longer a man, a father, or a human being—he becomes for the aggressor a living embodiment of evil, and therefore all is allowed. Many soldiers engaged in this bloody contest, on both sides, honestly believe themselves to be fighting on the side of righteousness against an enemy that is absolutely evil and absolutely corrupt. I truly believe that those who have committed terrible acts felt themselves not to be tormenting human beings, but to be tormenting "terrorists," abstract embodiments of everything wrong with the world. With that kind of moral piety, encouraged by the shallow theology of politicians, events like Abu Ghraib become possible. Moral surety is a dangerous thing. We do not question and we do not empathize. We do not dare imagine what the man on the other side might be thinking, or why he might be arrayed against us. We lose any sense of ourselves as flawed, limited human beings; we become avenging angels, righteous destroyers, and therein is the path to perdition.

I can talk about theology, I can talk about grand trends, but that's not really what I want to say about Abu Ghraib. I want to talk about the personal. I want to talk about the demons in my own heart, in the hearts of all human beings. If you've ever looked out your eyes at another person and truly wished evil upon them, then you are capable of Abu Ghraib. I am capable of it, I know this. In Iraq, there were many people who would have harmed me if they could. Don't believe for an instant that I am so moral and pure that I never harbored thoughts of harming them back. On the larger scale, America as a nation has many who would harm it. We feel threatened and not without reason. September 11 *hurt* us, it wounded our people and our nation in a way that affected our national conscience forever. We felt *personally* hurt, frightened, angry. As a nation, we wanted to lash out, to hurt those who hurt us, just as each of us individually has felt the need to retaliate against those who've hurt us. This natural desire to retaliate has been harnessed and exploited by those in power to lead us into a conflict that we believe is somehow about our safety. The instinct for vengeance, I believe, is as natural to our being as walking and breathing: part survival mechanism and part ego delusion. On the one hand, our biology makes us want to strike out at those who've hurt us because we want to be safe, not to be hurt again. On the other hand, we wrongly perceive ourselves as distinct and separate: a solitary ego floating above the world and apart from others. This is what Buddhists hold as *the* fundamental error: wrongly perceiving that our minds, our egos, are somehow real and permanent and separate from everything else. From this basic delusion arises the related delusions of greed, hatred, and ignorance; because we believe that we have a permanent, separate "self," we feel we have to accumulate material wealth to protect it, that we have to harm and denigrate others to preserve it, that we alone are real.

Without conquering this basic misperception of ourselves, real love, generosity, and wisdom will never be possible. No one lives for themselves or by themselves, we are all interconnected in a web of mutuality. I believe that to be a demonstrable truth: that you could go through your own life and see that nothing you are exists except in relation to other people, other experiences; that your very self and identity are the product of the interactions with the things around you. The idea that you arise independently, that there is any part of you that does not relate outward into the world, is an illusion. Once we perceive our interconnectedness, or begin to look for it, the idea of revenge becomes nonsensical. Harming others harms yourself, both in concrete terms and in spiritual terms. When you understand that you are no different from the other, the enemy, that you have the same wants, needs, hopes, and desires, then compassion becomes possible even in war. The Dalai Lama, head of one sect of Tibetan Buddhism, once said: *All human beings want the same things: to be loved and to be happy.* It sounds horribly trite, but this truth applies to Iraqis as well as Americans, to prisoners as well as guards, to violent antagonists as well as Buddhist monks. We all want the same things. If you can actually realize that and hold it in your heart, then you can prevent yourself from becoming someone of whom you would be ashamed. "All human beings want to be loved and to be happy"—it sounds like a lame bumper sticker or T-shirt message, but if you stick with it and focus on it without letting up, it becomes a profound truth. When I say that Abu Ghraib is a spiritual problem, I mean to say that the large problems, the dramatic moral failures, are really the multiplication of many individual lapses: that grand expressions of hatred, like wars, are the result of the many petty forms of violence in our own minds. The Tibetan monk Geshe Kelsang Gyatso said of war: *Without inner peace in the minds of living beings, outer or world peace will never be possible.* Wars and atrocities do not arise outside of human beings, they are not forces of nature as some would have us believe. They are the aggregations of all our inner demons.

When you look out at the prisoner, at the enemy, at the other, and you see your own face staring back at you, then you can never do the things that we call atrocities. That is why I never would have been a good fighter or a good killer. When I stood across the wire from prisoners in Tallil and prisoners in Abu Ghraib, I didn't hate them. I saw the men of my own company reflected back at me: young, poor, without options in life, forced to fight me as I was to fight them. Some of them were full of hatred for us, just as some of us were for them. They weren't abstract, they weren't black-cloaked terrorists, they were men who were struggling to make it through life with the options they'd been given from birth. I saw in them the same sort of faces that I saw everyday in Cairo, the same people who I knew as bakers and shopkeepers and teachers. I saw them as soldiers who didn't want to be at that prison any more than I did. That mirroring, that sense of recognition, preserved a part of my soul.

By mid-January I feel a burning envy of everyone I see going home on leave while I am stuck in Abu. Talking on the phone with Amy just isn't the same. I remember Tallil, and how the commander took my leave away just like that. For months I have been pestering

Sergeant Wallace, "Please ask the command about my leave. Please ask them if I can go on leave." I doubt Sergeant Wallace has ever really brought it up with much vigor. Every NCO in my support chain blames the decision on the person above them. I decide I have nothing left to lose. To hell with my support chain: I will use the commander's "open door" policy. They tell me I can't just walk up to the captain and start talking to him, I have to arrange a meeting. But one day I notice him duck behind the curtain that shields his cell from view and I follow. I catch him by surprise as he is unbuckling his flak vest. I ask if I can have a moment of his time. He smiles and says sure, falsely congenial as always.

"Sir," I begin, "I think you know that taking away my home leave is wrong. I'm a good soldier and I've been loyal to the unit; you have no right to take away my leave just because of my CO packet. I've been trying to handle this issue the right way, talking to my NCO support chain, but they haven't gotten any results. So now I'm talking to you directly. I want to go on home leave. I promise you that I will return when my two weeks are up. I'm not a flight risk and I'm not a traitor. You have insulted me and my character by implying that just because I'm a Buddhist I have no honor and would be willing to desert the unit."

"It's not because you're a—"

"Sir, the fact stands that my conscientious objection is based on Buddhism. Nowhere in the regulations does it say that you can take a negative personnel action like revoking leave just because I applied for CO status. I believe that this is a matter of religious discrimination. If you don't give me back my leave, I'm going to make it a huge problem for you. I will call the American Civil Liberties Union and the World Congress of Buddhists to let them know that you are punishing me because of my religious beliefs." This is a bluff and a bald-faced lie: the World Congress of Buddhists is a made-up organization, the first thing that pops in my head. "Sir," I continue, "there are some people who would just take this lying down. I'm not one of those people. I'm very comfortable writing letters and dealing with bureaucracy. I *like* writing letters. I will make myself heard. I will make this a huge headache for you." Wow, I think, this is either going to win me my leave or get me an Article 15 on the spot.

Success! The commander looks stricken and conciliatory.

"Look, Delgado, I know that you come from an influential family. I know how well-connected your father is..."

I laugh to myself and try to remember to tell that to Dad. Yes, my father is vastly powerful and influential... if you're a grape, a fig, or a dry-season legume. He's an agriculture diplomat, not chairman of the Joint Chiefs, but the commander doesn't have to know that. The captain seems to have softened his position, he's willing to work something out, he knows how much I want to go on leave and how much this means to every soldier.

"Look, talk to the sergeants in personnel and ask them to schedule you in the next round of leave."

"Thank you, sir! This means a lot to me. I'll come back, you don't have to worry, sir."

"You better, Delgado." Then he laughs and tries to engage me in a discussion about weightlifting or some other subject. I play along, so overjoyed with getting my leave that I can even fraternize with the commander. He thinks we're peers or something because we've both been to college. In another setting we might have been friendly with each other, but the deployment has put too much distance between us. Those two black bars are an unbridgeable gulf.

At the moment I couldn't care less, however—I've got it back. I've got my leave. In less than a month I'll see Amy again.

TAMPA INTERNATIONAL AIRPORT, FLORIDA

JANUARY 24, 2003 I step off the plane in my street clothes. A short tram ride takes me to the main terminal. As I walk across the concourse I see my friends in the distance and they spot me as well, grinning wildly. At the front of the small group, I see Amy. She stands before me in the flesh: brilliant, beautiful, shining, as if she had stepped out from a picture on my cell wall. We start toward one another, my other friends hanging back a respectful distance to let us have our reunion. I step forward into her arms and she into mine. I remember it so clearly: we're standing on a carpet patterned with circular shapes. A shaft of light falls directly onto us from a skylight overhead, illuminating us both in speckles of light. In the background, my friend Mateo smiles and I know he's thinking the same thing: the scene is absurdly picturesque, dramatic, so perfect it almost seems staged. Amy and I embrace in a column of light. We stand there together for what seems a long time before my other friends rush forward and encircle us both. I'm home. Not the ground, not the rooms, but this: these people make it home. They whisk me off into a car for the hour-long ride to Sarasota.

Our conversation buzzes: jokes, gossip, remembrances, words of thanks. Mateo and I laugh together as if we've never been apart. My arm is fastened around Amy the whole while, as if she might be plucked away at any moment. I don't remember a single word of what was said, but it was all good things. My friends are overjoyed to see me and I them. For the entire ride home, our car could as well have been sailing along on a cloud.

That night, Amy and I are alone together for the first time in nearly a year. At first, we're both so giddy that we hardly need to speak. I pull her close, feeling both the comfort of an old friend and the anxiety of first impressions. It's been so long since we've seen each other; I'm actually scared. I tell her how much I love her and how terribly I've missed her these past ten months. We're both on the verge of tears.

Now I'm sitting up across from Amy, neither of us saying a word. A silence lies between us. I feel such sadness and horror that I want to run from the room. Something is terribly wrong. I sit there, looking at her, and all I can feel is sorrow. Here is the very person I have longed for all this time, who I've dreamt about, and now that I'm with her I feel smothered. It's all too much. I'm not ready for this.

There is so much about the last year that I want to say but I can't make my mouth move. She'll never understand; she's never been there. She looks up at me with love and that breaks my heart even more, because I know that all she wants is to comfort me. I can't think of anything to say. We're only four feet apart across a linen bedspread, but there is suddenly a chasm between us.

At that moment, I know that things will never again be the same between us, and the grief of that realization is too much to bear. We lie side by side, holding each other and talking softly. We tell each other that it's just the anxiety and all the anticipation, that things will be the way they were before. But they won't, and I believe she feels it too. I hold her even tighter, trying to make myself forget. I miss her—even being there with her, I miss her. I feel guilty for being here and yet being distant. She's been so good to me: calling my parents to tell them I'm all right, sending me letters and packages, taking care of everything while I'm away from college. I'm disappointing her now. I feel utterly alone.

Being here with Amy I am filled with a terrible shame: I want to go home, to Iraq.

ABU GHRAIB PRISON

FEBRUARY 2004 The prison walls loom over me again. The transport convoy passes through that breach in the wall that serves as a gate. Stepping off the cargo truck, I jog back to the motor pool and our little corner of Abu Ghraib. Shoe and Sergeant Toro clap me on the back and welcome me home. "Sucks to be back, doesn't it?"

Yeah, I laugh with them, it sucks to be back. In truth, being back in the prison, back in the motor pool, back in my cell, feels safer and more real than Florida. The States had been a dream, a two-week holiday; this place is the reality. Bleak as it is, grim as it is, this is where I know what to do. There are people I care about here. In Sarasota I couldn't rest for even a moment because I knew I'd have to come back here. That knowledge poisons everything. There are only about two months left in my tour, and I have to finish what I began here. I don't want a holiday. I want all this to be over.

As I step back into my place in those blue and white walls, I realize that my return is more than just keeping my word to a man I couldn't care less about. I look around at the people in my unit and I realize that I'm probably the only Buddhist they're ever going to know, and someday I'm going to be the only conscientious objector they've ever known. That means something to me now. Four months ago I could have said to myself, "Who gives a damn what anyone in this unit thinks?" Today that's not true, because of what I've done, because of the way I've done it; I'm not just me anymore. I'm representing Buddhism. I'm representing conscientious objection. I'm representing everyone back home who knows this war is wrong. I have to uphold that. I have to represent Buddhism proudly and strongly and gracefully in everything that I do, so that when these other men look back years from now they'll say: "Yeah, I knew a Buddhist once."

My time in Iraq is almost up. Now I just have to be solid: like a stone buddha on an iron mountain.

Late one night, a tremendous explosion reverberates through the prison. If it was a mortar shell, it was a big one. Word comes down from the command that there has been some kind of attack on a patrol outside the prison; a team of mechanics are needed to go out and tow the vehicles back. Spangler and Sergeant Wallace are roused from their beds to go out with the wrecker recovery vehicle. They don't return until dawn.

In the morning there's an odd mood in the halls, quieter than usual. Rumors are flying about the ambush outside the prison. An announcement is made: one of the vehicles on patrol outside Abu Ghraib was struck by an IED, rockets and small arms fire. Two of the guys inside were hurt, one thrown from the vehicle and the other injured badly. The third never made it out. Our faces go blank, and the day's business is forgotten.

One day in Senegal, my brother and I were late for the bus after school. I made it, taking one of the last two seats. My brother just barely missed the bus, leaving that one seat empty. On the ride home, the bus got into an accident, a car struck it in the side. No other part of the vehicle was damaged but that last open seat, crushed into a jagged star of metal. I remember shuddering as I looked at that mangled seat, knowing how close my brother had come to being in it. I felt nauseous, and my hands were cold. *My hands were cold.* I think it's something we all feel when death passes close by us.

I feel it again now: cold nausea. These men lived down the hall from us. They were an MP unit just like ours, on a routine patrol just like we do. Some of our own men had gone on missions with them, riding along in the very same vehicle that had been struck. We all realize that these men could have been us, any one of us. Their fate is so terrible in its randomness: no warning, no hope of valor, just driving along and then...I didn't know the men, maybe I passed them in the hall a dozen times without realizing it. The truth is that death is never very far away at Abu Ghraib prison, we just forget about it. As a soldier, for this entire war, death has always been just a roulette spin away and yet it also seemed impossibly distant: no one I knew had ever been killed. This man's name was Ramirez. He was Hispanic, like me and half the members of my company. He lived just down the hall with the unit next door. I didn't know this man, and yet, only a few rooms away, his fate somehow seemed nearer.

On the day of the memorial service, the tiny stone chapel is packed to overflowing with every member of both units. At the front of the church is a rifle standing barrel-down, a helmet resting on it, a pair of desert boots at the base. We all stand to attention. An officer from the other unit, the 670th, steps forward and begins to speak, saying something about being a hero. My face tightens. He tells us something about the departed man: he just came back from leave. He has a wife and two young children, and one of his children is very sick. They offered him the option to stay home and not come back to Abu Ghraib, but he said no. He said that he had to come back because that's where his buddies are. Now, he leaves behind a widow with two young children. I feel my face burning; I'm trying to hold it back. Looking around I see almost every man in both units, trying to do the same: tightening their lips as their eyes go red. The women are weeping openly. I bite into my bottom lip. Hold it together. Don't make a scene.

His friends come forward one at a time to share remembrances of Ramirez. One man says that he was the kindest, happiest, funniest guy you would ever meet. A big bundle of joy. A woman steps forward and through her tears tells us how she used to laugh when she saw him lumbering through the halls in a towel, how he used to cheer her up. She tells us how much he loved *Star Wars*. She smiles at some private memory. Then she stops speaking, she can't finish. I am losing my composure. Tears threaten to break and roll down my face. I smother them furiously with my sleeve, trying not to draw attention to myself with this gesture. I look across the chapel and see Sergeant Toro and Sergeant Lewis, their faces contorted. I am about to break down. I feel his loss so acutely, the pain, the broken friendships, the lost family. Yesterday he was a name with no face, today he is a whole person to me: Ramirez, who had a wife and children and friends. Specialist Eric Ramirez, who was patient and funny, who smoked, who had thick, black hair and loved *Star Wars*. I never knew him, and yet I miss him. I grieve for him. This little island of stone and mortar seems poorer without him. Worst of all is the feeling of senselessness. He didn't have to die. This didn't have to happen. Were it not for the war, he would still be here. The hand of fate shows no mercy. They gave him the chance to stay home and like a brave man he didn't take it, he returned. A few weeks later he's dead, his wife widowed, his children fatherless. By the end of February, 541 soldiers and countless Iraqis have been killed in Iraq. It all seems so cruel.

The chaplain offers a prayer and I bow my head low. A man begins to speak, strongly and with feeling: the Christian prayer rises over me, ascending to heaven. Inside, my own words run through me as a mantra: *May he be happy. May he be freed from suffering. May his next life be a happy one. May his family be comforted.* The prayer ends. The two commanders call us to order and we render a salute. My arm slices the air in front of me, as rigid as an iron bar at my right temple.

Through the stone-slotted walls, a sharp tone pierces the silence: "Amazing Grace" on the bagpipes. I lose it. Tears flow down my cheek and drip onto my lapel. Seven rifle shots explode in three quick bursts. I cannot move, my hand stays locked at the side of my head. The bagpipes play on, and I hear the words of the song in my head: *Amazing grace, how sweet the sound, that saved a wretch like me...*

It's too much. My heart is bursting. *I once was lost, but now am found...*

Goodbye, Ramirez, be reborn with joy...*was blind but now I see.*

There is nothing more precious than human life. Nothing. All the flags, all the helmets, all the walls and towers don't mean anything at all. Life is the only thing that's important. Ramirez's life was important. It was irreplaceable. One more life snuffed out forever in this paroxysm of hate. I imagine how many funerals there must be in this war, how many soldiers, how many Iraqis: soldiers standing at attention with their arms up, stifling their emotions; Iraqis carrying the coffin by hand in a procession, releasing their grief and rage to the heavens. Pain envelopes me. None of this was necessary, none of it. This is all about human pride and human anger and human ignorance. We fight because we think that if we can just find all our enemies and kill them, we'll be safe, we won't have any enemies left, but that is a lie. We've all come to believe this absurd myth about the curative power of violence: that somehow if we kill and destroy enough then someday it will all be over and we won't have to fight anymore. Our heroes on the screen settle everything with a fight, and when the smoke clears the bad guys are destroyed forever. So we learn that a good battle is the solution to every dispute. I believed that once. I believed in the just battle that sets everything to rights. It's seductive. It makes you feel powerful. It makes you feel pure and uncompromising. It makes you feel purpose.

The ancient myths of the Greeks describe a monster called the Lernean Hydra. It was a terrible serpent with nine heads, and every time a head was cut off by some would-be hero, two more grew in its place. The more violence dealt to it the more powerful it became. The Hydra, like a vicious ideology, could not be conquered through force of arms. More terrible yet, one of the Hydra's many heads was immortal and could never be destroyed, only cut off and hidden. Like this mythical monster, terrorism and fanaticism have an aspect that is immortal: as long as hatred endures in human hearts, the seeds of terror and violence will always exist. You cannot destroy the immortal part by cutting off heads, just as you cannot extinguish hatred in the mind by slaughtering human beings. As the heroes of Greek myth learned: one does not defeat the Hydra by striking wildly at it, for this only makes it more terrible and strong. That's the secret of the Hydra, something that the ancients knew about war and revenge that we would do well to remember. The Buddha once said: *Hatred does not cease by hatred, but only by love; this is the eternal rule.* By harming those who would harm us, we do not make ourselves stronger or safer. We only turn the wheel another cycle: giving birth to new enemies by the very act of striking down the old ones. Terror, fascism, and fanaticism are ideas. A hateful idea cannot be burned, nor shot, nor pierced by bayonets, nor bombed into submission. An idea can only be overcome by a better idea.[17] A way of life without hope can only be overturned by the prospect of a better life.

Geshe Kelsang Gyatso once said: *Love is the only real nuclear bomb that destroys enemies.* The hardest truth is that violence doesn't end anything. Violence doesn't end. Retribution. Revenge.

Justice. Honor. Forever and ever. That's war, that's the price of war: another human life, infinitely precious, taken in the name of justice. Do not take that which you do not have the power to give back. The First Precept is to not take life: do not kill, do not destroy, not in war, not in anger, not for a flag, not for an idea, never. That is the teaching of Abu Ghraib, that is the sutra that I read inside those four stone walls: *Do not take life.* It's written in the powdered bones of the grave pit in Nasiriyah. It's written in the wet, pink brains of prisoners shot down at Abu Ghraib. It's written in the razor wire and the rotting food. It's written in the eyes of the soldiers who've turned, their hearts gone black. It's written on the lips of all those who smile to hear of another's cruelty. It's written in all the blank stares of innocent men caged like animals. It's written in that empty helmet and pair of boots that once held a human soul. At long last, after twenty-two years of life and a year of war, it's written broad and clear across my heart.

Now the chapel begins to empty. People shuffle out meekly, like somber ghosts drifting through the halls. Our unit is told to stand fast. The commander wishes to say something.

This is a moment that will live in infamy in the annals of the 320th Military Police Company for all eternity. This is the bottom, the lowest point. It's probably one of the moments when I have felt the most hatred in my entire life. The commander takes the floor and begins one of his speeches. We're all standing around like clubbed fish, still reeling with emotion, overcome by the solemnity of the occasion. The commander says he hopes we realize how serious this all is, and what a terrible thing it is to lose a man, as if we hadn't noticed. He goes on, reminding us about what he had personally promised our families.

"When we go home next month, I'm going to be able to say that I brought every single one of you back alive..." He steps forward and points in the direction of the other unit's barracks, and an odd expression comes over his face: something like a self-satisfied smile. "The 670th can't say that!"

The air in the chapel is suddenly charged. One hundred spines go rigid and two hundred fists clench into balls of rage. He's mocking them. He's mocking the unit that just lost a soldier. He's mocking them at that soldier's funeral. I look over and see Sergeant Lewis and a dozen others trying desperately to stifle their outrage. A stunned silence engulfs the assembly. Even the commander must feel this, realizing he's just stepped over a line that should never be crossed. I like to believe that he feels some shame, some recognition. To taunt another unit for losing a man is heinous, unforgivable. To taunt them at their own soldier's funeral goes beyond heinous into a realm that can only be called blasphemy. The commander has just uttered unholy words at the conclusion of a ceremony honoring a man who's just given his life. We're all still mourning him, still reeling from the reality of his loss, and the commander has the audacity to *brag,* to use his death as some kind of feather in his cap, a dig on a rival unit. His career, his pride, his unit above everything else; even another man's life.

Back in the halls after we've been dismissed, we cannot contain our rage.

"Can you believe what that motherfucker said?"

"He was making fun of the 670th for losing a man."

"I wanted to jump out and strangle the fat motherfucker."

Sergeant Toro adds, "I just thank God no one from the 670th was around to hear that."

By some perverse alchemy, all of the day's sorrow and pain is transmuted instantly to anger at our commander. Maybe it's a mercy to be able to channel all those feelings into something tangible. We turn our sadness into hate, and through that we are relieved of it for a time. Later, we talk about the memorial. We are cautious at first. In the Army, tears are the ultimate mark of weakness, of womanliness, of humiliation. Yet today each of us freely admits that they wept or were on the verge of doing so, and for once there's no shame in it. We all felt the same way. No one has the heart to go back to work, and even Sergeant Wallace tells us to take the rest of the day to ourselves. We shuffle off, cursing the commander so as not to think of anything else: not to think the name *Ramirez,* not to see the empty boots, not to hear the strains of "Amazing Grace."

MARCH 2004 At the beginning of the month all our thoughts turn to redeployment. There's still no word on the status of my conscientious objector application, and we're already beginning to shift to a return footing. Everything slows to a crawl as we begin to pack away tools and measure boxes for shipment back home. Guys tear their girls off the walls and begin to lug their TVs into shipping containers. Laboriously everyone starts to pull out their roots. We give everything we're not taking back to the units remaining behind. We tell them to stay in high spirits, that their time will come. None of it seems real. As the day of return draws nearer, my anxiety rises dramatically. After wanting it for so long, now the thought of returning home fills me with dread.

One day I turn to Sergeant Toro in the middle of his bench-press set and say quite abruptly, "Sergeant Toro, I need to talk to you. I'm not doing so good. I feel really, really bad. Depressed about going home."

He stops tinkering with the weights and turns to face me. He has a serious expression on his face. "Yeah, I know."

"Sergeant Toro, I feel more frightened of seeing Amy than I do of mortar attacks. I'm so scared of going back to college that a part of me feels like I want to stay here. I've been dry heaving for weeks, every day, from all the stress and anxiety. Everything feels meaningless, like nothing in my life matters or is worth doing. I don't have any enthusiasm for anything. Sometimes I wonder what's the purpose in me being alive."

I pause for a moment and then add hastily, "I wanted to talk to you about this for a while now, but I don't want you to go to the command and tell them I am suicidal or anything. I don't want them to think I'm crazy, it might affect my conscientious objection."

Sergeant Toro smiles. "You know I'm not going to do that. To tell you the truth I felt a lot of the same things you're feeling right now. The thing is this: you've got to realize that these feelings are just a phase that you're in right now and they'll pass. You'll go back to Amy and to college and to your friends, and you'll step back into your old life. Delgado, you've got to realize that you have so many things going for you: you've got college, and law school, and a girlfriend, and your whole freaking life ahead of you, man. The last thing you need to be thinking about is killing yourself."

"I'm not thinking about it, Sergeant Toro. It's just a way of talking about how I feel, like sometimes my life has no purpose."

"I know you're not seriously thinking about it, but it goes to show that you're feeling a lot of depression right now. Delgado, if you killed yourself, I would get so angry I would wanna choke you! Leaving me without a weight-lifting partner and depriving me of my closest friend."

We both laugh. The tension drains. Whenever Sergeant Toro tells a joke, he does it in this singsong voice that always cracks us both up. I feel a lump in my throat. Beyond going home, I know that the end of the deployment means leaving Sergeant Toro and my friends. I'm going to miss them so much. Just talking about it, just saying the words already makes me feel better. I know that Sergeant Toro cares and that this is something we're all going through. The aching pain fades away. Just expressing it made all the difference, it's manageable.

Sergeant Toro puts his hand on my shoulder, and presses it hard. "Everything will be all right in the end, Delgado. You'll see. You'll look back on this time and say, what the hell was I thinking? Wanting to stay in Iraq? I must have been crazy!"

We finish our bench presses, laughing and joking like old times. I don't know how I would have made it through Abu Ghraib without Sergeant Toro. Our friendship has become like air, a substance that infuses every moment of every day and enables me to draw breath. For all of us, the motor pool, through our shared hardships and experiences, is like a single entity divided into separate forms. We live communally. I am never apart from them or they from me. Their presence has become an unspoken assumption of life, at any moment we can speak or reach out and know that the others are there. I, a deeply private and reserved person, have forgotten how to live alone. The realization that we will be separated, that we won't live and work together, constitutes a large measure of my depression about going home. In Nasiriyah, with the whole of the deployment stretching out before us; life with my friends seemed eternal, our time together unlimited. Now, with the end of the deployment rushing toward us, we realize that our span together is finite. For myself, this infuses all the ordinary moments with an unspeakable poignancy: sitting with Shoe watching TV, listening to Patterson's Jamaican accent, watching Sergeant Wallace thumb through his little yellow notebook, even Spangler. These guys are my family; entirely different from one another, raised worlds apart, we have *become* family through struggle. Whatever darkness I have come through in Iraq has always been illuminated by the bonds of friendship, by brotherhood so simple and deep that it need never be acknowledged or spoken. Going home to Sarasota, each of us going our separate ways, will be like splitting my body apart.

With less ceremony than the occasion deserves, we mount our vehicles for the last convoy: the one headed south, the unraveling of the one we made so long ago that brought us first to Nasiriyah and then to Abu Ghraib. A resounding cheer, rising into a deafening roar, emanates from 140 throats as we prepare to step into our trucks bound for Kuwait. Each vehicle is laden with bags and parcels and televisions and all the myriad things we acquired in our tour and are loath to leave behind. Keepsakes. Apart from our bristling weaponry, we resemble a gypsy caravan all in drab. To say that it is a surreal moment is to understate it to the point of absurdity. The entirety of our existence, the whole of the world we've known for the last year is about to end and dissolve into memory. Our room, our cell, has been swept clean of any trace of our existence save for a single bottle of Shoe's spent tobacco juice. The hermit shell is vacant and ready for its next occupant, the new unit is already there, scouring over our rooms and abandoned belongings. At some point, I must have slammed the blue iron bars shut behind me for the last time and descended a last flight of stairs into the courtyard. The morning must have been bright and clear and beautiful, no matter the weather. Above, the sky would have been open and infinite with possibility. We are leaving, for real this time. In two weeks we'll be home forever and free of the Army. It's no exaggeration to say that the experience of leaving a yearlong tour of Iraq feels like dying. In a very real way, we are all dying today. The soldiers we are will soon be no more, we will become only civilians again, back to our regular lives and jobs. The identity of being a soldier, that all-consuming sense of belonging and purpose, is fading before our eyes. Passing through those gates on the way home will truly be the death of one person and the rebirth of another. There is no way to commemorate the moment: it feels like a funeral, a wedding, and a graduation day all rolled into one. A part of me will miss this prison, as the sum of my world for the last six months, the sun around which I and 140 other lives revolved. Another part of me wants to bury this place so deep in my mind that I never think on it again, never recall what happened here. That is my feeling upon leaving Abu Ghraib: a jumble of nostalgia for the place, relief, anxiety, and utter loathing all in the same moment. That moment, leaving, is still with me now. I can feel it, but I can't remember it.

I don't recall any of the details of our leaving: the noises, the sights, the smells, who did what or where. The only thing I recall clearly is the profound sensation of amnesia coming over me. The moment our vehicles left the gate and we could take in the entirety of Abu Ghraib at a glance, I could already feel the last month, the last six months, the last year becoming vague and indistinct. Did any of this really happen? It seems only days ago that we were living in the South, at Tallil, beneath Etemennigur. Abu Ghraib seems to have passed in a day and a night. All those moments that had crawled past in agony now seemed to have flown by at the speed of lightning. It was all a dream. Already Abu Ghraib and Iraq seem like something that happened to someone else, some other Aidan, a long time ago. I still don't know if my petition for conscientious objection has been heard or what my final fate will be. I have spent most of the last eight months doing nothing but agonize over it. Yet today it seems unimportant... for me at least, the war is over. Before the prison is out of sight, it's a distant memory.

Looking out over the prison, over the farms and roads that surround it, I am struck by a sudden feeling of crossing through an invisible barrier. On one side is the shimmering dream world: the prison, the walls, the towers, and the darkness; and on the other is the present moment: the wind running over my face, the feeling in my hands, the fear of the future. I am stepping out of a dream and into something far more terrifying: the unknown of home, of return, of the life that I left behind. Somewhere behind me there must be a line, a line separating Abu Ghraib from the rest of the world, a line marking the end of my time in that prison and the beginning of whatever else is to come for me. Further back still, there was another line: a line that is vague and shifting, a line drawn faintly in the sand. It's the sort of line that you don't see until you're standing right on top of it, and even then it's hard to make out clearly. This is the line that every one of us, every soldier, has to face. On the near side is the man you were. On the far side is a stranger; the far side is the man that war made you. We all come to this line, at one time or another, and we have to make a choice. No one can make it for us. We either see that line and turn back, turn back to our true natures, or else we step over it. This is the terrible truth: you don't always see it coming, you don't always know the moment when it happens, but once you step over that line you can never come home again. Your flesh may return, your body may return, but the man you once were is lost forever on that other side. How many are lost out there in the desert? How many never saw it coming and only realized too late that they had crossed that boundary which must never be breached? That's why you must always guard your steps. That's why you have to always be the protector of your soul and the ruler of your own heart. No one steps over that line for you and no one can push you across it. The door of oblivion is always open, as is the door of renewal and rebirth. Only you can say: this is as far as I go. When your time comes to face that line in the sand, you have to know in your heart what is right, feel it, and be ready to stand tall and die for it. Then...and only then...can you truly come home.

Epilogue
A KNIFE AT THE THROAT

FORT STEWART, GEORGIA

APRIL 2, 2004 I once again set foot on American soil. I actually kneel and kiss the tarmac at Hunter Army Airfield. Two weeks in Kuwait passed as if in a dream, everything else blotted out by the prospect of return. We occupy the same moldy, drafty barracks as before, only now they seem a mansion. This is America, where all good things are. Our unit goes through the events of a year ago, but backward, running through the bureaucracy of return: getting medical checkups, returning equipment, attending to the thousand other mundane tasks that separate us from total liberation.

The night we arrive at Fort Stewart, the company has a surprise for us: our families are here. They were told in advance when we would be coming home and have driven all the way from Florida to meet us. We are ushered into a huge auditorium and suddenly the lights go on and everyone is there, roaring and cheering and rushing for us in a human tide. Husbands and wives embrace, fathers and children, it's a time of celebration for everyone. I'm calm, knowing that my family is overseas. It's good, I think, I'm not ready to see them yet. I need some time to decompress.

Then Amy steps out of the crowd and sees me, and our eyes lock. My heart plummets into the soles of my feet even as she embraces me. This isn't right; I wasn't ready for this. I try to be happy for the half hour or so we are allowed together but I can't conceal my sorrow. The family reunion ends with the promise that we'll be allowed to see our families again at the company picnic tomorrow. Mercifully, we are separated and I have some time alone.

While everyone else is inside the hall, kissing and hugging and squeezing every drop out of this moment, I duck outside like a thief. In the crisp, cool Georgia night beneath a towering pine I weep so bitterly that I fear someone will hear me. It's all wrong. It wasn't supposed to be this way. I'm supposed to feel joy, unrestrained joy to be home and to see Amy again. Why do I feel so terrible? Why do I feel the same way I did back in Abu Ghraib, dry heaving behind a tent? Amy is here and she loves me, she's missed me. I love her and I've missed her, yet in her presence I feel like a traitor, like a monster. I have hung everything, every hope, every dream, every promise on this moment: the moment I return. The nightmare is over; my old life awaits. So why is my heart breaking?

We spend five more days at Fort Stewart before boarding charter buses back to St. Petersburg. These five days are consumed with the mind-numbing boredom of barracks life: standing in lines, filling out forms, sitting through lectures and mental-health briefings. The nights belong to us, and we fill them with a meaningless whirlwind of bars and strip clubs, staggering back to the barracks in the early-morning hours. I don't drink often, the bars and strip joints bore me, but this is about us, the soldiers, spending our last days together in something approximating happiness and freedom. I go to every bar and get dragged to every club and drink every round that someone buys because I want the guys in the motor pool to know that I love them and I'm with them every step of the way, in peace as well as war. We drink too much. I get sick. Everyone gets sick. It's too much of a good thing and we've earned it. We're flush with wages from a year without expenses, and prone to excess from a year without drink. We just want to spend a few more days in each other's company.

For the rest of our stay at Fort Stewart, no one says anything profound, but then we don't have to: every toast, every stupid joke told for the hundredth time, every meal taken in the dining facility, sitting side by side, is a silent farewell. It would be out of place to make grand gestures. Instead, we help each other pack our bags for the bus and lend each other batteries for our CD players. In these simple acts, invisible to outsiders, we are truly saying goodbye.

ST. PETERSBURG, FLORIDA

APRIL 8, 2004 To my horror, there is a large crowd waiting for us at the reserve center in St. Pete. I had hoped that this final part of the process could be dispensed with quickly and without ceremony. It is not to be. Crowds of family members and well-wishers fill the parking lot. I spot several high-ranking officers in full uniform. With a sinking feeling, I realize that there will be numerous farewell speeches. Over the cheers and whistles of the audience, the platoon sergeants call us to attention. We snap to it sharply, to impress the families. They applaud wildly again. The speeches begin. First an officer from our Reserve Unit chain of command that I don't recognize, then the first sergeant, who keeps it mercifully brief, and finally, of course, the commander. He always has to get in the last word. He goes on about how we're the best unit in the Army and how proud he was to serve with us and how much the families have been supportive. Naturally, he throws in a boast that he personally brought us all back alive, recalling for us his ill-fated words in the chapel, but we let it pass. We're all too close to freedom to give a damn about the captain and what he thinks of us or of himself. I take great satisfaction that this will be the last time I will ever have to sit through one of his speeches. Finally it ends. The last bit of nonsense ceremony that we couldn't care less about. With a thunderous shout, the commander cries, "Company dismissed!"

That's it. We're free. I make a beeline for my bags, and load them into the back of Amy's car, telling everyone that I don't want to say any more goodbyes, that I want to get under way as soon as possible. Turning back for one final look, I make eye contact with Sergeant Toro, Shoe, Patterson, and Sergeant Wallace, all rifling through the mound of baggage. I nod solemnly and turn away.

SARASOTA, FLORIDA

APRIL 2004 Friends let me stay in their dorm rooms. I drop my green duffel bags in the corner and spend my days hanging out. Their lives continue: they have classes, work, places to be. School is still in session but I'm not enrolled this semester. I'll go back in the fall, but for now I have nothing: no job, no college, no responsibilities of any kind. After the intense structure of the military, I don't know what to do with myself. I am accustomed to awakening every morning and literally having my activities dictated to me until I go to bed. Without that external pressure, I can feel myself collapsing into an inert mass.

At the end of the month a letter arrives from the office of U.S. senator Bill Nelson. When I see the blue-stamped return address, my heart skips. In all the emotion of coming home, I had nearly forgotten about my CO status. My father has been contacting every member of government he can get an address for, pressuring them for word about my conscientious objector packet, now long overdue. I tear open the envelope.

It is our pleasure to inform you . . .

I drop the envelope. I don't need to read further. I've won. My application has been accepted. I am now officially a conscientious objector, to be honorably discharged from the United States Army. It's over. I've been vindicated. It's a bit of an anticlimax: my feelings of being proven right, of being acknowledged as a CO and a Buddhist, do not compare with all the months I spent agonizing, waiting for this moment. The letter is a formality. In my heart I've been a conscientious objector from the start; they can't tell me what I already know. It's gratifying, of course it is, but it's also unnecessary. I fold the letter up and pack it away with the rest of my Army papers. I know who I am. I've known for a long time. The letter is simply the last page, the headstone on my military career.

SUMMER 2004 I sit upright in bed, sweating profusely in the dense summer night. Once again, I can't sleep. At night, especially, all the old feelings come back to me: that vague, insubstantial horror, the hopelessness, the sense of loss. What is my life now? Where are all my friends? I feel loneliness in spite of Amy's constant presence, her warmth, her effort. All the things that I desired so much, that I thought I desired, are painful to me now. Amy and I move past each other like shadows, without ever really touching. I get out of bed, walk over to the small refrigerator nearby, and twist open a Corona. Again.

At night when I stretch out to sleep, a sudden, intense thought always disturbs me. I cannot lie down with my throat exposed. I feel a sensation so intense that it borders on hallucination: as if someone were holding a knife to my throat. I can feel the phantom blade pressed against my jugular, the edge . . . I start to sleep with my head down, my throat covered, yet this feeling intrudes even on my waking life. Sometimes in the middle of the day I find my hand straying to my throat, defensively, as if to ward off this imaginary knife. All the pain, all the regret is compressed into this one intrusive sensation. Every time I feel nausea and depression rising in my stomach, I feel the knife at my throat. As if all the horror of the last year were compressing and flattening, sharpening itself into a knife.

FALL 2004 I return to college. Everyone seems happy to see me again and asks where I've been. I tell them flatly and quietly, hoping to change the subject as quickly as possible. But everyone's curious, of course, they press. The war? Oh my god! What was it like? I develop routines. I tell stories. I say things like, "It sucks." I smile and nod when they say welcome home. More than anything, I just want to avoid all talk of Iraq. I don't want to get into it with them, they're strangers, they wouldn't understand. It's not their fault, they're curious and concerned, the war's a big issue and they want to hear about it firsthand. I shouldn't blame them. Yet every time someone asks me about Iraq, asks me for the thousandth time if I killed anyone, I feel a splinter of pain go through me. How can I explain to them everything that's changed in me the last two years? I feel myself becoming a novelty, an oddity: that guy who went to Iraq. At parties, that's how they introduce me and it's the first thing people ask. I notice it in myself as well. I am reducing myself to a caricature. Sometimes the only thing I can talk about is the war; I even bore myself. I'm so tired. Tired of talking about it, tired of *being* it for everyone else, tired of listening to my same stories. No one wants to hear the real tale, anyway.

One day at school, I'm on my way to get coffee and a girl walks up to me. I don't know her that well, but she knows who I am. She strikes up a conversation, asking me where I've been. She tells me that her family is from Iraq. Something like shame goes through me. I feel responsible. Her hair is night-black and dense and it spills down her back. She is beautiful. I start to talk about Iraq.

For some reason, to this person I barely know at the time, I share some of the things that I've thought and felt in the last year. I tell her that I wish I could just tell everyone all at once and then never have to talk about it again, show my photos, tell my story, and be done with it. To finally let it rest. She says that people should hear what I have to say, that I need to tell them. She tells me that I should give a presentation; she would be glad to help.

I don't know why, but this moment changes everything. She gives me courage. I feel resolution forming inside me: I'll do it. I will hold a public talk and invite the whole college. I will show the pictures of corpses and the rot of Abu Ghraib. I'll tell them everything, and once I have, perhaps finally I'll be free of it.

I said before that all the great struggles begin with something inconsequential, something small and obscure as a strip of flypaper. And so it is now: an arbitrary meeting, a random conversation, sets it all in motion. Years from now, I will trace my activism back to this moment. She may never know the influence she had on me, or the ways my life has shifted because of that talk we had, on my way to get coffee. An avalanche begins with the rumbling of tiny stones.

DECEMBER 6, 2004 Tonight is the night. Before leaving home to drive to the auditorium I pour two large glasses of wine and drain them in two quick gulps. As I walk into Sudakoff Auditorium, an hour or so early, I can just begin to feel the wine coursing through me. Everything's arranged: rows of empty chairs, a projector screen, and a single podium on stage. Before the first audience members arrive, I have time to stalk down the rows of chairs, going over in my mind what I am going to say. I tried to write everything down but stopped after half a page; this won't be something I can write out. I will have to rely on myself to say the right thing when the time comes. I have given up on the idea of an outline. I will trust everything to the moment. My page of notes has only a disclaimer of liability for the college and a welcome to the faculty members before it trails off into blank space. At the bottom I have scrawled a quotation from Chekhov, from his short story "Gooseberries," that I will use to open and close the presentation:

> We do not see or hear those who suffer, and what is terrible in life goes on somewhere behind the scenes. Everything is peaceful and quiet and only mute statistics protest . . . the happy man is at ease only because the unhappy ones bear their burdens in silence, and if there were not this silence happiness would be impossible. There ought to be someone . . . reminding him that

there are unhappy people...and that life will sooner or later show him its claws, and trouble will come to him...and then no one will see or hear him, just as now he neither sees nor hears others.

It's a snippet I read two years ago in my Russian literature class and never thought much about at the time. When I returned to it later, the words had bite. *We do not see or hear those who suffer...* how true, even for me. Until Iraq, I had passed my life in self-focus, half-comprehending that somewhere *over there* were people struggling and suffering and dying. Only the experience made it real to me. That's what Abu Ghraib was: somewhere behind the scenes, a dismal backstage to all the pomp and glory of the war. Those who suffer, the prisoners, the soldiers, all do so out of sight. If people knew such things were happening in their name, if people could conceive of themselves being snatched from their homes and cast into a prison camp like that, well then they would have to say something. Silence and silent happiness would be impossible. I smile to myself, thinking that Professor Schatz, the Russian literature teacher, will be proud to hear me make use of Chekhov. I'm so nervous I could vomit.

Outside, the stars come out and the first people begin to trickle in: pairs and trios at first, then in a steady stream. They say it's worse to come early and watch the audience fill up, that it reminds you of how many people there are. I greet everyone I know as they filter in and take their seats. Suddenly, three familiar faces leap out of the crowd. They're members of the 320th, who live in different parts of Florida and have driven up to attend. They must have heard me on the radio earlier this week, advertising this talk. I smile and shake hands with each of them as I feel my knees go to water. They are speaking words to me but I can't hear anything, a jumble of sound rolls past me and I nod dumbly. One of them is the man who posed with a spoon over the corpse of a prisoner at Abu Ghraib. He's brought his wife and infant son along for the presentation. I'll be showing his picture tonight: spoon and all. I feel bile rise in the back of my throat. The room spins. They take their seats in the back of the hall, side by side, whispering to each other. The hall fills. Fifteen minutes after the start time, the four-hundred-capacity auditorium is full to overflowing and students are standing in the back and sitting cross-legged in the aisles. I'm milling about aimlessly at the side of the stage, clasping and unclasping my hands as I think of any reason to put off the inevitable...just one moment longer. Professor McDonald rises from his seat and walks over to me. He puts his arm around me.

"It's time. You need to start."

"But...Professor...there are members of my unit here. The guy in the photo with the spoon, and two others. I'm scared. They're going to rush the stage..." I'm desperate now, spinning desperately for any reason not to mount those stairs. Professor McDonald doesn't take one step or change his expression.

"Don't worry about them. I'll make sure nobody rushes the stage. You need to go up there and get this presentation started."

You can't foresee the moment you make a decision that changes the rest of your life. It is always ordinary and obscure, the smallest decision. In that moment you make the choice either to turn toward what you fear or to turn away. I look across the hall to the members of my unit. I look at Professor McDonald. I look out over the crowd: my friends, my professors, Amy, my brother. I think of my comrades: Sergeant Toro, Sergeant Wallace, Patterson, Shoe, and all the others. A half-delirious calm rises in me, bringing memories of a walk in the desert, handing in my weapon, standing defiant before the commander, and a hundred sleepless nights in Abu Ghraib. It's all so sharp. Everything I've been through surges past me in an instant: the pain, the loss, the friendship, the loneliness. I taste again ten thousand cartons of skim milk wrapped in plastic, ten thousand scoops of carrots mixed with peas from a B-ration. I see myself sitting in a red fabric chair, filthy, watching Shoe trying to cook popcorn. I hear Sergeant Wallace's voice calling us to work. I am standing in a makeshift gym and Sergeant Toro lays his hand on my shoulder and tells me everything will be all right in the end.

The memories crash over me and then they're gone, leaving only a profound stillness in their wake. Calm. Pause. Serenity. Our lives are not shaped by the broad strokes of our agency; rather they are the product of our unremarked-upon decisions, unplanned steps, feints that we make every hour of every day. *Sometimes the tide of a great battle can shift with the actions of a single soldier.* I take a long, slow breath and let it out, as is my custom. The world turns on the tiniest and most delicate of hinges. I face the stage.

Mounting the stairs in one step, I take my place behind the rostrum and lay the single sheet of paper down in front of me. The dull murmur of the audience withers and dies. Silence comes over the hall, and then a rising tide of applause. I raise my hand in recognition and the hall becomes still once more. I reach out and take hold of the podium with both hands, clinging to it so hard that my fingertips blanch. I begin to speak.

He who conquers himself is greater
than he who conquers a thousand times a thousand
on the battlefield.

THE BUDDHA

Acknowledgments

Here I pause. I am hesitant in writing these acknowledgments, only because there are so many who have played a role in the creation of this work that I fear I'll leave someone out. In truth, if I were to thank everyone who has made this work come to life, I should never be able to end it.

I would like to thank Beacon Press. I cannot express my appreciation for all the courtesy and faith they have shown to me. It was *A Buddhist Bible* from Beacon Press that I carried with me in Iraq, the book that helped me to win my freedom, and so I feel profoundly honored now to be able to tell my story through them.

I would especially like to thank my editor, Christine Cipriani, for her patience and dedication throughout the long journey that this book has been. I would also like to recognize Melissa Dobson, Lisa Sacks, Tom Hallock, Helene Atwan, and the rest of the team at Beacon Press, not only for believing in my history enough to give me the chance to tell it, but also for their tireless efforts in turning this collection of half-told stories into a real narrative.

I would like to thank Amy and Emiliano for treading back through the memories with me, correcting me, reminding me, guiding me, and as always for being my dear friends. Without their support I would not have been able to tell this story, and beyond the telling I can never thank them enough for the parts they played in it, sustaining me through one of the dark times of my life. Thank you, Amy, and thank you, Sgt. Toro.

To my brother, mother, and father, who have never stopped telling me that I could do it, who read the drafts and laughed with me and told me they were proud of me. To my family, who has always believed in me.

I am profoundly grateful to Professor Pat McDonald for always encouraging me to speak out, helping me find my voice, and guiding me every step of the way from returning soldier to activist; also to Professor John Newman, for the invaluable assistance he provided in writing about Buddhism as well as for all the things he has taught me in the last five years.

At the last I would like to thank everyone else who in one way or another has been a part of this story and whom I have not specifically named. I am so grateful for everything that you have given me since I came home, and I bow in deep respect to you all.

Notes

1. The Five Precepts, in Buddhism the five most important moral guidelines, in their simplest form: (1) to not harm any living thing, (2) to not steal, (3) to not commit sexual misconduct, (4) to speak truthfully, (5) to abstain from intoxicants.

2. The Wat Phrathat temple, atop Doi Suthep in Chiang Mai province.

3. Excerpted from chapter 1, "The Sorrow of Arjuna," *Bhagavad Gita* (New York: Barnes and Noble, 1995).

4. The reference is to Stevens, who had taken emergency leave from the unit and had not returned.

5. Not my exact words, but close enough in meaning.

6. A misunderstanding; my parents lived in the Philippines before I was born.

7. The English translation of *abu ghraib* is somewhat unclear. The word *abu* is a common Arabic prefix meaning "father of," but the second word, transliterated into Roman script as *ghraib* or *ghurayb*, is a form of an obscure root (gh-r-b) that has several meanings. It has been variously translated as "foreigner," "banished," "exiled," "strange," "small raven," and "the West." *Ghraib* is also a fairly common place name in Iraq, so the prison's name may simply be a proper noun or a reference to the surrounding area. Mine is an idiomatic translation that corresponds to the building's role as a prison and death camp, the "father," or source, of banished persons.

8. The Taguba Report, "Findings and Recommendations," Part 2, section 34, subsection i: "24 November 03—Shooting of detainee at Abu Ghraib (320th MP Battalion)," p. 29.

9. The Taguba Report, Annex 69, February 10, 2004.

10. The Jones/Fay Report, "AR 15–6 Investigation of the Abu Ghraib Detention Facility and 205th Military Intelligence Brigade," pp. 56–57.

11. "Report of the International Committee of the Red Cross (ICRC) on the Treatment by the Coalition Forces of Prisoners of War...in Iraq during Arrest, Internment, and Interrogation," February 2004, section 5: "Disproportionate and excessive use of force against persons deprived of their liberty by the detaining authorities," subsection 45.

12. ICRC report, section 1: "Treatment during Arrest," subsection 7.

13. ICRC report, section 1: "Treatment during Arrest," subsections 6, 8.

14. The Taguba Report, "Findings and Recommendations," Part 3, section 7, p. 29.

15. In addition to the iconic photos released to the media, there are some ninety video files among the evidence of detainee abuse at Abu Ghraib. The Taguba Report, in "Findings and Recommendations," mentions the videotaping of nude male and female detainees, incidents of forced masturbation, and sex (rape) between a male MP guard and a female Iraqi detainee. At Abu Ghraib, we first heard rumors of the videos; only later did the photographs take center stage. Some of the former have been viewed by members of Congress, but none was released to the public. According to the military these videos are "too graphic" and "depraved" to be viewed by the American people.

16. Sergeant Joseph Darby of the 372nd Military Police Company provided a CD of these photos to an Army Criminal Investigation agent, essentially blowing the whistle on prisoner abuse at Abu Ghraib. According to subsequent news reports, after the scandal broke in the United States, Sergeant Darby and his family were subjected to threats and harassment and ultimately entered military protective custody. In 2005 Sergeant Darby was awarded the John F. Kennedy Profile in Courage Award.

17. Paraphrased from a quotation by the American journalist Dorothy Thompson: "The only force that can overcome an idea and a faith is another and better idea and faith, positively and fearlessly upheld."